CLASSIC CLIMBS

—— of the ——
Northwest

Alan Kearney

ALPEN
BOOKS
PRESS

Published by AlpenBooks Press, LLC
3616 South Rd, Ste C1
Mukilteo, WA 98275 USA
(425)290-8587

Manufactured in the United States of America
Maps and photo overlays: Gray Mouse Graphics
Book and cover design: Marge Mueller, Gray Mouse Graphics
Cover photo: *Climbers on the West Ridge Route of Forbidden Peak in Washington's North Cascades. Moraine Lake below, and Eldorado Peak in the distance*
All photos by Alan Kearney unless otherwise noted

ISBN 0-9669795-5-9

Contents

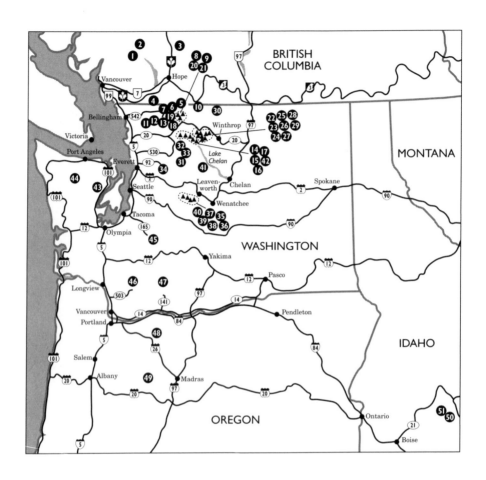

Oregon

Idaho

Mark Houston on the East Ridge of Forbidden Peak. Mount Buckner in the distance

Foreword

IF THE CRITERIA FOR A GOOD CLIMBING GUIDE is that the author be a good climber, *Classic Climbs of the Northwest* has to be one of the best guidebooks ever written. Alan Kearney has been in the forefront of the North American climbing scene for nearly a quarter of a century. Not satisfied with just repeating the hardest established routes, Alan has the extra fortitude to attempt first ascents and hard new routes. When he does these, you can be sure the climb is accomplished in good style— i.e., no fixed ropes, the minimum of permanent anchors, the maximum of free climbing, and leaving the mountain as he found it.

For a while, Alan had the opportunity to impart this philosophy to others when he taught climbing and guided trips during the 1980s. He once told me, "I try to be safe in the mountains and have a good time. I always feel that if you get too serious you are probably not having enough fun." I can attest to that sentiment with first hand experience. Alan, my son Nik, and I survived an adventurous all-night drive from Seattle to Yosemite one summer. Then we had great fun climbing some of Yosemite's famous, terrifying vertical routes.

Long before I met him, I heard of Alan's alpine accomplishments. Locally, these included hard free routes on Prusik Peak, Big Snagtooth, Dragontail, and Inspiration Peak. Farther afield, in Alaska and the B.C. Coast Range, he put up impressive new routes on Mount Hunter, Kichatna Spires, and Mount Combatant. Not the least of his remarkable accomplishments was the 150-mile circumnavigation of Mount Foraker, Alaska, on skis. I stood on the summit of that great mountain one time, and can appreciate what an alpine adventure that must have been! His numerous expeditions to Patagonia, Nepal, and Pakistan are only partially covered in his first book *Mountaineering in Patagonia*.

We've had Steck and Roper's *Fifty Classic Climbs* around for a long time, and I'm sure we have all found it very useful. However, it describes only six "classic" climbs of the Cascade Range. This volume focuses on over fifty outstanding routes throughout the Northwest, as well as extols the beauty of the wilderness and the joy of climbing. As such, this book is long overdue.

Alex Bertulis
Seattle, Washington

Luna Peak and Sourdough Ridge in winter

Preface

I HOPE THE READER WILL DISCOVER throughout this book that the reason people climb in the Pacific Northwest isn't necessarily to seek out the hardest climbs on perfect rock or vertical ice. The rock here is often not perfect, and the ice (when vertical) might be rotten or could be gushing water. A hike to the base will usually not follow a neat short path lined with cairns or markers, but might constitute an involved adventure through brush, up and over ridges, and across glaciers. People climb in the Northwest because many of the peaks are situated in a pristine setting; finding a hard line is often a secondary objective in a land with a short climbing season and often abominable weather.

Despite this (or because of it) the Northwest ranges have produced many admirable performers who went on to embrace the field of super-alpinism. Climbers such as Carlos Buhler, Steve House, Sean Isaac, Steve Swenson, Mark Twight, and many more first learned their trade on the varied faces of Northwest mountains. Encountering all types of weather, in every season of the year, they climbed wet and dry, hot and cold, and everything in between. Sometimes the exasperated Northwest climber, eager to be active year-round, moved to a sunny climate to keep his or her upper body in shape. For the rest of us who are still active, an occasional trip to the desert, and more frequently the indoor rock gym, has had to suffice.

It is also a well-known fact that although Northwest climbers in the 1950s and '60s were somewhat insulated from techniques and trends in other parts of the country (Yosemite especially) some pretty damn good climbers came out of that era. Seattle climber Don McPherson had started what might have been the country's first climbing school, The American Climbing School. He held a rock seminar at Squamish, British Columbia, and invited Royal Robbins up to teach. During the session Robbins, a masterful crack climber, struggled up the off-width Tantalus Crack at the base of the Chief. McPherson recalls, "Robbins got his knees all chewed up and he asked me how hard it was [the crack]. It shows I had an ego. I think it's kind of a tough 5.8. We thought 5.8 was about our limit. We didn't realize we were doing stuff that was 5.10a and 5.10b sometimes. When Robbins came down he was really pissed at me; his legs and knees were all chewed to shit."

Aside from a number of scruffy rock walls, what we do have up here in the Northwest are the quintessential summits that climbers and poets have written about for decades. These craggy peaks and spires shrouded in mist, mantled by riven fields of ice and guarded by a sea of lesser mountains and deep valleys are what gives this place its charisma. To claim that any one area is better than another is hardly relevant, since we do not have perfect granite walls, nor does Yosemite have glaciers and remoteness. Every mountain range and cragging area throughout the country has its own special quality. I have climbed in many of these wonderful places in the past three decades, savoring red sandstone, crunching over blue ice, pulling up on small feldspar crystals, or soaking in an expanse of unpeopled solitude.

And what makes a climber? Is an alpinist measured by his or her technical accomplishments? Yes, often that is the case. But, I feel the best climbers are not only the ethical ones—the ones who are friendly to their fellow man or woman, who return a lost piece of gear to the owner when they find it, who freely give out information about routes when asked, and who have fun practicing their sport. The other climbers that I respect are those who love the mountains and the sport and continue to pursue it to the best of their ability (when their personal life permits) and on into their twilight years. Who of us has not been impressed by the senior climbers that are out there "still doing it?" I only hope I still will be able to do so.

Alan Kearney

Acknowledgements

I WOULD LIKE TO THANK all of the climbers who agreed to interviews and who shared their stories with me. Bob Kandiko read the entire manuscript and gave helpful advice. A special thanks to Cliff Leight for his photos of Dome Peak and Liberty Bell, Joe Catellani for his image of Big Four Mountain, and to Brett Baunton for his photo of Mount Olympus. All of the other photographs are by me. A special thanks goes to Marge Mueller for her expert editing, helpful advice, and patience with my numerous text changes.

I am grateful to my parents for introducing me to the outdoors and encouraging my writing and photography for the past twenty years.

Alan Kearney
Spring, 2002

Introduction

FOR ME, THIS PROJECT HAS BEEN A LONG ONE that involved climbing a lot of routes, taking notes, asking others what climbs they liked, and so forth. A number of routes came highly recommended, but did not pass the grade when I climbed them. The North Buttress of Chamois Peak, the North Ridge of Black Peak, the Northwest Arête of Shuksan, the Northeast Face of Goode, and the Northwest Face of Forbidden were just not, in my opinion, all that great, even though I enjoyed them. Some climbs that I wanted to include, but didn't get around to completing, were: the North Buttress of East McMillan Spire, the North Ridge of Mount Blum, the East Face of Chianti Spire, and the Springbok Arête on Les Cornes.

What constitutes a "classic climb" is, of course, subjective. In Steck and Roper's original *Fifty Classic Climbs*, they listed their criteria for picking the routes in the book: The peak had to have a striking appearance, a significant climbing history, and excellent climbing. They then decided that "excellent climbing" should outweigh other factors when in doubt about a climb's inclusion. To this day I have never agreed with their choice of the Price Glacier on Mount Shuksan. My one experience attempting it involved racing across slopes to avoid toppling séracs, and much of the route above looked like the same scene—far too much traversing over unstable ground. However, some friends climbed it in November and had a great time, as it was cold and firm. So much of a person's opinion of a route depends on whether they had a good experience that day. Maybe the person hadn't been out climbing in a while and was so jazzed about being on a mountain, that they overlooked those obvious elements that would not put a route in the "classic" category.

A number of climbers felt the West Arête of Eldorado Peak was a good route, but when they were nailed down they admitted it had very rotten rock. My rules for picking the best routes included the attractiveness of the peak, interesting climbing, rock quality, charismatic name, and remoteness. To a certain degree, I weighed the peak in its standing historically and for who first climbed it. First ascensionists are not always objective about their

Opposite: *Kathy Zaiser near the summit of Mount Bardean*

pet climbs (myself included) and they sometimes tend to inflate the quality of the route they did. I took a particularly hard look at my own new routes and selected only five.

In the Washington Cascades alone there are eleven hundred peaks that fill Fred Beckey's three volumes of the *Cascade Alpine Guide*. It is difficult for a climber to sort out which routes to climb in the Northwest, and it is especially difficult for a climber living out of the area. Locals can find out from friends which climbs are the better ones. This book does not pass on hearsay about any climb; I feel the only way to judge if a route is worthwhile is to do it personally. I hope that by having climbed each of the routes I can provide useful insight for avoiding most pitfalls as well as current approach and descent information.

Of the hundreds of routes that Fred Beckey first put up, sixteen are included here. We have all been influenced by Beckey's drive and pioneering spirit; his *Cascade Alpine Guides* have set the standard for what constitutes a good guidebook. Many of us have picked out new lines to climb from the photos in his books, and commended or cursed his route descriptions. Information is only as reliable as its source and accurate route details can be hard to come by.

How To Use This Book

The climbs in this book have been arranged roughly from north to south. Many share common approach routes. Traveling farther along the same highway or trail brings you to another route. Alternate approaches are listed when appropriate, along with useful references. Because many glaciers have dramatically receded in recent years, it has been necessary to describe alternate starts for some routes.

Ratings of snow and ice climbs are classified by maximum steepness and roman numerals I, II, III or IV, indicating length. The difficulty of these routes varies greatly with conditions; you can experience powder snow, slush, firn, water ice, or rime. For rock, the Yosemite Decimal System is used from class 1 through class 5 and aid. Class 5 is subdivided into 5.1 to 5.11. For the gradations of 5.10 and 5.11 a minus and plus is used. 5.10- is equivalent to 5.10a or b, 5.10+ to 5.10c or d, and 5.11- to 5.11a or b. For overall difficulty and time, rock routes range from grade I through V.

Because the level of fitness of individuals can vary so much, and route conditions can change, I have foregone specific times for route completion. Wet and iced rock is not uncommon in the Northwest. Expect it in crummy weather.

Directions are given as if you are facing the cliff, or snow slope, or approaching the peak on a trail. Pitch numbers are in bold face square brackets, difficulty is in parentheses.

Throughout the text I mention a "standard rack" for rock climbs; my standard rack is as follows:

> several tiny steel nuts
> set of 8–10 Stoppers
> 1 each, small camming units
> 2 each, 1-inch, 1½-inch, 2-inch, and 2½-inch cams
> 1 each, 3-inch, 3½-inch, and 4-inch cams
> 40 carabiners
> 6 quick draws
> 8–10 shoulder slings

I use a 200-foot (60-meter), 10 or 10.5mm lead rope for alpine rock climbs and sometimes carry a 200-foot 7-mm line as well for hauling and rappelling the longer, harder routes. A nut cleaning tool is useful and prevents the buildup of unsightly fixed protection. Many of the climbs will require experience with an ice ax and crampons. One of the best snow anchors is an ice ax buried in a deep T slot, with a long sling girth-hitched to the shaft (similar to the diagram on page 80 of *Glacier Travel and Crevasse Rescue* by Andy Selters).

The following abbreviations used throughout this book:

> *AAJ*: *American Alpine Journal*
> *CAG*: *Cascade Alpine Guide* (three volumes)
> CFM: Canadian Federal Map
> *CHGSWBC*: *Climbing and Hiking Guide to Southwest British Columbia*
> *CGOM*: *Climbers Guide to the Olympic Mountains*
> CM: Climbing Magazine
> RMNC: Recreation Map of the North Cascades
> NPS: National Park Service
> *OH*: *Oregon High: A Climbing Guide*
> USFS: United States Forest Service
> USGS: United States Geological Survey. All USGS maps listed as references are 7½'.

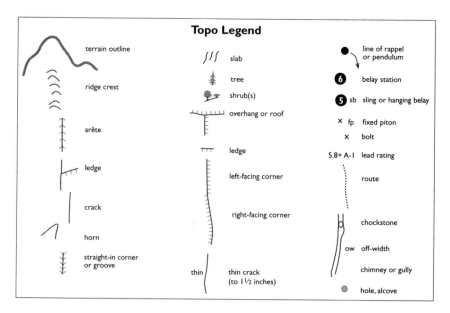

Topo Legend

terrain outline

ridge crest

arête

ledge

crack

horn

straight-in corner or groove

∫∫∫ slab

🌲 tree

🌿 shrub(s)

overhang or roof

ledge

left-facing corner

right-facing corner

thin | thin crack (to 1½ inches)

● line of rappel or pendulum

6 belay station

5 sb sling or hanging belay

× fp fixed piton

× bolt

5.8+ A-1 lead rating

route

chockstone

ow off-width

chimney or gully

● hole, alcove

Mountain Safety

Every climb in this book is an alpine route and is on a mountain. Mountain hazards in the Northwest include avalanches, icefall, lightning, rockfall, crevasses, and weather. The latter two are especially prevalent since our region has so many glaciers and such capricious weather.

Unless you are absolutely sure you're not on a glacier, and you really understand the differences between seasonal snow, firn, and glacier ice, you should rope up and know how to prusik and extricate your partner(s) from crevasses. Useful reading on the subject is Andy Selter's *Glacier Travel and Crevasse Rescue*.

Weather moves in quickly; forecasts are not reliable. Summer storms in the mountains are incredibly wet, and often have temperatures right at freezing. If you're wearing cotton when caught in one, you've had it. Recommended reading on the virtues of other natural fabrics vs. synthetics is *Secrets of Warmth* by Hal Weiss. I use an umbrella for trail walking, waterproof rainwear for wet weather, and a light nylon windshirt to cut the wind when the weather is dry.

I never wore a helmet in the Cascades until I nearly dropped a good-sized flake on my partner's head in 1987. Now I look on helmets as cheap insurance, especially when you are often far from help in the alpine realm.

It is best to climb the volcanoes in winter or spring when their surfaces are snow covered, since the rock is lousy. For other routes the season normally runs from May to October, depending on how that year's snowfall has affected the access. Many climbers have been turned back by snow-covered rock and cornices on Triumph's northeast ridge in mid-June. North and east faces will be the last to dry out, and some routes can only be climbed in July or August.

It has been shown that accidents tend to recur in the same places. Crevasses on the descent route down Mount Baker swallow unroped climbers every year; climbers frequently slip in the gullies of Fisher Chimneys on Shuksan, séracs clobber climbers on Rainier, and the descent route off Mount Hood has been the scene of many weather-related disasters. Learn proper skills, be prepared, and adopt an attitude of complete self-reliance.

Cell phones do not take the place of good judgment, and don't always work, even in the high mountains. Imagine there is no one to help you in an emergency and you will likely live longer. There are many occasions in the mountains when it becomes pointless and dangerous to continue. Be able to make a judgment call; learn to know when to retreat. Keep abreast of current conditions by consulting with other climbers, and have a rewarding alpine experience!

Wilderness Ethics

According to Tom Patey, "An efficient mountaineer need fulfill only three criteria. He must not fall off. He must not lose the route. He must not waste time." I would add a fourth. He must leave the mountain as he found it. As an author, I have identified these special routes; as a climber and camper it is your responsibility not to mess them up!

It may be naive for me to imagine these climbs will not have more traffic on them after publication of this guide, but to say that degradation must also follow is ridiculous. Make the extra effort to carry out all your garbage and litter. Always have a cigarette lighter handy to burn your toilet paper (or carry it out during times of high fire danger). When accidents of the bowels do occur, deal with them—use a bag if you have to. In addition, follow all of the wilderness guidelines established by the National Park Service and the U.S. Forest Service for minimum impact camping and travel. If these routes get trashed, you and I are jointly responsible.

Access and Permits

There are a lot more climbers, hikers, bikers, hunters, and anglers visiting the mountains than there were several decades ago when the first guidebooks were published. Climbers, as such, are an anarchistic and independent bunch of individuals who don't like swallowing rules, paying fees, or obtaining permits instituted by government agencies.

The fact is, there are so many more people on the planet now that we, as humans, have a greater impact on the land. For example, if trails weren't regulated, hikers and climbers might find themselves sharing paths with motor vehicles. Some kind of designated usage and protection is essential for the preservation of the mountain environment. The North Twin Sister, near Mount Baker, and the mountains of southern British Columbia have virtually no usage protection. They are on, or accessed through, privately owned timber or mining land. I think that most backcountry users would agree that these beautiful peaks would be better off than they now are if they were within the boundaries of a national park or forest.

I feel the real issue is not whether areas are regulated, but what services are provided by the money spent on fees and permits. On Mount Rainier several years ago Cliff Leight asked the ranger at Paradise what the money from the $15 climbing fee provided. The reply was, "The money goes to provide climbers with information about conditions on the mountain." When asked about the current conditions, the ranger had no information.

Leight was curious and pursued the matter with the Forest Service by talking to a head ranger in Darrington. The ranger admitted that the USFS was no longer getting as much revenue from logging and "wanted to get into the recreation business." The trail park pass is their toehold for collecting more money from recreation users. There is documentation on the web showing that (thus far) fees collected do little more than pay the salaries of employees collecting them.

It is not my position to advise a climber about abiding by all the rules, paying all the fees, or conversely, aggressively opposing them. But people do need to know the facts and have the option to choose their course of action. Many climbing and publishing organizations (which have become bureaucracies themselves) would have us all submit to every new rule and fee that appears. Bear in mind however, if we, as recreation users, become a significant source of revenue to the managing agencies, our usage may take priority over other, more damaging, uses of the resource.

This book provides the reader with all the necessary contacts to organize a trip into the mountains through the proper channels, or to further research fees and permits.

The website for the Washington Trails Association is http://www.wta.org. At this website you can click on Outdoor Links to access the National Parks, National Forests, Wilderness Areas and the specific areas in British Columbia, Washington, Oregon, and Idaho that you want to visit.

Useful telephone numbers for the climbs are as follows:

Climbs 1 and 2: Canadian Forest Products Ltd.
Harrison Mills, B.C. (604) 796-2757

Climbs 5–9 and 13 –21: North Cascades National Park
Marblemount, WA (360) 873-4590

Climbs 10, 22, 29, 30: Okanogan–Wenatchee National Forest
Twisp, WA (509) 997-2131

Climb 11: The Campbell Group
(360) 336-9733

Climbs 12 and 34: Mount Baker/Snoqualmie National Forest
Glacier, WA (360) 599-271 and Verlot, WA (360) 691-7791

Climbs 35–40: Okanogan–Wenatchee National Forest
Leavenworth, WA (509) 548-6977

Climbs 31–33 and 41: Glacier Peak Wilderness
Darrington, WA (360) 436-1155

Climb 42: North Cascade National Park
Chelan District Office (509) 682-2549

Climbs 43 and 44: Olympic National Park
Port Angeles, WA (360) 452-4501

Climb 45: Mount Rainier National Park
Longmire, WA (360) 569-2211 x 3317 or (360) 569-4453

Climb 46: Mount St. Helens National Volcanic Monument
Amboy, WA (360) 247-5800

Climb 47: Mount Adams Wilderness
Trout Lake, WA (509) 395-2501

Climb 48: Mount Hood Wilderness
Zigzag, OR (503) 668-1704

Climb 49: Mount Jefferson Wilderness
Mill City, OR (503) 854-3366

Climbs 50 and 51: Sawtooth National Recreation Area
Stanley, ID (208) 727-5000

DISCLAIMER

Mountain climbing is an inherently dangerous activity. Although the author has taken pains to be accurate in his descriptions of the routes contained herein, he is only human, so errors could have occurred. In addition, conditions in the mountains frequently change due to weather and other natural forces, so it is likely that some route differences will be encountered. In addition, editing and printing errors can occur in any book. Therefore, you are forewarned that you will be using this book at your own risk, and that the author and the publisher of this book disclaim any responsibility or liability for any injuries or death that might occur to you. Be careful—instead of relying solely on the descriptions contained in this book, use your own good judgment (it had better be good, or you have no business climbing). Also, the routes described herein vary in difficulty. Please make sure you have the experience, physical health, and mental state to undertake the climb you are considering. You are on your own.

Friends & Climbers

MOST OF THE HISTORICAL INFORMATION FOR THIS BOOK was obtained from climbing journals and magazines. When those sources dried up, I consulted climbers personally or tried to remember scraps of information from early encounters with the first ascensionists. It is hard to recall the details of a climb you have done two or three decades ago, and unless you take notes or write an account of the climb for publication, certain memories fade.

The majority of climbers do not pursue new routes. While some of us return again and again to the same peaks, picking off secret lines, another contingent is busy climbing every mountain in the range. Their information about approaches, quality routes and priceless stories is invaluable. The following paragraphs also describe many excellent climbers who have contributed to our sport, but who are virtually unknown.

These brief biographies are of a few of the Northwest climbers who have contributed much to the exploration of the mountains. Two-thirds of these climbers have joined me on a rope. Some of these people are well known; however, many are excellent climbers who have never given slide shows nor published their exploits. I wanted to share with the reader a little about their backgrounds and their beginnings in the sport.

FRED BECKEY has accomplished far more than most of us will if we have several lifetimes to do it and, in fact, his many climbs seem to blend into one another when he is asked about details. No one peak is more significant to him than another, as I discovered when I first met him in Canada in 1974. I was climbing in the Valhalla Mountains of southern British Columbia in August and had put up a new route on Prusik Peak earlier that year, in May. I was real excited about Prusik Peak and related the ascent to him and *Beckey, for all his ambition, passion, and eccentricity has demanded the ultimate of his partners* George Ochinski, his youthful climbing partner in tow. Beckey had just completed a new route on the nearby West Molar and strolled into our camp on a warm afternoon attired in blue air force surplus wool flight pants with big

Fred Beckey. (Photo by Cliff Leight)

padded knees—just as good as knickers and far cheaper.

I said the rock was outstanding, and Fred's reply was, "Oh, yeah, I guess it was." When I explained how Chuck Sink, Jay Foster, and I got off route on the South Face of Prusik in 1973 I pried him for pointers on where we went wrong. "Oh, just follow those cracks up the face," he answered. "Yeah! Whatever the guidebook [his guidebook] says." After a discussion with Fred, your brain always feels emptier and your questions remain unanswered. He didn't have time to chat as he and his partner planned to hike the ten miles out to the car that evening and drive to another range of peaks in B.C. I was impressed then by his energy, and I still am.

Beckey, for all his ambition, passion, and eccentricity has demanded the ultimate of his partners from all over North America. While working on Shiprock in 1965 with Eric Bjornstad, Beckey had encountered harder climbing than he expected, as well as sandstorms, and cold temperatures, and consequently he had suffered a decline in enthusiasm. During his "morale boosting" sessions in the nearest town he used a bar room phone to persuade Alex Bertulis to join them. Bertulis had a steady job and couldn't just take time off on a moment's notice to go climbing. Beckey was adamant. "This is such a great route." he raved. "With a strong third climber we can do this thing much faster."

When Bjornstad abandoned Beckey and the fixed ropes, Bertulis caved, asked his boss for a raise, didn't get it, and quit his job. Way out on the proverbial limb, Alex flew to Las Vegas, met Fred, and joined him on the searing 1500-foot walls of Shiprock. (Typical of the desert, the temperatures had shifted from freezing to boiling.) The difficult climbing did not relent, and with a lot of wall gear the pair was moving slowly. After several days going alpine, they were within a couple hundred feet of the top, although they could not actually see the way clear and were very low on water. As if a fine-tuned and indomitable machine had suddenly had a spanner wrench thrown in it,

Beckey refused to climb any higher. When Bertulis questioned him, Beckey launched into a diatribe about all the deaths he had witnessed climbing. Arguing with him was like trying to talk to a rock. Says Bertulis, "Fred's stubbornness is legendary, and he was not about to give in to a young upstart like me."

Their shouting reached ear-splitting proportions, with Bertulis threatening to continue on alone. "If you do, I'm not waiting for you. You'll die," Beckey wailed.

And so they retreated together, with Beckey later relating their tale to an unbelieving group of Navajos, and Bertulis, by dint of luck, returning to the job he quit. It is one of those stories that will be retold for years to come, and it only proves that we climbers are some of the craziest bunch of misfits and whackos on the planet.

Being sent to a war orphanage in 1947 might have been a sentence for a kid eight years old, but for Lithuanian **ALEX BERTULIS** it became the beginning of his love for the mountains. "The orphanages were in these incredible monasteries up in the Austrian Alps. Some of the older kids would take off on the weekends and hike the local summits and I would tag along," Alex relates. Three years later he emigrated to the United States and wound up in Los Angeles. Forays into the Sierras with Boy Scout troops further piqued his interest in climbing. When in college, he transferred to a university situated close to mountains, Washington State University in Pullman. As Bertulis, laughing, tells it, "Because I already had some climbing experience when I arrived, they immediately made me chairman of the climbing club."

Alex Bertulis

Later, he transferred to the University of Washington in Seattle, and did the Picket Traverse in the summer of 1966. "Fred Beckey found out about it and that's how I got on the list of Fred Beckey partners, because he was always looking for younger partners that could keep up with him." He soon met Eric Bjornstad and Ed Cooper, ". . . and there was this whole new world of 'everything we do is a first ascent' because there was a gold mine here [the Northwest] of first ascents."

Bertulis did many fine climbs in the 1960s and 70s on some of the most forbidding north faces in the range. As a younger climber I held these dark steep faces in awe, especially the two routes Bertulis put up with Soviet climbers on Bonanza and Inspiration Peaks. Through an exchange program several elite mountaineers from Russia showed up, intent on doing first ascents or new routes. Alex relates, "In the process of rambling through the Cascades I picked out some potential routes and said, 'Wow this hasn't been done!'" In 1970 Bertulis stormed into Bonanza Peak with Mark Fielding in the hopes of doing a big unclimbed north face on the southwest peak. After one look at the ominous face Fielding said, "I ain't doing that!" As Bertulis tells it, "You've been there, you give them the pitch, pump them up with a few more beers and they get enough courage, and okay, we're gonna go. Then when they get there your partner says, 'Oh, Jesus!'" Bertulis and Fielding did end up doing an unclimbed snow couloir adjacent the big face, but they didn't publish anything about it.

"I kept it quiet, like Fred Beckey, keeping this for myself," Bertulis explains, "so when the Soviets came over and they said, 'So, Alex (we were drinking vodka), we really want to do some new route here. You know the mountains?' I said, 'Yeaaaah, I think I have a new route for you guys.' I said nothing else—didn't show 'em pictures or anything. Sergei Bershov led most of it and Slava Onishchenko was his belay partner. It was the era when rock shoes hadn't fully been introduced, but the Russians already had these little galoshes like EB's. We ended up bivouacking three-quarters of the way up, and the next morning we finished off the climb. They were happy because it was aesthetic, and we named it the Soviet/American Route."

One year later the Americans went to Russia and were provided many opportunities for new routes and enjoyed plenty of vodka. Then, in 1977, the Russian climbers came back, and Bertulis took them to the Pickets, knowing they had the whole expanse of north faces to choose from. Mark Fielding more than redeemed himself on the North Face of Inspiration Peak, where he paired off with the strongest Russian climber. "Mark had just come back from Yosemite, having done six or seven grade VI's that summer," said Bertulis. "You should have seen his body, it was rippling with muscles. I mean, he was in the top shape of his life. I would say, 'Mark, go!' and he would lead anything."

One of the excellent younger free climbers who is not afraid to strap on a big pack full of hardware and hike far into the mountains is **BRYAN BURDO**. In 1987, with Andy Cairns, he climbed a grade IV 5.10 route on the north face of Davis Peak near the southern Pickets. In addition, he has established a slew of new routes at Washington Pass and in the Wine Spires over the last decade. Bryan is always fit, helped partly by working at the Vertical World (an indoor rock gym), and is always eager to disseminate information about good climbs in the area.

Bryan Burdo. (Photo by Pete Doorish)

Recently, I met him in Seattle and asked him about several of his new routes in the range. Bryan was a bundle of energy, especially when it came to describing first ascents, and there was hardly a need to ask questions since the stories rolled out on their own. Throughout it all it was apparent Bryan wanted to establish new lines in good style and knew the difference between a quality route and a substandard one. We talked about future aspirations and, although his sights are higher than mine, the Northwest still has plenty of room for his exploration.

CHRIS COPELAND grew up in Kentucky, Texas, Connecticut, and on the East Coast. He went to college at Dartmouth from 1975 to 1980, and it was during those years that he discovered climbing in the White Mountains and Shawangunks. Ice climbing, especially, required additional expensive gear that Chris didn't own. He was on financial aid at college, so he walked into the aid office and said, "I want to start ice climbing but can't afford a pair of boots." The clerk asked how much they cost; Chris winced and said, "$150." The office believed that no Dartmouth student should be denied access to social and sports activities, and wrote him out a check for a pair of Galibier Peutereys. If I had tried that at Washington State University, they would have laughed at me.

"In the final two pitches there was not one solid anchor, even for the belays. If we had fallen, we'd have died."

Chris used the boots and the ice climbing experience he subsequently gained to climb in Peru in 1977 with Peter Kelemen. They attempted a new difficult route on 21,000-foot Santa Cruz, and made it to within 1000 feet of the top. Chris was an energetic climber when he moved to Seattle in 1980 and discovered the Cascades. With Josh Lieberman he climbed the Northeast Buttress of Slesse, the complete North Ridge of Stuart and made the sixth ascent of the terrifyingly steep North Face of Nooksack Tower. Of that climb he said, "In the final two pitches there was not one solid anchor, even for the belays. If we had fallen, we'd have died." I was curious about the quality

Chris Copeland

of Nooksack Tower, and later spoke to Alex Bertulis, who, with Scott Davis put up the route in 1973. He assured me they encountered no rotten rock or desperate runouts. Clearly Chris and his partner had erred, another testimony to the seriousness of routefinding in the mountains.

In 1987 Chris joined me on the South Face of Big Kangaroo where we climbed an eight-pitch new route close to the one I put up in 1984. Chris has tremendous enthusiasm for alpine climbing, but he recently called a timeout to raise a family and work at becoming an outdoor writer. His wife Mo teaches physics and Chris juggles caring for his two kids at home with writing at his computer. I look forward to the day his entire family can visit the mountains and he and I can do more climbs together.

▲▲

When I met **DAVE DAILEY** at Midnight Rock in 1976 he had been climbing for thirteen years, with ten of those at a high standard. Dave and his wife Diana noticed my battered '66 Mustang was a car they once owned, and wanted to meet the new owners. From that encounter Shari Kearney [a former spouse] and I joined them for a climbing trip to the Wind Rivers in August of the same year.

Dave has spent a lot of time on Yosemite walls, and climbed the West Face of Leaning Tower with Charlie Porter in 1969. Porter wanted to climb The Nose also, but instead Dave got on his ten-speed and biked 900 miles back to Seattle. He's returned many times and eventually climbed The Nose

Opposite: *Mike Lee on the Southeast Route on Mount Despair*

and Salathe Walls on El Cap and the Northwest Face of Half Dome with Diana. Back home, Dave did the third winter ascent of the Nisqually Icefall on Rainier with Julie Brugger and Bruce Carson.

Also, in 1970 Dave first met his future wife, Diana, climbing with another party on the north side of Rainier. Niels Anderson and Dave had climbed partway up the Brumal Buttress of Willis Wall when a big avalanche cut loose and nearly creamed them. The pair scurried across the slopes to Thumb Rock on Liberty Ridge, where they met Diana, Warren Bleser, and Bruce Carson climbing the ridge. All five climbers did the ridge and then came down the Emmons Glacier, but Dave didn't want to traverse the long way around the mountain and hike back out the Carbon River. Instead, Dave, Diana, and Bruce hiked down the White River and hot wired a telephone to call a friend to pick them up. Dave and Diana have been a team ever since, and were married in 1972.

The couple joined Jim Nelson in 1975 for a climb of Mount Lituya in southeast Alaska; it's the closest to being in an epic that Dave will ever admit to. Lituya was unclimbed by any route, and Seattle friends said it looked like a straightforward snow climb up a 6000 foot North Ridge. A Juneau bush pilot dumped the trio off on a glacial lake near Cape Fairweather and they spent one week hiking to the mountain. They had brought only a three-week supply of food, and cached some at the landing site. With mostly snow flukes for pro-

tection they found themselves on fifty-degree water ice on a huge mountain. Dave later wrote in the *American Alpine Journal*, "No belays with only one ice screw. Company policy: nobody falls."

They spent three days making the first ascent of the mountain, and a week hiking out to the lake, where they ate the cached food and waited. In another week the pilot finally showed up and said, "You know, I didn't think you guys would be here."

Dave teaches high school physics in Everett and Diana teaches math in Seattle. With their summers off, the couple has climbed in Alaska, Nepal, Pakistan, Peru, Russia, and of course the Northwest. Several summers ago Dave and Diana led an expedition to 8000-meter Broad Peak, in Pakistan, where two of their party

Dave Dailey

reached the summit. Diana injured her back on the trip and Dave exited base camp with her while the others went to the top. They have plans to return to Pakistan and possibly try Hidden Peak in the next several years.

Dave has an incredible memory for details and can regurgitate descent routes off Cascade peaks from twenty years ago. Although Dave is serious about climbing, he knows where to draw the line. If he hasn't talked to a friend in a long time he will say, "Let's get together and belch, fart, and tell lies." He follows it up with a loud schoolboy laugh.

Upon first meeting **DAN DAVIS** in 1984 I was unsure how to get the discussion started. He was extremely quiet, and when I asked him a question a great deal of time expired before he answered me. "Did I say something wrong? Does he want me to talk at all?" were thoughts I had. Dan weighed my comments carefully and then slowly made a reply. Finally he asked me if I wanted a beer, and this helped immensely, for I felt it would loosen his tongue. Mostly it helped to put me at ease, for our conversation proceeded at exactly the same pace.

Dan Davis

Davis was very involved in first ascents in the 1950s and 60s in the Cascades and Canada, and put up the North Face of Mount Robson with Pat Callis in 1963. My primary mission that night was to ask him if I could make a photocopy of a black and white print of Forbidden Peak he displayed with two other prints inside a tall glass frame. The photo had been taken by Steve Marts, who had lost the negative. There was a very long pause during which I swallowed my remaining beer in a single gulp and awaited his answer. "You're not the first person who has asked to copy this print," he said. I responded, "How about if I make you a 4x5 copy negative and an additional print so you don't have to take this frame apart ever again?" This seemed to satisfy him and we spent the remaining time talking about photography, which he's greatly interested in, and cycling, of late his preferred activity to climbing.

Subsequent meetings with the lean and fit-looking Davis have gone better, with a greater exchange of information in a shorter period of time. One has the feeling Dan could step right back into hard alpine climbing and pursue it at his former level with ease.

▲▲▲

When Todd Skinner came to Index Town Wall and free-climbed City Park he remarked that it was perhaps the hardest climb in Washington State. Local climber Charlie Hampson pointed at Mount Index and said, "Forget it, buddy. The hardest climb is over there across the road." Climbers in the Northwest still hold the alpine routes in high esteem, especially when they are the ones establishing the climbs.

Pete Doorish. (Photo by Bryan Burdo)

PETE DOORISH climbed the twenty-three-pitch North Norwegian Buttress on Mount Index in 1985 with Hampson and Dale Farnham, adding it to his long list of first ascents in the range. Doorish is a big quiet guy, in his early fifties, who is still a very active climber. As a social worker, he is able to get sizable chunks of time off for mountain trips. Several summers ago he put up a hard route alone on the North Face of Mount Baring.

I spoke with him at his home in Seattle and my many questions included queries about his trips to Bear Mountain. I was impressed to learn that he had made five successful climbs of the peak, four of which were new routes. Pete is clearly an admirer of mountains, and often, when he takes a trip to a foreign country, he simply carries a light pack and hikes around, instead of being obsessed with getting up a summit.

Throughout the conversation we talked about solo climbing and the peculiar mind set it puts one in. He asked if I still climbed and I said, "I like to think so." But it was definitely a discussion that left me humbled when I totted up Pete's many fine ascents.

▲▲▲

SUE HARRINGTON was my companion in marriage for eight years. A New York native, she grew up in Buffalo and went to college in Rochester where she studied nursing. The nearby Niagara escarpment provided Sue and a few friends the environment to learn rock climbing, and the White Mountains offered winter camping opportunities. When she moved to Oregon in 1979 mountaineering became a more important part of her life.

She climbed the West Buttress of Mount McKinley with several Portland climbers in 1982 and scaled Orizaba, in Mexico, with Rachel Cox in 1985. The two women chose a more challenging route up the peak, to the awe of locals they encountered on the summit. Once she relocated in Seattle, workouts on "Husky Peak" (the practice rock on the UW campus) honed her rock climbing even more, and the Cascades sharpened her snow and ice skills.

Sue Harrington

In addition to the routes in this book that Sue joined me on, she has maintained a solid climbing partnership with several competent women climbers including Cathy Cosley, Rachel Cox, Julie Hirsch, Deb Martin, and Kathy Zaiser. The Entiat Icefall on Mount Maude, the North Face of Burgundy Spire, the North Ridge of Mount Sir Donald, the Northeast Buttress of Mount Goode, and th e complete North Ridge of Mount Stuart are some of the climbs she has done with other women. She has remarried and has become an avid, quite skilled, sport climber.

A native of Ohio, Alabama, and New York **BOB KANDIKO** moved to the Northwest in 1976 after attending Cornell. He and a friend got out a road atlas and noticed that Vancouver, B.C. was flanked by mountains and glaciers—and they had never seen a glacier. He applied to graduate school at the University of British Columbia where he eventually earned a Masters degree in forestry. Upon arriving at UBC, Bob immediately joined the British Columbia Mountaineering Club and began to learn climbing skills on the nearby peaks.

Bob thinks of himself as one who pursues mountaineering for its scenic value, rather than technical challenges, and is modest about his accomplishments. He did many excellent trips with mountaineering clubs, including the third ascent of the Caternary Ridge of Mount Logan in 1979, the first ascent of the North Face of Blackfriar Peak in B.C. the same year, and he climbed a

Bob Kandiko

new ice route up the North Face of Mount Munday, near Waddington, with Joe Catellani in 1981. Also, in 1981 he climbed the Cassin Ridge with Mike Helms where, from the top of the route he downclimbed the ridge in a foodless and stormy ten-day epic, accompanying an exhausted climber from another party.

Since a trip to Peru in 1984, he and his wife Karen Neubauer have used their summers off from teaching marine science and special education to climb in the Wind River Range, Tetons, and North Cascades and have paddled much of the British Columbia and Alaska coast in sea kayaks. The sheer volume of peaks they have climbed is staggering, and when asked about an approach into a specific mountain Bob can list several, including how some went in winter.

Bob's icy wit can cut right through the thickest egos and remind people who take climbing too seriously to lighten up. In my case he scrutinized one of my new routes, which I wanted to include in this book, and asked me if the climb was truly a classic, or did I just want another route to my credit? The words he chooses in the role of critic are analytical, and are always followed by a hearty laugh.

SHARI KEARNEY and I were married for five years, during which time we climbed many fine routes in Yosemite, Alaska, the Sierra and the Cascades. We made ascents of El Capitan, Half Dome, put up a new route on Mount Hunter, and climbed throughout the western states; eight of those climbs are described in this book.

In almost every adventure we alternated leads on rock, snow and ice. In 1979, when we received a brochure in the mail asking us to contribute money to an all-woman Dhaulagiri expedition to Nepal, I remarked that she was more experienced than the climbing team members listed in the brochure. I said, *"You should be on this expedition."*

Shari went to Nepal in 1980, and although she did not make the summit of Dhaulagiri, participated in four more expeditions to Ama Dablam, Mount Everest, Annapurna, and Pumori. She led two of the trips and reached the summits of Ama Dablam and Pumori. Shari made it to 27,500 feet on the West Ridge of Everest in 1983 without oxygen.

She began working for National Outdoor Leadership School in 1981 and moved to Lander, Wyoming, that year. She now lives just outside of Lander on twenty acres where she owns three horses. When she's not resupplying NOLS basecamps in the Wind River Mountains, she likes to fly fish and sea kayak.

Shari Kearney

▲▲

PETER KELEMEN would like to return to the Northwest, where he first learned mountaineering in the Cascades. Currently, as a geologist at Woods Hole Oceanographic Institution Peter nurtures his career and pays the bills. "Do I have to abandon my job to move back to Seattle or can I get work at the University of Washington?" he asks.

Originally from Armington, Delaware, Peter read all the expedition books in the public library and wanted to move west and climb mountains. In 1972 he did his first roped climbing while working with the Student Conservation Association trail crew in the North Cascades. In the summer of 1974 he and a friend loaded an Oldsmobile up with food and came out to climb in the Cascades for eight weeks. They did several of the high traverses and many obscure summits, where they seldom saw other climbers.

He began college at Dartmouth in 1974 and was frustrated to find the climbing school full. Peter sat on the instructor's steps late on a Sunday night waiting for him to return from the weekend in order to wrangle his way into the class. The instructor showed up and asked Peter, "You know how to tie a figure eight right? You know how to tie a bowline?" "Yes," Peter replied. "You're an instructor!" came the response.

In 1976 and '77 Peter made two trips to Peru, picking off new routes on Quitaraju and Artesonraju with his Dartmouth mates. However, he didn't

Peter Keleman

make it up a big unclimbed route on Santa Cruz and for a time afterward became despondent about mountaineering. He concentrated on short rock and ice climbs in New England while finishing up his geology degree.

He moved to Seattle in 1981, where he began graduate studies at the UW and undertook geological field mapping in the North Cascades (probably just a disguise for a climbing trip). Peter met Rachel Cox in 1983 and together they concentrated on mountaineering for the next couple of years. In 1985 the pair climbed the Northeast Buttress of Slesse and in 1986 put up the sought-after twenty-eight-pitch Direct North Buttress of East McMillan Spire. Rachel and Peter were married in 1987 and Peter got his doctorate in geology the same year. Since then the two have climbed in India and the Alps, and are always eager to visit the Northwest for short climbing trips with old friends.

▲▲

STEVE MARTS left Kansas with his parents at the age of eighteen and came to the Northwest. He had always wanted to climb mountains, and he made an ascent of The Brothers with his older cousin. From this beginning he took up skiing, began practice climbing on rock, and met several older climbers including Sean Rice, Bob Swanson, and Eric Bjornstad. There were many fine unclimbed routes in the Cascades in 1960 and Marts had an active role in pioneering these for more than a decade, until he focused on expedition cinematography.

Steve Marts. (Photo by Alex Bertulis)

During an interview in his home his teenage daughter was having a birthday party and between the party-goers' squeals of laughter I learned about Steve's mountain adventures. Many of his first ascents were done at Washington Pass where, with other partners, he climbed a half-dozen grade IV and V routes. Shooting movies is Marts' living, and during my questions about the Cascades he queried me about filming in Patagonia. We exchanged ideas on photography. Later, over the phone, I gave him the necessary information for him to find his way around in Chile and Argentina.

▲▲

When black clouds began boiling over the top of Sentinel Rock in Yosemite Valley, **Don McPherson** and Jim Bridwell continued up to the base of the rock. "We started up the West Face of Sentinel together and it rained," McPherson recounts. "Well, we're used to rain up here [in the Northwest] and we went down and he [Bridwell] didn't want to go back, but he said I could use his ropes. So I went up with this Englishman [Mike Costerlitz]. I knew we were going to have a hanging bivouac up there, but he didn't realize we were going to be in hammocks. He was surprised, wondering where the ledges were, when I dug out an extra hammock and handed it to him."

McPherson racked up a lot of experience on Yosemite walls while going to college in southern California. Although many climbers of that era favored the Kronhofer gray suede rock

Don McPherson. (Photo by Alex Bertulis)

shoe, McPherson liked his Italian-made Cortinas. It would be another twenty years before sticky rubber showed up, and climbers had to fit the shoes real tight for good performance. McPherson felt he was pretty fast on aid until he and Jim Madsen were in the Bugaboos one summer and discovered someone faster. Says McPherson, "Jim and I watched Steve Roper cleaning a [aid] pitch on the East Face of Snowpatch Spire. Shit! Did that open our eyes on how to clean a pitch. He clipped a carabiner into the pin and then bam, bam, bam, and ping!"

If McPherson could label anyone as his mentor it would be Madsen. The 220-pound climber impressed everyone with his incredible drive and motivation. But it was more than that. As Don tells it, "He also got us into a spiritual realm; he would get high through the mountains and spirituality." In 1969, while checking on a couple of overdue climbers on El Cap, Madsen rappelled off the end of his rope one pitch below the top. No one knows exactly what happened. "When Jim Madsen fell off El Cap I quit climbing for fifteen years," said McPherson during my interview. His eyes misted over and he took a long silent pause to wipe off his glasses. McPherson moved to Canada that same year. "I had to get away from the culture to where there was nothing around me. I've always kind of pushed the climbing. Seven of my buddies had died by this time. I was probably coming up on the list pretty soon."

Lowell Skoog. (Photo by Cliff Leight)

I finally met **LOWELL SKOOG** in February of 1995 when, with his brother Carl, we carried overnight gear and skis up to Church Mountain just north of Mount Baker. All the Skoogs are hot skiers, and brother Gordy was a nationally-ranked freestyle skier in the early 1970s, but didn't want to embrace the ski bum, on-the-road lifestyle. Love of snow, and the graceful way of traveling on it, was passed down from their father Dick Skoog. The senior Skoog grew up in Saint Paul, Minnesota, and with his friends became aeronautical engineers, after being inspired by Charles Lindbergh's flight across the Atlantic. He migrated to the west coast and got a job at Boeing and continued to pursue downhill skiing and ski jumping.

As Lowell tells it, "Our father got us into skiing when we were pretty young. I started when I was maybe six, and I was kinda late for our family. We gradually got into climbing on our own later, and I think Gordy was the first to get involved. He took a climbing course at the UW." Lowell, especially, was influenced by Harvey Manning's ethic wherein, "One makes a respectful entry to the North Cascades . . . involving a full day of valley hiking before you even get to timberline. Timberline—that's the icing and you gotta experience the lowlands." The brothers did their share of valley entries to the peaks and put up a significant number of new alpine routes in the range. When

I think of how hard it is for me to get an alpine start in the morning with coffee, I ponder how the Skoogs did all these trips without caffeine. But they continue to do it—and with style.

JEFF THOMAS began climbing at the age of sixteen in the Alps. His family was living in Europe and Jeff enrolled in the Meiriegen climbing school. The following summer Jeff was back and got more training in Leysin, Switzerland, where he met Don Whillans. Once back in New York he further improved his rock climbing skills in the Gunks, which shaped his style of climbing. Jeff moved to Oregon in 1970 to attend college, and undertook the first of many expeditions to Alaska, where he forged new routes on Mount Hunter, the Kichatna Spires, and Mount Huntington.

Jeff Thomas

I first met Jeff in the mid 1970s and began doing routes with him. After a spell of climbing in Yosemite in 1976, Jeff began methodically eliminating the unclimbed lines at Smith Rock and putting up the hardest routes at that time. Our trips into the Cascades have been the greatest adventures, seeking out unclimbed routes in the shortest possible time. Every summer I try to lure him up my way for a mountain climb, but often I go south to Oregon and get in some cragging instead.

Jeff is thorough when it comes to climbing or writing and has put up nearly a hundred first ascents or first free ascents on Oregon rock and is the author of three guidebooks to Smith Rock and Oregon. He doesn't like to talk of his accomplishments, since his climbing isn't as frequent, presently. The fact is, until lately, when I have gone climbing with him I can hardly keep up.

1 MOUNT BARDEAN
The Tuning Fork

VIEWED FROM MOUNT BAKER, THE LOW ROCK RIDGES of the Chehalis Range belie the great northern walls concealed there. Only from the indigenous northerly peaks such as Mount Grainger are the impressive rock buttresses, arêtes, and beetling overhangs revealed. Mount Bardean's Tuning Fork (named for its similarity to the instrument), with excellent climbing, is one such fine feature in this group of mountains.

Vancouver B.C. resident Don Serl explored the area extensively in the late 1970s and 1980s. From the summits of Mount Clarke and Viennese Peak he picked out the fine unclimbed lines of Mount Bardean's north side. According to fellow climber Mike Down, a plot was hatched in a pub one night to show rival Calgary climbers what great climbing the B.C. Coast Range boasted. The pub con-

Elzinga gracefully powered his way up a wide crack with little pro, shattering the coast climbers beliefs that Rockies climbers couldn't handle granite.

versation went, "Those Calgary climbers think they're so hot, throwing their names and exploits around as if they were the only real climbers in the country. If they only knew what we've got down this way!" "Yeah! They can keep their slimy limestone and crumbling mountains all to themselves. We've got the real stuff—granite!"

Down and Serl invited Calgary climber Jim Elzinga as their granite guinea pig, thinking the limestone expert could not possibly master the intricacies of climbing on "good" rock. The trio set off up the brushy approach on a July weekend in 1980 after barely outfitting themselves with alpine gear, since they had planned on only lowland rock climbing. A half day later they were parked on a boulder below the chosen route and consulting Serl on what gear to take up. "Free climbing all the way," was Serl's credo. He claimed that Chehalis rock is studded with rough holds and edges that line the profuse shallow cracks and small corners typical of the area.

Opposite: *The Tuning Fork Route on Mount Bardean*

With that information the climbers left behind aiders, Jumars, extra pins, and any bivy gear. Even so, high cirrus clouds had arrived in the morning, and, as with all Northwest climbs, they added that element of anxiety to the climbing. For a group of three, they moved quickly and allowed one person to lead three pitches consecutively before turning the sharp end over to another. Elzinga gracefully powered his way up a wide crack with little pro, shattering the coast climbers beliefs that Rockies climbers couldn't handle granite.

Five pitches up, the climbers were engulfed in a thick mist that, as they described it, ". . . cut us off from the outside world in a muffling envelope of wet gray rock and wet gray air, its bleakness broken only by the snaking luminescence of our 'radioactive rope.'" With visibility down to a couple hundred feet, Serl wove his way through a series of improbable-looking small overhangs to where the route became straightforward again.

As the light faded, the climbing became wet and steep just below the summit. Elzinga led through some loose blocks to where it was obvious the three climbers would have to bivy without the luxury of any spare clothing or sacs. "Mercifully, the impending monsoon held off during a fitful night crammed on a tight ledge," he later related. "But with first light the murky heavens tore loose with a downpour. Now conditions were closer to true Coast climbing form. We were drenched even before beginning the long descent down Bardean's west flank."

Once back at the route's base, the climbers retrieved their bivy gear and continued the descent and brushwhack out. Serl and Down chose a different line out, following the creek bed, while Elzinga continued on the route the group had initially used. The B.C. pair were further deflated to find that Elzinga reached the car an hour ahead of them. So much for showing up their Interior rivals!

In September of 1995 Kathy Zaiser and I did two climbs in the Chehalis: one a grunge fest on the north side of Viennese and the other The Tuning Fork. With prior knowledge of the approach we gained from a soggy hike in 1992, we made the base of the climb, with light to spare, on the first day. With excellent first ascent information, we chose to climb with a single 200-foot 9-mm rope, a standard rack, one hammer, a few pins, and no ice axes or boots.

The climbing was slightly chossy down low, but as we gained elevation the plants dwindled. Climbing with Kathy is always a joy, since she has such a solid background in crack climbing from her years exploring the American desert. Never one to hesitate, she simply looks upward, slots in some gear, and goes. As a small team we climbed fast and didn't linger at the shady belay stances chilled by autumn air.

Because of alternating leads, I wound up with the hardest crack pitches and found myself breathing hard at the start of pitch eleven. Several small cams in a row alleviated my nervousness, not wanting to splat on the belay ledge. Higher, I popped into the sun and really began to appreciate the magnificent surroundings of the Coast Range with its bristling peaks, glacier-carved

Kathy Zaiser high on the Tuning Fork

U-shaped valleys, and verdant ridges. As beautiful as mountains are, companionship is even better. Bardean was the last alpine climb I did with Kathy, since our climbing paths have not crossed again.

Mount Bardean: The Tuning Fork

First ascent: Mike Down, Jim Elzinga, and Don Serl; July 1980
Difficulty: Grade IV, 5.10-
Equipment: Standard rack up to a 4-inch cam
Access: From the town of Mission, B.C. take Highway 7 20.8 miles to the Hemlock Valley turnoff. Drive 0.2 miles, then turn left onto the Chehalis Main Line logging road. This road may be closed during times of high fire danger; check with the logging company (604-796-2757). The road parallels Chehalis Lake. At 21.4 miles from the beginning of the gravel road keep left; do not cross the river. At 24.3 miles cross the bridge over the creek flowing out of Statlu Lake and park. An old overgrown road goes up the north side of the creek for 0.3 mile. You can drive about another 0.2 mile of this road if your car has clearance. From there,

a trail leads to Statlu Lake and around its north shore. At the west end of the lake brushwhack along the south side of the creek flowing into the lake from the west. Eventually, you can gain rockslides and talus, then traverse to a fresh rock gully coming down from Bardean's northeast ridge. Zigzag up through brushy ledges on the west edge of the gully to gain a large right-trending brushy ramp. Follow this ramp up and right to slabs leading to the base of The Tuning Fork.

Kathy Zaiser on Pitch 11 of the Tuning Fork

Route: **[1]** From the left side of the buttress toe, climb cracks on the light wall (5.8) to a belay stance. **[2]** Climb up and right across the face (5.5) to gain the buttress crest. **[3]** Scramble up for 600 feet on the crest past small trees; the last bit is up cracks and small pillars (5.7) to a ledge. The Tuning Fork route goes up and left, Flavelle-Beckham route up and right. **[4]** Traverse left and up for 75 feet to gain cracks just left of long, left-facing corners (5.7). Follow these crack systems for four pitches **[5]** through **[8]**, ranging from (5.8–5.9). **[9]** Climb thin cracks on a short steep wall (5.10-) to regain the buttress crest. **[10]** Climb a crack on the crest, traverse right to another crack (5.9) and follow it to a ledge at the base of a vertical right-facing corner. **[11]** Jam and stem a steep corner (5.10-) to a ledge at the base of a chimney. **[12]** Climb the chimney and then scramble up and right to the summit. The climb is possible in twelve pitches with a 200-foot rope (60m).

Descent: Downclimb Bardean's west side to the Bardean-Ratney col. Climb the east side of Ratney, continue over the summit, and downclimb and rappel the North Ridge. Traverse the Stave-Statlu divide northward until it's possible to rappel down to the glacier and slabs leading back to Bardean and the base of The Tuning Fork.

Map: CFM: Chehalis North 1:50,000
Reference: *CHGSWBC* and *CAJ 1981*

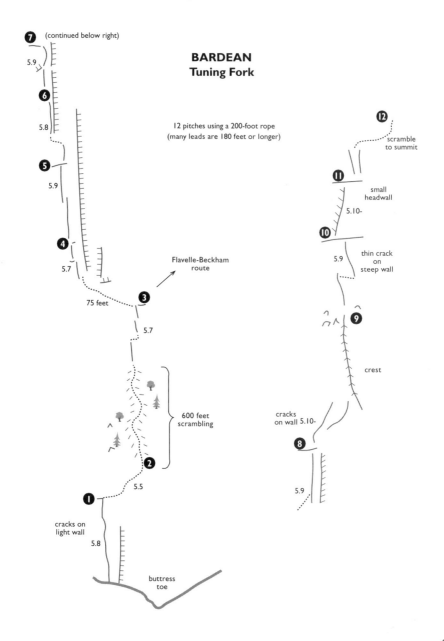

BARDEAN
Tuning Fork

12 pitches using a 200-foot rope
(many leads are 180 feet or longer)

Flavelle-Beckham route

scramble to summit

small headwall

5.10-

thin crack on steep wall

crest

cracks on wall 5.10-

600 feet scrambling

cracks on light wall

buttress toe

2 MOUNT GRAINGER
J Crack

SIXTY MILES NORTHEAST OF VANCOUVER, B.C., the compact Chehalis Range of granitic peaks boast excellent alpine rock climbs. While the recent extension of logging roads has improved access to the peaks, the subsequent cutting has removed the adjacent forests. Although clearcuts are commonplace on the brushy approaches, alpine solitude is still several hours from the car.

"Every branch of slide alder or tangle of berry bush was sworn to impede my progress, but Fred glided through effortlessly."

John Booth, Walter Cadillac, Art Dellow, Tom Fallowfield, and Les Harrison made the first ascent of 7207-foot Mount Grainger in August of 1942. Following a four-day approach from Harrison Lake, the climbers ascended the East Ridge and northeast flank of the peak.

No new route activity occurred until 1977, when the Southeast Gully and South Ridge were put up. Six more routes were established between 1982 and 1985, including J Crack. Fred Beckey arrived on the scene in August of '85 with James Martin and Jim Nelson in tow. Beckey realized Canadians (with Don Serl driving them) had climbed three new routes on the peak that year and he carefully threaded a new path up, across, and between the existing lines.

According to Martin, the approach was still fairly brushy when they hiked to the peak. "Every branch of slide alder or tangle of berry bush was sworn to impede my progress, but Fred glided through effortlessly," he related. Once at the route's base, Beckey was unsure what line he had attempted years before when stormed off. Finally, Nelson picked a classic crack and corner pitch and started up, reached a good ledge, and brought the others to his stance.

Higher, the buttress was seamed with many good cracks, but Beckey felt they might have already been climbed. He persuaded Nelson (in the lead)

Opposite: *Mount Grainger from the south, showing the J Crack Route*

to traverse rightward onto new ground. In several more pitches of quality climbing the three climbers made the summit, where Beckey shared his intimate knowledge of the surrounding peaks.

⎯⎯⎯⎯⎯⎯⎯⎯ ⛰ ⎯⎯⎯⎯⎯⎯⎯⎯

After hearing rumors about the Chehalis since arriving in Bellingham two decades earlier, I made an exploratory trip in 1992 with Sue Harrington. A friend gave us a crude topo and recommended J Crack as a good climb. We

loaded the Subaru wagon on a clear Saturday morning in June and headed north. In a little over two hours we reached the end of a thirty-mile dirt road, beat the dust off our packs, and started hiking through salmonberry bushes.

From a camp at the head of Eagle Creek, we climbed smooth slabs and a long snowy talus slope to the base of Grainger's south face. A chilly wind numbed our hands as we jammed and laidback perfect cracks several pitches up the climb. Sue asked me how hard the next pitch was, as it was her lead. "I don't know if we're even on the right route!" I replied. Actually, I suspected she was about to lead the crux pitch, but if I'd told her so she might have backed off. After a little complaining about scarce pro, Sue reached the belay and brought me up. "I think you just led the hardest pitch," I told her. A huge smile filled her face at the realization of this news.

We reached the summit in several more leads of reasonable climbing up flakes and cracks. Beyond snow-mantled ridges to the south rose the great north faces of Mount Clarke and Viennese

The author halfway up J Crack. (Photo by Sue Harrington)

Peak. We would have to allocate several future weekends for those peaks, now that we had "discovered" this nearby playground.

Mount Grainger: J Crack

First ascent: Fred Beckey, James Martin, Jim Nelson; August 1985
Difficulty: Grade III, 5.10-
Equipment: Standard rack up to a 4-inch cam
Access: Approach as for Mount Bardean, described previously, and at 26.8 miles go left and uphill just before the road drops and crosses Eagle Creek. Follow the road on the west side of the creek for 1.8 miles, making a right at 0.7, a left at 1.2, and another right at 1.8 miles, where a spur road ends. A path (possibly flagged) begins in brush and goes through salmonberry and into a patch of old growth timber. When the trail exits the forest, it climbs left, then up talus to just below cliffs. The trail contours through slide alder and talus, drops 200 feet, then climbs back up into forest. Once in the upper valley, huckleberry, swampy meadows, and talus lead to the cirque. From talus beneath a cliff band climb a slabby gully to talus below Grainger. (The gully is the third one on the right, adjacent a pinnacle and large snag). From this gully, ascend slabs directly up from the notch behind the pinnacle to gain talus leading to the base of the South Face.
Route: [1] Begin climbing in shallow grooves and a hand crack leading to a small roof. Undercling this roof left (5.9) and lieback up to a belay stance. **[2]** Climb cracks and a corner for 60 feet (5.9), then exit right onto a ledge. Climb behind a large flake, then go 30 feet higher to a ledge. **[3]** Diagonal right and up to gain an arête. (5.8). **[4]** Climb cracks and flakes on this arête (5.9). **[5]** Continue up the arête for 60 feet to a sloping ledge below a short overhanging wall (last move 5.10-). **[6]** Climb a short, steep crack and a corner above, then continue with easier climbing to a large ledge. **[7]** through **[8]** Scramble pitches up a ridge to the summit.
Descent: Downclimb and rappel the south ridge, then traverse back to the base of the south face.
Map: CFM: Chehalis North 1:50,000
Reference: *CHGSWBC*

3 YAK PEAK
Yak Crack

LIKE SOMETHING TRANSPLANTED FROM YOSEMITE'S Tuolomne Meadows, the 6600 foot top of Yak Peak is the culmination of classic exfoliation slabs so characteristic of granitic domes. Yak is part of the Anderson River Group, and the Needle Peak Pluton is responsible for its appearance. A plum such as this, so close to the highway, is hard to pass up. One can only imagine what the alpine area was like before the opening of the Coquihalla Highway in the mid 1980s.

Although some climbing activity occurred on Yak Peak and the adjacent summits of Guanaco, Vicuna, Alpaca, and Zoa in the 1960s and '70s, things livened up with highway access. (Prior to the paved highway you could reach the peaks via the gravel Coquihalla River pipeline road.) The East Face was climbed in 1979 by Roman Babicki and Alfred Meninga, the West Ridge in 1980 by Scott and Keith Flavelle, and a slab route on the southwest side in 1982 by Ross and Margaret Wyborn and Peter de Visser. Then, in 1985, Jack Bennetto was working for the highway department and living in a shed near the pass. He realized other climbers would soon discover the south face, so he phoned Rick Cox and told him to get up there fast.

The climbing, although not super hard, held their attention, especially since a leader fall would have been a long one.

Bennetto and Cox both agreed on the line to do: an obvious and striking diagonal crack system that cleaved the white granite from above a hand-shaped feature of rock. They felt the problem might be the smooth rock and the giant exfoliation slabs, some of which appeared crackless. Cox described their dilemma right at the start. "For the next few hundred feet it looked like a walk," he said. "But we had not anticipated the eons of polishing that had occurred because of the way the slope of the rock had drained all moisture into the corner. The corner was compact, pro was scant, and the belays were not the best."

Opposite: *The Yak Crack Route on the South Face of Yak Peak*　　　• 49

Joe DeMarsh leads the crux on Yak Crack

The climbers looked upward at the wide slot behind the hand-shaped flake. "Above us was an unprotectable chimney that was over half-a-rope in length," Cox relates. "As with so many things in life, the thought of it was worse than actually doing it." He was able to lieback the big flake more easily than chimneying inside, and on later ascents climbers discovered a perfect hand crack going straight up the outside of the feature. From the top of the "hand" the pair followed a diagonal crack and seam that sometimes simply vanished as though an invisible eraser had been at work.

On that August day Bennetto and Cox found an occasional pin they drove under the big slabs to be the only protection for some distance. The climbing, although not super hard, held their attention, especially since a leader fall would have been a long one. The pair were aiming for a big dihedral near the top of the peak, but after groveling up a rotten groove they had to stop beneath a crescent-shaped overhang without a clear idea of where to go next.

Bennetto led up a sketchy corner to get a view of the route above. As on so many climbs where the line isn't obvious, he was pestered by questions from the belayer, who was experiencing his own anxiety. "Well, can you see over the lip?" Cox queried. "Yeah, it's a featureless sea of rock," was the reply. Not the greatest news anyone wants to hear nine pitches up a smooth granite wall. Cox felt there had to be a way of reaching the sought-after corner. "Not real sure where we were, but the big D wasn't above us," Cox said. "It was not on the left, so that meant it was probably somewhere to the right. There was a shoulder of rock that was just beside the belay and I set off for a look, frictioning around this shoulder. Bingo!

Above and to the right, about a rope length away, I could see the corner—our ticket outathere!"

As the shadows began to lengthen, the climbers increased their speed in a rush to avoid getting benighted. Cox was leading the last pitch and got a cam stuck in the crack, and when Bennetto reached it he was determined not to leave it. "We usually split the cost of gear," Cox relates, "but I said, forget this one, Jack. It's on me. Did it help? Forty-five minutes later it was really starting to get dim and he finally gave up, much to my relief. We stumbled to the top, shook hands, and started down." After one day off exploring, the pair put up another new route on Yak Peak, which they named the Porcelain Chicken—some eight pitches with big cracks.

My first experience with Yak Crack came in 1992, when, with Mark Price (the youth), we drove to the pass the night before, slept on the ground, and awoke to pouring rain. The grooves and corners of Yak Peak were soon sprouting waterfalls and streams everywhere. It reminded me of being washed off the Mammoth Terraces of El Cap in 1974. Back then my partner and I had to do ten or twelve rappels with our drenched haul bag; this time we had only to drive home and make popcorn.

Five years later I was back at Yak with Joe DeMarsh and Deb Martin from my home town. Without a cloud in the sky the only obstacle seemed to be mosquitoes, and of course completing the climb. We car-camped in a big gravel parking lot near the peak, popped open cold beers and downed prepared sandwiches for supper. Several Bellinghamsters had already climbed the route and their gear beta was invaluable. Sorting the night before, we added triples of the ¾ to 1-inch small cams to our rack. Our friends claimed these would be useful in protecting the undersides of the giant exfoliation slabs. They were right.

With a fine morning for climbing we were soon scrambling up smooth granite to a rope-up point below the hand crack on the hand-shaped flake. A few mosquitoes attempted to follow us, but were discouraged by our speed and a slight breeze. The setting on Yak Peak was fabulous, with rocky domes punctuating the verdant horizon, and the noise of weekday traffic minimal. It didn't seem possible that we were only a two-hour drive from home. These would have been hard-won views for explorers and climbers venturing in before any road existed. It almost seemed like cheating to not be wading icy creeks, swatting mosquitoes, parting the brush, and grimacing under shoulder-rending loads.

We swapped leads up the soaring ramps. Although I was climbing well, I did not feel as free as the swallows that dipped in and out of the wall. My mind and heart still held a great weight of loss; it had been barely two months since my friend Steve Mascioli was killed by a huge falling cornice on Mount Hunter, in Alaska. How fine it would have been were he by my side at that moment, sorting gear with his infectious laugh and smile. The only thing that seemed to replace the hollowness (if only momentarily) was the pure joy of climbing on perfect rock with great friends.

The shadow passed, as did the fleecy clouds overhead, on that warm August day. Joe traversed around the corner and disappeared from view up a vertical smooth rib. A few little grunts and gasps were the only indication he was experiencing difficult climbing. Deb and I, in turn, struggled up the short pillar and scrambled onto a ledge where Joe belayed. Above rose a giant left-facing corner, the left side of which appeared polished from storm runoff.

For most of the climb I had been absorbed in the climbing, attentive of the connecting rope that maintained our safety, or enjoying the view. I allowed those other thoughts and feelings to infiltrate only at belays, when not moving. Now, high in the steep corner, I didn't seem to be climbing well. The moves didn't feel very hard, but I wanted the pro right by my waist, or fumbled and fumed because I lacked the right piece. Once at the top, I couldn't put my finger on the cause of my behavior until another swallow took one last dive at the rock.

It might be quite a long while before (if ever) I could be outdoors without thinking about Steve. I was very glad to have friends like Deb and Joe who were patient and caring. The presence of life and the immediate absence of it is often incomprehensible. Buddhism, like other religions, sometimes helps us to cope and appreciate our time on this planet, and I recently read a statement that seemed appropriate: "You have to go through the darkness to truly know the light."

Yak Peak: Yak Crack

First ascent: Jack Bennetto and Rick Cox; August 1985
Difficulty: Grade IV, 5.10-
Equipment: A standard rack up to 3½-inch with extras in the ¾ to 1-inch

small cams. Although pins were used on the first ascent, there is no advantage in having any along. A 200-foot rope may be useful in reaching better anchors.

Access: From the town of Sumas, Washington, drive B.C. Highway 1 for 48 miles to Hope. At Hope take Highway 5 (the Coquihalla Highway)

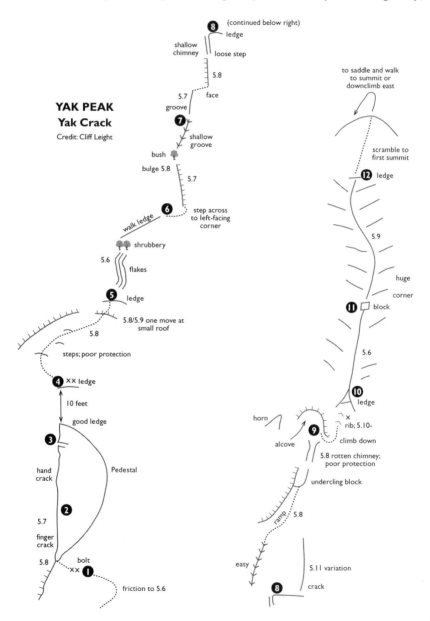

YAK PEAK
Yak Crack
Credit: Cliff Leight

and follow it for 25.5 miles to the Boston Bar Summit. Because the highway is divided, you will need to drive another 2.5 miles and take the Falls Lake Road exit (last exit before the toll gate), then drive back west and park on the right (north) side of the highway below Yak Peak. From directly below the right side of the peak's south face, hike through a swampy forest and up a timbered strip left of an avalanche path (possibly flagged). Continue up to a huge concave ledge and then scramble left and up to gain the route.

Route: The object is to reach the large hand-shaped flake low on the route. **[1]** Climb slabs leftward (5.6) to a bolt belay below the big flake. **[2]** Climb up and onto the outside of the big flake (5.8) to gain the hand crack on the face. **[3]** Continue up the hand crack (5.7) to nearly the top of the flake and belay. **[4]** Climb past the top of the flake and friction up to a ledge and belay bolts. **[5]** Now, ascend the line of weakness on the face (indistinct at first) by climbing up and left and then back right (5.8), surmounting several exfoliation flakes. Pass a small roof (5.9) and continue up to a ledge. **[6]** Ascend flakes (5.6) to a low-angle ledge and scramble up it rightward. Belay where the face steepens. **[7]** Step across to reach a left-facing corner (5.7) and climb up over several bulges (5.8) and then up a groove to a belay. **[8]** Continue up this groove (5.7), face climb right and then climb a right-facing corner (5.8) to a shallow chimney. Belay on a ledge at the top. **[9]** Continue up a corner and work right to reach a slab (5.8) beneath a right-facing and leaning corner. Climb this slab rightward to a block. From the block, climb a rotten shallow chimney (5.8) at the start (not a squeeze) with no pro, to a belay on a ledge. **[10]** From beneath a crescent-shaped overhang, climb down a bit and step out right and climb up a vertical rib (5.10-) with one bolt. Continue on a short way to a ledge and belay. (Belaying any higher creates too much rope drag). **[11]** Climb up the giant left-facing corner (5.6) and belay at a block. **[12]** Continue up the big corner (5.9) and eventually belay on a ledge. Scramble to the top.

Descent: From the summit scramble and walk east and down into meadows. Continue down near the base of slabs, then head eastward (climber's left) and down brushy gullies until it's possible to work back right below the start of the route.

Maps: CFM: Spuzzum 92 H/11

Reference: *CAG 3: Rainy Pass to Fraser River*

4 SLESSE MOUNTAIN
Northeast Buttress

ON A CLEAR DAY IT'S GREAT FUN IDENTIFYING CASCADE SUMMITS. A newcomer to the range will have a lot of questions. During my mini-lecture I pause as our eyes sweep toward Canada. Inevitably my climbing partner will gasp and say, "What peak is that?" "That is Slesse Mountain" will be my reply.

Far to the north, the 7800-foot dark tooth of Slesse stands alone. Our discussion takes the obvious turn—my mate desperately wants to climb the mountain. The striking appearance of our Northwest peaks has often been the sole reason climbers have sought them out, hence Slesse's magnetism is difficult to resist.

Slesse was guarded by brush-choked valleys, the contents of which often included the spiny devil's club and iron mesh-like vine maples.

Slesse was first climbed on August 10, 1927 by Stan Henderson, Mills Winram, and Fred Parkes, who blazed a route up a couloir, ledges, and a chimney on the Southwest Face. They reached the summit that day and retraced their approach down to Slesse Creek on the west. Fred Beckey got a close look at the peak in 1950 from a plane.

In 1956 an airliner smashed into the mountain during a violent December storm. It was six months before a climbing party, led by Elfrida Pigou, discovered the wreckage and the remains of the sixty-two passengers some 200 feet below the summit. Pigou was out for a weekend climb, not really searching for the lost plane or the $80,000 in cash that Chinese businessman Kwan Song was carrying.

When Pigou led searchers, including Paddy Sherman, to the crash site, they found bits of currency and large fragments of the plane barely clinging to the east wall. The rescuers retrieved no bodies, because of the dangerous terrain. For some time the government made the mountain off limits to everyone; even touching the wreckage carried a fine of $5,000 and a year in jail.

Fred Beckey, Ed Cooper, and Don (Claunch) Gordon put up the Northwest Face route on June 21, 1959. For the most part they found the climbing enjoyable, except for the final pitch which they described as a vertical wall of loose bricks.

Slesse Mountain. The Northeast Buttress is the sunlit crest on the right

Like so many unexplored north faces in the Northwest, Slesse was guarded by brush-choked valleys, the contents of which often included the spiny devil's club and iron mesh-like vine maples. Beckey made several forays trying to reach the great northeast side until he heard of a logging operation on Middle Creek (now Nesakwatch Creek). He and Steve Marts reached the Northeast Buttress in July of 1963 and climbed halfway up the 3000-foot wall before a thick fog enveloped them at a bivouac. Uncertain how to push the route higher, they rappelled the buttress, following their pre-placed stone cairns. Beckey and Marts left two fixed ropes at the base, over the hardest pitches, with the intention of returning as soon as possible.

In August, Eric Bjornstad joined Beckey and Marts for a second attempt. On the list as an alternate climber was Seattle architect Alex Bertulis. But, getting asked on a climb that was a Fred Beckey brainchild was not so easy. When I asked Bertulis if he had been on any of the attempts he said, "No, I was sitting on the edge of my chair waiting to be invited. When Eric came in and said, 'Well, Alex, you know they didn't make it and they're gonna recruit another guy or two' I knew it wasn't Eric's decision. It was up to Fred, and you didn't dare make a suggestion unless you were asked. And I was there with my tongue hanging out, but they went off again. Of course they came back successful . . . and that's how close I came to taking part in a great climb."

Beckey, Marts, and Bjornstad did the approach on the first day and made it to within four pitches of their previous high point. On the 27th they climbed steadily up difficult terrain, finishing a tricky pitch with aid moves in the dark. Marts was stuck below in stirrups while Beckey and Bjornstad sat on a comfortable ledge and fought off "snafflehounds." Although the pair sat on their packs, the rodents chewed the shoulder straps and their boots. The next day they reached the summit in several moderate pitches, where they celebrated their achievement.

By August of 1976 the route had been climbed perhaps ten times. Jeff Thomas, Shari Kearney, and I drove my battered Dodge van to within a mile of the face. At that time the road was barely passable, but by coaxing my van we saved a lot of walking. With no idea how to reach the buttress, we plunged into the brush and clawed our way up into the basin. All about lay rotted shoes, scraps of aluminum, and a landing gear from the 1956 airplane crash.

Vegetated slabs and a gully led to the pocket glacier, which we crossed

Sue Harrington traverses the crest of the
buttress on Slesse

to gain the buttress a half-dozen pitches above the toe. At the time it seemed the logical and fastest way to go. Cracks and corners ended on a large tree-covered ledge just at dark. With minimal bivy gear, we squirmed for comfort during the cool night.

In the morning I laced up my blue Robbins shoes as Jeff coaxed his still-recovering frostbitten toes, injured earlier in Alaska, into red PA's. The route looked dry; I was dismayed when Jeff poured his malted milk mix into our only remaining quart of water. Quenching my thirst that day with brown sludge would be impossible.

The climbing went smoothly, with the leader draped in hexes, Stoppers, carabiners, and shoulder slings, while the followers carried large day-packs. Jeff led the crux pitch of potato-chip loose-flakes and poor pro, but Oregon rock had well prepared him for that terrain. Above, difficulties eased and the three of us simultaneously climbed for 500 feet until the buttress again steepened. The sun was beginning to drop as I grabbed the hardware from the leader, raced up a pitch, slammed in a couple of nuts and yelled, "Off belay!"

Shari led a hard pitch just at dark. I cleaned it, then joined her and Jeff on the summit where we parked close to a snowpatch with a tiny drip. With a parched throat, I spent an hour under the trickle spooning water into bottles. All through the night we were tormented by several large-eared, long-tailed rodents that chewed mercilessly on our gear. The critters were probably bushy-tailed woodrats *(Neotoma cinerea)* which are known to shred clothing and steal anything from a watch to a bottlecap. I tried beaning them with rocks, but Jeff told me to go to sleep. Just after sunrise I awoke to loud cursing. The ankles of Jeff's PA's were in tatters.

We descended the Northwest Face in a series of rappels and downclimbing, after nursing a bit more water from our snowpatch. A long traverse out a ridge northerly led to snowfields on the east, then steep brush back down to Nesakwatch Creek and the van.

Slesse Mountain: Northeast Buttress

First ascent: Fred Beckey, Eric Bjornstad, Steve Marts; August 26–28, 1963

Difficulty: Grade V, 5.10- (via the pocket glacier) and 5.10- from the toe

Equipment: Standard rack up to a 4-inch cam. Take additional small wires and cams if climbing the route from the toe. Ice ax and crampons.

Access: From the Trans-Canada Highway (B.C. 1), take the Sardis/Chilliwack exit and drive south to Vedder Crossing. At the Chilliwack River, turn left just before the bridge onto the Chilliwack River Road. Drive 19 miles, then turn right onto the Chilliwack South logging road. Go right in 0.3 miles, then drive another 1.5 miles. (At this writing [2002] the spur road was being reopened; it may extend to nearer Slesse in the future.) From the end of the spur road hike an old overgrown road to a deserted cabin and cross a log bridge over Nesakwatch Creek. Follow the brushy spur road up into the basin below Slesse. Once in the meadow, stay on the left side and go up a rotten gully near a waterfall. Scramble left to avoid active ice, then cross the pocket glacier (seasonal snow on smooth slabs that disappears late in the year) and gain a buttress low in an obvious book.

Route: Gaining the buttress from the pocket glacier avoids the toe and the first six to eight pitches of the route. From the toe, begin climbing in an open book, then climb left through small overhangs and mossy cracks (5.10-). Climb a slab with moss and cedars, then follow a long lead up slabs. Climb a rounded buttress in a sloping open book. Move left out of the book, then go up low-angle ground for several pitches (the shrubby part of the buttress, where you can access the route from the pocket glacier). Stay on the crest through a steeper section up cracks (5.8),

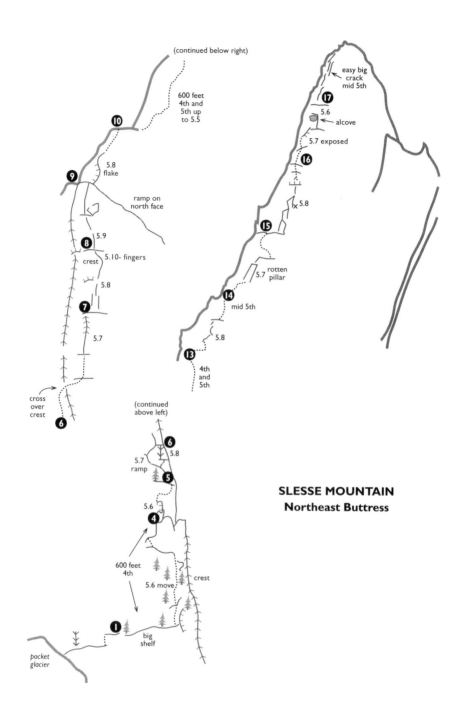

(continued below right)

600 feet
4th and
5th up
to 5.5

easy big
crack
mid 5th

17

5.6

alcove

5.7 exposed

16

x 5.8

10

5.8
flake

9

ramp on
north face

15

5.7 rotten
pillar

5.9

8

5.10- fingers

crest

5.8

14

mid 5th

7

5.7

5.8

13

4th
and
5th

cross
over
crest

6

(continued
above left)

6

5.8

5.7
ramp

5

5.6

4

SLESSE MOUNTAIN
Northeast Buttress

600 feet
4th

5.6 move

crest

1

big
shelf

pocket
glacier

then climb slightly right of the crest up thin cracks in corners (5.10-). At this point, ramps farther right can be climbed to avoid this section.

The midsection of the buttress is 500 feet long and easy climbing. The final 700 feet consist of four hard leads on steep rock. Stay on the crest to a good ledge and a leaning pillar. From a hanging belay, traverse 50 feet right (5.8), then climb grooves to the right of a pillar crest for 80 feet up to a grassy belay ledge. Then, ascend right-slanting grooves and ramps to the base of a vertical wall. Cracks lead past a bolt and through a small overhang onto a narrow belay ledge. An easier pitch leads to a cave; a short lead above ends on a sandy terrace. Continue up the crest to the summit. There are good ledges at one-third and two-thirds of the route for bivouacs; the latter contains snow until late in the year.

Descent: Descend the Northwest Face, then traverse a ridge north over numerous small peaks to where snowfields or talus lead down into the basin below the buttress. This was the descent I used in 1976. You can also descend the Southwest Face and go out Slesse Creek. For the latter descent, downclimb halfway down a sandy gully, then traverse out of it to the south. Continue down to a steep wall 150 feet above the Giant Gendarme and rappel off a block. Downclimb again, then do a 40-foot rappel onto a step. Below the top of an open gully, rappel off a great block 150 feet to a terrace. Traverse this sloping terrace north, away from a gendarme, and descend the gully 180 feet. Then, make an upward 150-foot traverse onto a grassy slope to a horizontal block.

Downclimb a left-hand wall on a descending traverse (class 3) to just below a notch. Descend a prominent gully adjacent to the main summit face, then descend a bowl near the west rim. Continue down the bowl to a rocky, tree-covered ridge, then on down to 5800-foot campsites. From 5800 feet, cross a saddle with dead trees, then go south over a knoll to a ridge and pick up switchbacks of the Slesse Mountain Trail. Descend the trail 2000 feet to Slesse Creek and the end of the Slesse Creek Road. Either do a car shuttle, leave mountain bikes here before the climb, or hike the road out 6.4 miles to the Chilliwack River Road and hitchhike back to your car. Although this sounds complex, it avoids beating the brush back to Nesakwatch Creek and the approach.

Maps: CFM: 92 H/4 Chilliwack. RMNC

References: *CAG 3: Rainy Pass to Fraser River; CHGSWBC*

5 MOUNT REDOUBT
Northeast Face

THE MASSIVE FORTRESS OF MOUNT REDOUBT, three miles south of the Canadian border, rises above other peaks of the Chilliwack group in a series of sweeping ridges and buttresses. B.C. climbers Jimmie Cherry and Bob Ross made the first ascent of the 8956-foot peak in 1930, most likely up the south side.

The great flying buttress on the southeast forms a colorful wall of shattered Skagit Gneiss. Geologists Roland Tabor and Dwight Crowder, in their 1968 book *Routes and Rocks in the Mount Challenger Quadrangle*, explained the striking bands. The book said, "Layers containing different amounts of light-colored and dark-colored minerals, and the platy streaky look of the rocks is caused by parallel alignment of the minerals, especially mica."

"The route elegantly shot up a narrow ice crest to the upper rock wall."

On the mountain's north side, 1700 feet of glacier, snow, and ice to 50 degrees, and a couloir lead to a saddle on the East Ridge 300 feet below the summit. In July of 1971 Fred Beckey and John Rupley made the ascent, primarily on snow, from an approach up Depot Creek. A heavy winter snowfall enabled them to walk on top of much of the brush from the head of the creek to the mountain's base. Although belay anchors on the snow were non-existent, on the upper portion of the climb they hammered pitons in the rock along the side. They traversed under a drooping cornice to, where, as Beckey described it, "The route elegantly shot up a narrow ice crest to the upper rock wall."

Twelve years later I joined Debbie Martin and Bruce Pratt for an August ascent of the Northeast Face. Luckily for us, Canadian climbers had recently brushed out the Depot Creek path, enabling us to reach a comfortable camp above timberline in one day. The mosquitoes were bad during dinner, forcing me to retire into my headnet in an attempt to sleep. Debbie and Bruce

Opposite: *The Northeast Face Route of Mount Redoubt*

had a homemade "impotent" with no netting. For them it was a stuffy and hot night, for me a noisy one.

On our way early, we cramponed up the glacier and were climbing the face by dawn's light. We moved together, with only an occasional picket or fluke adding some security to the climbing, which mostly demanded care. Near the top, a nice looking rock rib lured me out of the couloir, but then it blanked out. Bruce wisely persuaded me back onto the snow. We soon gained the notch below the summit. From there it was necessary to descend a scree-covered ramp and traverse west a hundred yards to gain easier climbing up south-facing gullies and ribs to the top.

The mist swirled in and wiped out any views of Bear Mountain, which would have been outstanding from that perspective. We hung out and snacked, hoping the clouds would part, but the soup only thick-

Bruce Pratt on the Northeast Face of Mount Redoubt

ened. The descent of the south slope, and the trek east to the Redoubt Glacier, was a pleasant walk over a snowy expanse that led us back to our camp for an early supper.

On the last day the rain held off until we made it down into Depot Creek, where the heavy water caused slide alder to droop over the path. At the car, I poured a pint of water out of each of my leather Super Guides.

I had a great time climbing with Debbie and Bruce and was eager to do more trips with them. Sadly, Bruce died of pulmonary edema eighteen months later while leading a climb of Aconcagua.

Mount Redoubt: Northeast Face

First ascent: Fred Beckey and John Rupley; July 1971

Difficulty: Grade III, snow and ice to 50 degrees and low 5th class rock

Equipment: Snow and ice anchors and some rock protection. Ice ax and crampons

Permit: A permit for overnight use is required in North Cascades National Park when approaching from Canada. Contact the NPS, Skagit District, Marblemount, WA 98267 (360-873-4590).

Access: Same as for Slesse, described previously. Turn left off the Chilliwack River Road at 31.4 miles onto the unmarked Depot Creek Road. The logging road extends for 2 miles along the north side of the creek and may be gated. Keep left at both Y intersections and walk the last bit of overgrown road to the trailhead. From the road end the trail parallels the north side of the creek through slash, then bears back to the creek. For 2 miles the path keeps within 300 feet of the creek. The brushy headwall with waterfalls steepens at 3500 feet. Where the path ascends the headwall the rocks are slippery and dangerous during high runoff. Talus leads to a 4300-foot small saddle; a descent leads into an open basin. Cross a brushy marsh area, then ascend talus and moraines to 5700 feet. There are good campsites near the glacier, below the Northeast Face.

Route: Climb the left edge of a snow-ice apron to a sharp snow crest. Climb the crest, then do a rising traverse into a snow couloir to gain the col. From the col drop over to the south side, traverse west and descend, then climb to the summit on the south face.

Descent: Descend the south slope to 7600 feet, traverse east to a 7760-foot saddle and cross over onto the Redoubt Glacier. Traverse the glacier northeast, then descend north to 6000 feet and traverse below the long Northeast Ridge of Redoubt.

Maps: Green Trails: Mount Challenger No. 15; USGS: Mount Redoubt; RMNC; CFM: 92 H/4 Chilliwack

Reference: *CAG 3: Rainy Pass to Fraser River*

6 BEAR MOUNTAIN
North Buttress West

THE 7942-FOOT SUMMIT OF BEAR MOUNTAIN is hardly visible from anywhere in the Cascades except from Mount Redoubt, two-and-a-half miles to the northeast. Bear's rocky southern flanks are timbered and brushy, little resembling most craggy Northwest peaks. But, on the north side the massif has been cleaved away, forming a 2500-foot wall. The west side of this wall is granodiorite of the Chilliwack Batholith, while the east side of the wall is a metamorphosed rock where there is contact with gneiss. Four impressive buttresses and several ribs rise above small remnant glaciers are obvious attracions for exploratory mountaineers.

Bertulis and Stewart discovered an abandoned mining trail that was the start of an excellent approach route.

Initial climbing activity began in August of 1939 with the first ascent up the south side by Calder Bressler and Will Thompson. A group of seven climbers scaled the East Ridge in 1964, while in 1967 Fred Beckey and Mark Fielding bagged the North Face after much trail preparation and hauling of heavy loads.

In the early 1970s Dan Davis and Mike Heath made an attempt on the left side of the North Face, where they encountered poor rock and found few good cracks. While hiking through Bear Creek they made a rare (for Washington) sighting of a grizzly bear. In 1973 Alex Bertulis and Tom Stewart tried the buttress left of the North Face. On that trip Bertulis and Stewart discovered an abandoned mining trail that was the start of an excellent approach route to the mountain via Ruta Lake and a ridge between Bear and Indian Creeks. Bertulis and Stewart climbed seven pitches up the wall, where they ran into a sizable section of crackless wall, which, as they judged, would have required numerous bolts. The pair rappelled off, spent the night at the base, then hiked to their car in seven hours the following day.

approach

Bear Mountain. Direct North Buttress Route, left, and North Buttress West, right

During August of 1975 Chuck Sink and I reached the base of the North Face via Hannegan Pass, the Chilliwack River Trail, and Bear Creek. Not only was the face intimidating, but we discovered all of our slings were missing. We retreated.

In September of 1977 I returned with Shari Kearney, Ed Newville, and Jeff Thomas. We approached up the Little Beaver Trail, then brushwhacked the pathless alder and vine maple of Pass Creek south of Bear Mountain. Under clear skies we ate lunch above Bear Lake and studied Bear's north wall. We chose to attempt what I now call the 2000-foot North Buttress West (Beckey refers to it as the North Face West Buttress in his *Cascade Alpine Guide*).

The Buttress was an excellent climb of seventeen pitches. We began in the early evening with 400 feet of scrambling to reach a bivouac. The next day we climbed a chimney up and left, then followed cracks and face climbing toward the left edge of the buttress. An improbably smooth face ended under small overhangs; this provided the hardest climbing and poorest protection on the route. Climbing through the overhangs, we worked back up and right to gain the crest and follow easier terrain to the top. The buttress ended neatly atop a broad ridge below the talus and class 4 blocks of Bear's summit.

We bivvied on the ridge at sunset, rustling about and telling stories to delay the onslaught of the autumn cold that would penetrate our bivy sacs. The following day we scrambled to the summit, then thrashed out Bear Creek, unaware of the Ruta Lake route.

The second-ascent party informed me they had not found any hard climbing on our route, so there undoubtedly are other variations on the buttress.

Bear Mountain: North Buttress West

First ascent: Alan Kearney, Shari Kearney, Ed Newville, Jeff Thomas; September 1977

Difficulty: Grade IV, 5.9 (depending on the line)

Equipment: A standard rack, including small wires and a 4-inch cam

Permit: A permit is required from the NPS, Skagit District, Marblemount, WA 98267 (360-873-4590).

Access: Approach as for Slesse, described previously, then continue on the Chilliwack River Road 1.4 miles past Depot Creek to Sapper Park, at the south end of Chilliwack Lake. (At present this last 1.4 miles of road is closed to vehicles, but is still hikeable.) Begin hiking south along the east side of the Chilliwack River. (The trail is quite overgrown, as the NPS doesn't want to encourage hikers to use a trail so close to a foreign border.) In 5 miles reach Bear Creek and Bear Camp. An old trail begins uphill from Bear Camp and fades after about 1000 feet. Continue up through old growth forest and brush to the open ridge shoulder at 5286 feet (Ruta Lake, 5040 feet, is below this ridge to the east), then continue south along the west side. Traverse below and on the south side of a knoll at 6824 feet to a saddle at 6480 feet above timberline. From here, descend the broad gully into Bear Creek and make a short traverse east to the base of the route.

Ed Newville cleaning a pitch low on the North Buttress West Route

Route: The climb begins slightly left of the very toe of the buttress and involves 400 feet of scrambling to reach a prominent chimney system on the left edge. Chimney climbing ranges from 5.6–5.8. From the chimney top, climb cracks and slabs to just beneath obvious overhangs (5.9). Work up and right to gain the buttress crest and follow it to the top (some 5.7 and 5.8).

Descent: Once up, the buttress it is just a scramble to Bear's summit; return to the buttress top and easily descend northwest to the 6480-foot saddle

Maps: Green Trails: Mount Challenger No. 15; USGS: Mount Redoubt; RMNC; CFM: 92 H/4, Chilliwack

References: *CAG 3: Rainy Pass to Fraser River*; *AAJ*: 1978, page 522

7 BEAR MOUNTAIN
Direct North Buttress

DURING MY 1977 ASCENT OF BEAR MOUNTAIN with Shari Kearney, Ed Newville, and Jeff Thomas, we kept gazing at the central North Buttress, thinking it would be a worthy objective, even though it had already been climbed. In 1967 Beckey and Fielding climbed the recessed North Face, traversed onto the North Buttress, climbed three pitches on the buttress, then exited off into a gully/chimney. When my research revealed that very little of the actual buttress had been scaled, I was eager to return.

The exposure was incredible and the views stunning.

When I mentioned climbing Bear Mountain to Bobby Knight he was less than enthusiastic. He had just completed the 1980 summer season as an Outward Bound instructor, and didn't relish carrying any more huge packs through brush. I convinced him that from the summit I truly had spotted a better route into the peak, though at that time I didn't know it had been used in 1973.

Over Labor Day Bobby and I hiked into Bear Camp in the pouring rain and strung our Gore-tex bivy tent between two trees. At breakfast the next morning, as the sun penetrated the stately old growth forest of fir and cedar, I gave Bobby a sly wink. Northwest weather!

By noon we were on the high open ridge above Ruta Lake. That evening we descended to the base of the Direct North Buttress. Our one mistake was taking too much gear and food, which made for slow climbing, but we had no idea what the weather might do. It is the only climb I've ever done where I slept warm and ate well.

Our progress the next day was discouraging, and frequently we hauled our heavy packs. I used a bit of aid to overcome a chockstone several pitches above the glacier. (In 1985 Yann Merrand and Bryan Burdo repeated our line and freed the two small sections of aid on the route.) A short way above the chockstone Bobby set up a belay in an alcove of loose sharp flakes, one of which nicked the rope. After another rope length we bivvied on a sloping ledge, munching apples and sardines.

Bobby Knight at the start of the Pitch 7 traverse. Mount Redoubt in the distance.

The next day we put a lot of pitches below us and finally reached the narrow part of the upper buttress. The exposure was incredible and the views stunning. We spent the night on the flat top of a huge pedestal at a point where Beckey and Fielding traversed onto the buttress from the top of the recessed glacier. Mark Bebie and Lowell Skoog repeated that 1967 line in 1985 and confirmed what I thought that evening—that the terrain from the glacier to the buttress was dirty, loose, and poorly protected.

The following day I led a great pitch up to the base of the flaring squeeze chimney that, by Beckey's account, had given Fielding so much trouble in 1967. Fred related, "Several times Mark slid down a move after struggling up it. Protection was a major problem." If any of the four of us had looked around the corner to the right we would have found an easier, and protectable alternative that bypassed the chimney. Bebie and Skoog discovered this pitch in 1985—a useful piece of information for those parties wanting to avoid offwidth squeezes.

The weather was changing quickly, with dark clouds blanketing Mount

Redoubt. Precipitation was inevitable. Bobby climbed rapidly up a long finger crack on the twelve-foot-wide buttress crest; in two more pitches we were sitting on level ground with 2500 feet of wall below us. That day we reached our high camp on the ridge as it began to pour. I actually enjoyed hiking down through rain-soaked huckleberries with a monster pack. We had barely pulled off our new route in-between storms. We felt very happy.

Bear Mountain: Direct North Buttress

First ascent: Alan Kearney, Bobby Knight; September 9–11, 1980
Difficulty: Grade V, 5.10-
Equipment: A standard rack that includes a 4-inch cam. Ice ax and crampons are needed to reach the rock; we left them at the base for later retrieval.
Permit: A permit is required from the NPS, Skagit District, Marblemount, WA 98267 (360-873-4590).
Access: The buttress is ¼ mile due south of the North Buttress West.
Route: Ascend the glacier up and left of the buttress to below a prominent left-facing corner. **[1]** Climb slabs up and right above the glacier (5.5). **[2]** Continue up slabs to a chimney (5.7). **[3]** Climb a recess (5.7) to the base of the prominent corner system. (In some years it may be possible to reach this spot more directly via glacier ice or firn.) **[4]** Climb the corner past a chockstone and small roof (5.10-). **[5]** Continue stemming up the corner (5.8) to beneath a large roof. **[6]** Move left and climb a short chimney (5.8). **[7]** Climb a corner and crack (5.8) to a good ledge. **[8]** Traverse up and right to grassy ledges (5.9). **[9]** Traverse up and right again (5.4) to a ledge. **[10]** Climb up a ramp (5.6). **[11]** and **[12]** Ascend class 3 and 4 rock to a giant ledge with a snowpatch. **[13]** Jam a right-leaning crack on the buttress crest (5.8). **[14]** Continue up cracks on a blocky face (5.8). **[15]** Traverse left (east) on a large ledge and then climb a corner with a fist crack (5.9) to a ledge. **[16]** Climb a crack and groove to a belay beneath a small roof (5.6). **[17]** Face climb, then move left and up a rib (5.7) to a good ledge. **[18]** Climb an obvious chimney offwidth (5.10-) or climb a short way up, step around the right side, and climb the face and cracks to a ledge (5.8). **[19]** Continue up the crest (5.7), then up a wandering face and crack (5.9) on the crest. **[20]** Jam a long thin crack (5.10-) to a small stance. **[21]** Climb upward on the face (5.8), then traverse right on a catwalk. **[22]** and **[23]** Two pitches

(5.6) on the west face of the buttress lead to the buttress top. Scramble to the summit from there.

Descent: Same as for the North Buttress West, described previously.

Maps: Green Trails: Mount Challenger No. 15; USGS: Mount Redoubt; CFM: 92 H/4 Chilliwack

References: *CAG 3: Rainy Pass to Fraser River; AAJ: 1981, pp. 120–122*

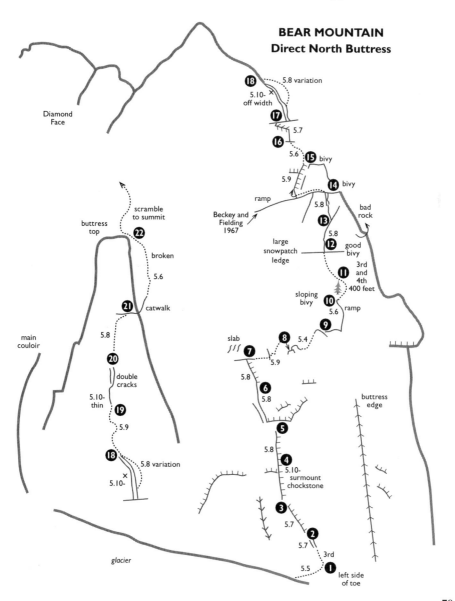

BEAR MOUNTAIN
Direct North Buttress

8 MOUNT CHALLENGER
Challenger Glacier

CHALLENGER'S 8236-FOOT SUMMIT IS THE LANDMARK PEAK of Washington's Northern Pickets. It can be reached in a long day of trail walking and another day of off-trail and glacier travel. Its broad northern glacier and summit pinnacle are visible from Mount Baker, twenty miles to the west.

"One thing that impressed us all was the shimmering white cleanliness of the immense three-mile-wide, deeply crevassed glacier."

Phillip Dickert, Jack Hossack, and George McGowan made the first ascent in 1936, using an approach from Hannegan Pass, Easy Ridge, and Perfect Pass. The trio planned for a rock assault; Dickert was surprised at what they encountered, stating, "We were confronted with a major glacier climb, except for the final rocky summit. One thing that impressed us all was the shimmering white cleanliness of the immense three-mile-wide, deeply crevassed glacier."

They began their climb at 6240 feet, leaving Perfect Pass, dropping 200 feet, and heading across and up in a southeasterly direction. The major difficulty was a bergschrund they surmounted by chopping a ladder of hand and footholds in the ice. Once above the 20-foot wall they scrambled up a rock outcrop, then tackled a 50-degree firn slope by hewing steps for 100 feet. From the top of the slope they worked between the snow and rocky face of a pinnacle, then descended to the base of the summit ridge. They then traversed the spiny crest to the quartz diorite top, which Dickert liked. He wrote, "This was ascended with the use of a piton and proved one of the best parts of the climb."

The climbers spent a long time on the highest point, checking the elevation with a barometer and identifying surrounding peaks. After recording their ascent in a record tube, the group descended to camp in three hours.

⛰

In 1973 my college chum Dave Neff suggested a traverse of the Northern and Southern Pickets for early fall, and Mount Challenger was on the way.

Opposite: *Mount Challenger from Whatcom Pass*

Dave Neff ascends steep snow on the Challenger Glacier

We packed food for seven days, a 120-foot rope, a small selection of nuts and carabiners, and three ice screws. I wanted to take four but Dave was fanatical about weight and insisted on only three. In those days everyone wore boots for both trail walking and climbing; they caused me excessive pain and suffering on the climb.

We approached the range from Hannegan Pass, the Chilliwack River Trail, and Easy Ridge. Below the west face of Whatcom Peak we were forced to descend a maddeningly long distance into the brush before climbing back up to Perfect Pass. The pass was a pristine spot of heather benches, tarns, and clean rock slabs. Although there was daylight left, we chose to camp.

In the morning we crossed the Challenger Glacier under clear skies, then threaded our way between crevasses to the base of the short steep firn slopes leading to the top of the peak. After dumping our packs, the climb was fun! We had only to swing the ax and kick the crampons in without the burden of our loads. By noon we were at the base of the summit; we quickly climbed the exhilarating rock pitch to the top.

With Challenger bagged, we descended the eastern portion of the glacier and camped on the edge of Luna Cirque. The north face of Mount Fury dominated the glacial bowl, and we heard an occasional sérac and sporadic rocks crashing 3500 feet to the bottom. Although our intention was to climb Fury and finish the traverse, the peak looked distinctly more difficult than Challenger. I wasn't sure I was up for it.

Mount Challenger: Challenger Glacier

First ascent: Phillip Dickert, Jack Hossack, George McGowan; September 1936

Difficulty: Glacier travel and steep snow, with one pitch of 5.4 or 5.5 rock

Equipment: Snow anchors, some nuts, and slings. Ice ax and crampons

Permit: A permit is required from the NPS, Skagit District, Marblemount, WA 98267 (360-873-4590).

Access: Approach as for Slesse, Chilliwack River, and Bear Camp, described previously. From Bear Camp, hike 5.3 miles to the Hannegan/Whatcom trail, then go left 5.2 miles to Whatcom Pass. From the pass follow a path south to talus and a steep timbered slope on the east side of the ridge. As the path fades, angle steeply up through woods, heather, and huckleberry. The path reappears and contours over to the Whatcom Glacier. Cross the glacier below the upper icefall, but above the snout (5600 feet), then descend and traverse class 3 slabs around the east side of Whatcom Peak. Continue on a rising traverse toward Perfect Pass, then ascend the glacier southeast toward Mount Challenger. If the glacier is impassable you can also climb directly over Whatcom Peak via the north ridge and descend to Perfect Pass.

Route: It is best to traverse the Challenger Glacier clear across to the east side, then ascend one firn slope to the rocky summit, which is climbed up the west side.

Descent: Retrace the climbing route.

Maps: Green Trails: Mount Challenger No. 15; USGS: Mount Challenger

Reference: CAG 3: Rainy Pass to Fraser River

Mount Challenger and the Challenger Glacier

9 MOUNT FURY
North Buttress

MOUNT FURY IS THE GUARDIAN OF THE PICKETS and the quintessential North Cascades summit. It is shielded by a two-day approach, large north face routes of moderate difficulty, and unpredictable Northwest weather. Bill Cox and Will Thompson made the first ascent of the 8288-foot East Peak in September of 1937, going up the Fury Glacier and the East Ridge.

The two traversed the glacier, eliminating a thousand feet of climbing from the bottom of Luna Cirque.

The easiest route up the mountain was established in 1958 by Tim Kelley, Dale Kunz, Tom Miller, and Franz Mohling from the Luna–Fury saddle and the Southeast Glacier. The Beckey brothers climbed the Fury Glacier in 1940; on that trip Fred was intrigued by the 4000-foot North Buttress (it's actually a ridge).

Fred returned in July of 1962, with Dan Davis. At 3:30 in the morning of the 15th, the two traversed the glacier below Crooked Thumb, Ghost, Phantom, and Swiss Peaks, eliminating a thousand feet of climbing from the bottom of Luna Cirque. (Due to the receding glaciers and lower snowfalls this approach is now dubious.)

Beckey and Davis gained a deep notch in the ridge via snow slopes, then ascended the crest. The climbing involved steep snow patches and class 3 and 4 rock with harder pitches. Not far above the notch Beckey's boot blew apart. They stopped briefly while Davis punched holes in it with an awl and tied the leather up with cord.

They reached the summit after nine hours of climbing, then spent six more hours descending the East Route to Luna Cirque and climbing back up to their Challenger Arm camp as rain began.

More climbers have expressed a desire to climb Fury's North Face (which includes the Northeast Face and North Buttress) than any other wall in the range. My first try was in 1973, when, after climbing Challenger with Dave

The North Buttress of Mount Fury, showing access from the east and west

Neff, we descended Luna Cirque to the base of Fury. Thoroughly intimidated, we ruled out climbing the Northeast Face (or at least I did). Once on the other side of the mountain, we had planned to traverse over to the Southern Pickets, but we didn't know where the route went. As we gazed down into the lost-world jungle of McMillan Cirque, Dave suggested rappelling brushy cliffs to the bottom, then climbing out the other side to finish the traverse. I was not keen about this plan.

Twelve years later Josh Lieberman and Chris Copeland climbed the

Mark Price pays out rope from a comfy stance on the North Buttress

Northeast Face of Fury in a snow-storm, enduring a wet bivy below the summit. The next day they descended the backside glacier, then followed streams and steep slabs. Where water-falls severed the route, they rappelled off nearby trees to gain the bottom of the cirque. They traveled only four-and-one-half miles in two days to reach the Big Beaver Trail. Copeland fumed over their rate of progress. "At times our feet never touched the earth," he said, "and in one section we figured it took an hour to go 125 yards." Perhaps I was psychic, but I wanted no part of McMillan Cirque. Dave and I turned back retracing, our path.

We finally reached Whatcom Pass, out of food and with nearly twenty miles of hiking left to reach Dave's VW bug. With only one peak to our credit, our first trip to the Pickets had been a humbling experience.

I made four more unsuccessful at-tempts to climb Mount Fury: in 1975, 1988, 1991, and August of 1992. It was not until September of 1992 that I finally set foot on the mountain. The weather was unstable that month, but Fury by now had an unshakable grip on me.

Mark Price and I left Bellingham on the 19th, drove to Chilliwack Lake and hiked to Whatcom Pass. The next day brought strong winds and heavy rain. We passed the hours sipping hot drinks and reading books. The sky cleared on the 21st as we climbed over Whatcom Peak with full packs. To the south lay the Challenger Glacier, its ridges bristling with craggy summits. Mark was smitten, just as I had been nineteen years earlier.

That evening we reached a campsite in Luna Cirque and sorted gear for the climb. Food, cams, Stoppers, small pitons, pile jackets, and raingear filled our packs. We didn't bring bivy sacks, but I tossed in a stove, pot, and drinks at the last minute.

In the morning we opted for an eastern approach to the buttress, as recent rockfall and scant snowfields ruled out the easier western side. Our route followed a huge gully and chimney that led toward the buttress crest. When Mark fiddled too long trying to lead over a chockstone I said, "Bzzzzz! Time's up. My turn." These young purists. I just slotted a steel nut and grabbed it.

Higher on the buttress the climbing was great and the rock solid when it needed to be. We may have been off-route in one spot, but we found a beautiful long hand crack that was tricky with plastic boots on. As the light faded, I zoomed up the final crest of firn, put in a fluke, a screw, and topped out on the summit ridge at dark.

Though we were happy with the climb, and made a bivouac under a large rock overhang, Fury was not happy with us. An impenetrable black cloud produced rain for most of the night. At one point a packrat used Mark's head to climb the wall above. We spent the following day descending the East Route in a full blown storm, rested a day at camp, then traversed out Luna Cirque on fresh slippery snow. Our clothing and bags were soaked and our food was nearly gone.

I decided we should try to rappel the wet brushy slabs just north of the Challenger Glacier's toe, a line I had spotted the year before. This was a semi-desperate maneuver, but due to our wet gear we hadn't slept in three nights. I wanted to get below the snowfall level. Mark nodded wearily as we downclimbed and rappelled near-vertical brush in a downpour. The wall ate slings, pitons, and Stoppers as water filled our sleeves and boots.

We reached the talus at dark and bivvied in the slide alder by Little Beaver Creek. The next day we hiked to Chilliwack Lake with feet squishing the whole way. We were two days overdue and our friends were about to call out a rescue. The Pickets, and especially Mount Fury, had humbled me even more.

Mount Fury: North Buttress

First ascent: Fred Beckey and Dan Davis; July 15, 1962
Difficulty: Snow and 5th class rock to 5.6, if done in early season
Equipment: A light rack of rock gear up to 3-inch cams and a few small pins. Some snow and ice protection. Ice ax and crampons.

Permit: A permit is required from the NPS, Skagit District, Marblemount, WA 98267 (360-873-4590).

Access: Approach as for Challenger, described previously. From the east side of the Challenger Glacier, descend north to a 6720-foot saddle, then continue east down the glacier arm. From a 5900-foot camp below the Challenger Glacier make a gradual descent into Luna Cirque, keeping above cliffs and below the glacier. After 1 mile, go down a long talus slope to the bottom of the cirque and cross to the base of Fury.

Route: Early in the season, with more snow, it might be possible to reach the buttress crest from the right or west side. That was a dangerous option in late '92, so we ascended a deep gully/chimney on the east side, with climbing of 5.8 or 5.9. Other parties have climbed easier slopes between the Northeast Face and the North Buttress to gain the buttress about midpoint; however, the Northeast Face is also quite broken. Try to get the very latest conditions from someone who has recently been on the route or had a close look at it.

From the avalanche chute below and west of Luna Lake, climb polished slabs up and west. Cross beneath the Northeast Face, then ascend a huge gully/chimney nearly to its top. Beneath a wet overhanging chimney, climb left across a steep face, then go straight up to finally gain the buttress crest. Follow the crest up to a deep notch and do two rappels. From the notch, drop a short distance on the west, then climb cracks and blocks up onto the crest again. Stay generally on the right side of the crest, or on the crest up to two pinnacles. Pass between these spires, then climb a snow/firn ridge to its top. Climb east to the true summit, over a rocky sub-summit and up a ridge.

Descent: From the summit descend a snow arête eastward and then follow a face downward to the top of the southeast glacier. Once over the bergschrund, continue down to the 7400-foot level where it is possible to traverse off the glacier and go east to the top of a snow couloir. Descend this couloir 1000 feet or so and then traverse slopes northeast (the backside of Luna Cirque) for 2 miles or more to pass 7040 feet below Luna Peak. From here descend slopes to Luna Lake.

Maps: Green Trails: Mount Challenger No. 15; USGS: Mount Challenger

Reference: *CAG 3: Rainy Pass to Fraser River*

10 CASTLE PEAK
North Buttress East

ONE MILE SOUTH OF THE CANADA BORDER and 2.8 miles west of the Pacific Crest Trail lies seldom-visited Castle Peak. It is one of several solid granitic peaks in the Pasayten Wilderness that offer fine climbing and, sometimes, an escape from west side precipitation. The mountain's north face rises 1500 to 1700 feet above a rapidly receding remnant glacier; it boasts three major buttresses and three lesser ones, only two of which have been climbed.

Members of the U.S. Geological Survey climbed the peak in 1904, up the south side, and surveyed the mountain's height at 8306 feet. Beckey led trips in 1973 and 1979 to the north side and established routes on the west side and the north face. These ascents approached Castle from the Pacific Crest Trail and Crow Creek.

Sue Harrington and I attempted to reach the mountain in 1986 via the Crow Creek route. I was dismayed by the brushy appearance of the creek, so we chose to scramble up Mount Winthrop instead. From the summit of Winthrop we had a good view of Castle Peak and a high open ridge leading toward Frosty Mountain. I was convinced that hiking in from Manning Park, in Canada, was the easiest way to reach the saddle between Crow Creek and Pass Creek.

Just as we thought the line might not go, a crack or holds would materialize.

The following summer Sue and I drove to Lightning Lake and hiked up the Frosty Mountain Trail. We contoured around Frosty, then followed meadows and talus slopes on the east side of a ridge leading to Castle. Late in the day several patches of krummholz (weather-gnarled stunted pines) slowed our progress, but we made the meadows below the peak and fixed dinner under a light nylon tarp.

As it was a nearly twelve-mile hike to camp, we had left behind crampons and boots to save weight; we used only trail shoes for the approach and hoped to chop steps in any ice leading to the base of the climb. In 1987

The North Buttress East Route on Castle Peak

there were still many unclimbed lines to chose from, including the far left buttress on the North Face. So far, the weather had been perfect, but even in the Pasayten you could never be sure.

Sue and I got an early start the next morning, scrambling across talus to the bottom of the buttress. Leaving one ax in the talus, I hacked steps over 200 feet of low-angle ice to gain the rock. We cached the other ax and our trail shoes at the start of the rock climbing. Slabby clean rock led upward to a small corner in the center of the face, where small wires and RP's came in handy. From there we found the route very interesting and reasonably free of lichen for a northern exposure.

Several pitches sported small roofs and overhangs. Just as we thought the line might not go, a crack or holds would materialize. As the day progressed, high thin clouds began to move in from the west. We didn't carry much gear for bad weather; each of our small fanny packs had a pint of water, candy bars, and a light raincoat. With only one headlamp between us we were getting anxious about the fading September light.

After the steep portion of the buttress ended, we climbed quickly up four or five pitches of easier ground, then squeezed up a chimney

Sue Harrington jamming clean granite on Castle Peak

onto the East Ridge. I wanted to scramble up the talus to the summit but ruled it out since dusk was upon us. Being without crampons, we chose to descend the route and rappel a shorter buttress just east of our ascent route. We made it back down the easy pitches just before the sun winked out.

Having one headlamp in the inky blackness was bad enough, but a mysterious fog rose up from the valley giving the whole place a spooky feeling. We groped down a short arête to where I thought we should begin rappelling, but the headlamp revealed only swirling mist and vertical rock. Where was the bottom of the wall? I slung a small tree and started down, hoping it was the right way. With still no sign of the bottom, and at the end of the ropes, I anchored myself and yelled for Sue to start rappelling.

Without a light she could only clip in and feel her way down. I tried to describe the various overhangs she would encounter, and kept the end of the ropes anchored to my stance. In another hundred feet I thankfully lowered onto the talus and could barely make out our buttress nearby. I was wise to have left one ax in the talus, as our steps had melted completely away. I spent an hour re-chopping them to reach the cached gear. In retrospect, we should have brought crampons.

We finally reached camp at 1 A.M. as the fog turned to drizzle, but the front was a weak one, and on the third day we hiked out in shirtsleeve weather. Surely the west side had received a lot more rain over the weekend. We were happy to have pulled off a new route in a remote area.

Castle Peak: North Buttress East

First ascent: Sue Harrington and Alan Kearney; September 12, 1987

Difficulty: Grade IV, 5.10+

Equipment: A standard rack up to a 3-inch cam and extra small wires and small cams. Two ropes. Ice ax and crampons optional.

Access: From Hope, B.C., drive Highway 3, 49 miles to Manning Park Lodge. Just beyond, turn right on Gibson Pass Road and drive 2 miles to the northeast end of Lightning Lake. Hike the Frosty Mountain Trail for 6 miles to the shoulder east of, and below, the summit. Contour around the south side of Frosty, drop into meadows and do a rising traverse southwest toward the international boundary cut. Traverse below the east side of Peak 7540, cross over a saddle at 7320 feet, then descend gullies and slabs on the west side of Peak 7520. Drop 600 feet, then traverse south to the pass at the head of Crow and Pass Creeks. There is good camping at this pass, and easy access to the route.

Route: [1] Climb slabs (5.7) to gain a small right-facing corner system on the left side of the face. [2] Climb a right-facing corner to its end and traverse rightward on small holds (5.10-) to a ledge at the base of a corner. [3] Climb the corner for a long lead (5.9) until able to exit left, then climb a thin crack through a small overhang to a belay stance. Directly above this belay are large roofs, with less formidable roofs up and right. [4] Jam a tiny left-facing corner to a small ledge (5.10-). [5] Climb a small overhang using a thin crack (5.9) and belay in an alcove. [6] Work up and left on face holds (5.10+), then turn a small overhang. Climb a long finger and hand crack that ends on a ledge (5.9). [7] Traverse right for 50 feet, then go up and right into a large corner system on the west side of the buttress (5th class). [8] Climb the corner system to the top of the steep part of the buttress (5.8). [9] through [14] Climb easier ground, then ascend a squeeze chimney on the right side of the block to gain the East Ridge (4th and 5th class).

Descent: Either downclimb and rappel the buttress just east of the route, or descend the East Ridge to a deep notch and small glacier to the north.

Maps: Green Trails: Jack Mountain No. 17; USGS: Castle Peak; CFM: 92 H/12 Manning Park

Reference: *CAG 3: Rainy Pass to Fraser River. AAJ*: 1988, pp. 128–129. *CHGSWBC*

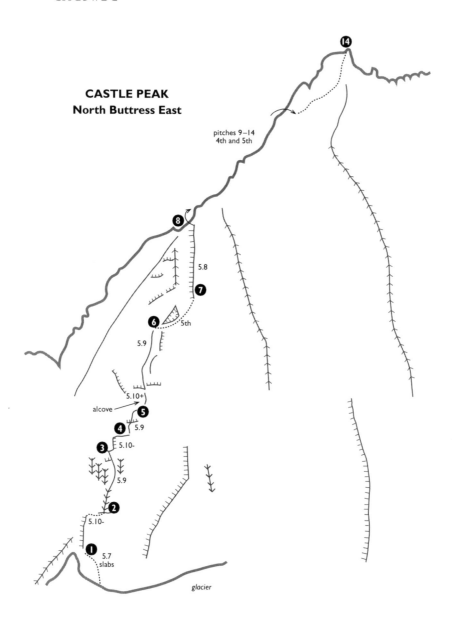

**CASTLE PEAK
North Buttress East**

pitches 9–14
4th and 5th

5.8

5th

5.9

5.10+

alcove

5.9

5.10-

5.9

5.10-

5.7
slabs

glacier

11 NORTH TWIN SISTER
West Ridge

FRED WEIL OF THE MOUNTAINEERS WROTE in 1916: "Terrific chasms and cleavages compel attention in this section. Mountains are sliced away for precipices and watersheds." He was not referring to the far off great ranges, but instead to the 6000-foot summits of the Twin Sisters. These reddish-brown craggy peaks ten miles southwest of Mount Baker provide enjoyable climbing on sound rock in an alpine environment.

The Sisters are composed of dunite (a dense igneous rock with a high content of olivine). It is coarse and gives good grip in wet or dry weather. The texture is not unlike limestone I have climbed on in the Canadian Rockies. Unfortunately, olivine is a mineral silicate used as structural material in cement and the Olivine Corporation operates a quarry low on the north side of North Twin Sister. Since the mountains are not protected by either a wilderness area or a national park, logging is rampant on the west and north sides of the range. These blemishes aside, you can have a great alpine experience in an hour's walk from the last skid road.

Back then, the approach involved a hike of eight miles to the Middle Fork of the Nooksack River, then several miles of trailless wooded ridge.

The 6570-foot North Twin was first climbed in August of 1898 by a party of nine. Back then, the approach involved a hike of eight miles to the Middle Fork of the Nooksack River, then several miles of trailless wooded ridge to reach the peak.

Presently, you can get to the North Twin in an hour's drive from Bellingham, depending on the status of the logging roads. (Gates are sometimes locked due to fire hazard or the whim of timber companies.)

⏶

I have climbed the West Ridge several times, including an autumn ascent in winter conditions. On a crisp fall day the frosted summits of the Twins can persuade even the most dedicated worker to call in sick and load up the day-pack with ice ax and crampons.

North Twin Sister. The West Ridge Route follows the right skyline

One October I left Bellingham in the morning in hopes of finding a little ice climbing on the West Ridge. I was able to drive within two miles of the mountain, and found myself wading through light snow in the forest below the ridge. Once beyond the woods, the ridge (for the most part) was scoured bare of snow by wind, but had enough rime ice for good cramponing. A few windswept pines clung to the ledges, and a cool breeze whipped about. The climbing was tricky, and in spots a rope would have been helpful.

When alone in these situations I fall back on the words of the Scottish climber Tom Patey, " One: The leader must not fall. Two: The leader must climb as if the rope was not there. The first commandment is self-evident. No useful purpose could be served by a leader falling except to provide his followers with belaying practice. For the second commandment, there is only one way to ensure that a leader climbs as if his rope was not there—take away the rope." I have found this to be true so long as I'm not too close to my physical and mental limits.

The climbing on icy rocks was exhilarating, but not sustained. In fifty minutes I scrambled carefully across snow-covered boulders toward the true summit. This was a strange place, where drifted snow barely covered large cracks and holes between the rocks, some of which looked fifteen to twenty feet deep. A surprise here might end in death or, at the least, a twisted ankle.

The ax was helpful when probing. When possible, I climbed up and around the holes on bare rocks. I soon reached the top and paused for a candy bar in the cool autumn sun. There is something very satisfying about climbing alone. From the North Twin I could see, to the south, many more challenges for the lone climber. South Twin, Skookum, Little Sister, Slab, and Nancy Peaks offered plenty of reasons to play hooky.

North Twin Sister: West Ridge

Difficulty: Grade II, Mostly class 4 and a bit of class 5

Equipment: You may want a rope and some pro for belaying inexperienced members, and ice ax and crampons in early or late season.

Access: From Bellingham take Highway 542 for 17.2 miles to Welcome. Turn right on Mosquito Lake Road and go 4.8 miles south to the Porter Creek Road (Road No. 38). Turn left on Porter Creek Road and parallel the Middle Fork of the Nooksack River for 4.9 miles to a Y intersection. Go right at the Y and drop steeply downhill, crossing the Nooksack River at 5.2 miles. (At this point the road can be gated by the olivine mine owners. If so, mountain bikes are useful for reaching Dailey Prairie.) After crossing the bridge over the Nooksack, keep left at 5.6 miles, right at 5.9 miles, right at 7.5 miles, and right again at 7.8 miles. Drive 0.2 mile and park on the right. From here, the road is undriveable; hike or bike another 1.5 miles to Dailey Prairie. (If the gate is locked on Nooksack River it will be 4.3 miles to Dailey Prairie.) Just as the road begins to drop into Dailey Prairie bear left and up on an unmarked skid road. The skid road switchbacks up a clearcut to a wooded ridge on the northwest. Hike a short way through slash and pick up a path on the wooded ridge that leads up to the West Ridge. For road conditions contact the Campbell Group, Box 456, Mount Vernon, WA 98273 (360-336-9733).

Route: Climb easy terrain on the right side of the crest to where a corner leads up and left to the crest. Climb right from a small notch, then continue climbing again on the right side of the crest up to a small headwall. Climb the headwall on the left, then continue up to the false summit. Climb along the crest, mostly on the north side, to the true summit.

Descent: Downclimb the ridge, or in early season descend snow on the north side and traverse back west to the start of the ridge.

Maps: Green Trails: Hamilton No. 45; USGS: Twin Sisters Mountain

Reference: *CAG 3: Rainy Pass to Fraser River*

Nancy Noble traverses the West Ridge of North Twin Sister in May

12 MOUNT BAKER
North Ridge

MOUNT BAKER IS THE MOST STRIKING of our Northwest volcanoes, particularly when viewed from the southwest. Its 10,778-foot summit forms the apex of the second largest mass of ice in the state, with twelve glaciers blanketing the peak. In 1981 the Coleman and Roosevelt Glaciers alone contained twenty square miles of ice—nearly half of the mountain's total— though they have since dramatically receded. The northern latitude, high elevation, and heavy precipitation cannot abate the melting.

Edmund Coleman, an Englishman living in Victoria, B.C., made three attempts to climb the mountain, starting in 1866. In 1868 he led David Olgilvy, Thomas Stratton, and John Tennant to

Most notable was Joe Morovits' solo climb of the Park Headwall with a rifle butt for balance and a wood ax for hacking steps!

the summit via the now popular Coleman–Deming Route. The group climbed the final slope with homemade crampons and much step chopping.

Three more new routes were established over the next eighty years: the Boulder Glacier in 1891, the Park Glacier Headwall in 1892, and the Easton Glacier in 1908. Most notable was Joe Morovits' solo climb of the Park Headwall with a rifle butt for balance and a wood ax for hacking steps! Ed Loness and Robert Sperlin made the first ski ascent in May of 1930; eighteen years later Fred Beckey and Ralph and Dick Widrig climbed the North Ridge.

The then-25-year-old Beckey had a good idea the ridge would go from a reconnaissance and ski ascent the year before. He returned with the Widrigs in August of 1948 to climb the ridge and overcome the ice wall at 9600 feet. For 1600 feet the trio climbed steep névé to the base of the ice wall, where Beckey later described the first lead: "Ralph anchored to an ice piton at the vertical wall's base, belaying as I chopped steps on a left traverse across the now knife-edged arête. Chopping in blue ice all the way, and once placing a [serrated ice] piton, I climbed sixty feet and anchored to another piton."

Opposite: The North Ridge of Mount Baker rises above the Roosevelt and Coleman Glaciers

Today, with modern tools and protection, a climber with a bit of skill can ascend the route safely and more quickly, since cutting steps is unnecessary. Most of the climbing is up 35- to 40-degree snow slopes, with the exception of two leads up the ice wall that are between 50 and 60 degrees. Most climbers may find threading their way across the crevassed Coleman Glacier to be more difficult than climbing the ridge.

⠀⠀⠀⠀⠀⠀⠀⠀▲▲

From 1980 through 1989 I spent much of my summer time teaching ice climbing and guiding routes on Baker. During that period, I guided a single client up the North Ridge. Mark Shahly and I carried gear for one night and bivouacked on rock slabs below the Cockscomb Ridge, thirty minutes from the base of the North Ridge.

During the night a single black cloud produced lightning and a brief rainstorm. I thought we'd been had, and our trip was over, but the next morning was perfect. We brewed instant coffee, ate some pastries, and quickly packed up. We detoured around several crevasses, then cramponed up perfect moderate slopes toward the ice wall. Climbing on the North Ridge, you are never beneath unstable ice séracs, as you are on the Roosevelt or Coleman Headwall routes.

Our front points bit into solid water ice just as the sun hit the peak. The climbing was enjoyable; a couple of ice screws made it much safer. Photographing Mark as he attacked the face, I watched the flying chips of ice sparkle in the morning light. We complained when the steeper ice lasted just two pitches, and not more. After a section of moderate snow, we walked across

Ruthard Murphy on good ice of the North Ridge

gentle slopes toward the summit, then proceeded down the long descent to our base camp on the Coleman Glacier.

Mount Baker: North Ridge

First ascent: Fred Beckey, Dick Widrig, Ralph Widrig; August 1948

Difficulty: Grade II, with ice to 55 degrees or more

Equipment: Several ice screws, flukes, and pickets. Ice ax and crampons

Permit: At this writing, usage on the mountain, which is in the Mount Baker Wilderness, is under discussion. In the future, a permit for overnight use of the area and for climbing the peak may be required from the USFS Ranger Station in Glacier, WA 98224 (360-599-2714).

Access: Approach as for the Twin Sisters, described previously, and continue east on Highway 542 for seventeen miles to Glacier. In 1 mile turn right onto the Glacier Creek Road. Drive 8 miles to the Mount Baker Trail. Hike 2.3 miles, then go right up a steep climbers' path to the edge of the Coleman Glacier at 6000 feet. (If you miss the sharp right turn, you will come to the end of the trail at 5200 feet, overlooking the lower lobe of the Coleman). From 6000 feet continue up the glacier to 7000 feet, then veer left, contouring across the Coleman and weaving around crevasses to the base of the ridge. To avoid any rock, traverse around the ridge's base to the Roosevelt Glacier and begin the climb 600 feet above the toe on the east side. If the upper Coleman is badly broken, an alternate approach is to go left at 2.3 miles to the Coleman overlook at 5200 feet. Cross the compression zone of ice at 5000 feet, then ascend talus and rock slabs on the far side to gain the Roosevelt Glacier. Do a rising easterly traverse across the Roosevelt and gain the North Ridge from the east side.

Route: From the east side start, climb onto the ridge crest and follow it up, then left, to the toe of the ice wall. Ascend ice slightly right of the crest for two pitches to reach the snow slopes above. At the final bergschrund, traverse left toward the summit plateau.

Descent: It is easiest to downclimb the normal route (Coleman–Deming Route) to 7000 feet, then retrace the approach route.

Maps: Green Trails: Mount Baker No. 13; USGS: Mount Baker and Goat Mountain.

Reference: *CAG 3: Rainy Pass to Fraser River*

13 MOUNT SHUKSAN
Fisher Chimneys

IN 1907, PHOTOGRAPHER ASAHEL CURTIS referred to Mount Shuksan as, ". . . a beautiful mass of igneous rock, with cascade glaciers flowing outward on all sides." Actually, the 9127-foot peak is mostly greenschist, a metamorphosed basalt. There are eight glaciers in all; two, the Hanging and the Upper Curtis, continually calve off great blocks of ice.

They could hardly have imagined that in a couple of decades there would be a path worn in the heather slopes from so many climbers.

Clinging ice sheets, steep walls, and sharp ridges give the mountain an almost-foreign appearance. Plastered with fresh snow, the fluted North Face of the summit pyramid takes on a Himalayan look, while other parts of the mountain resemble the Weisshorn near Switzerland's famous Eiger. While in Switzerland in 1999 I observed the similarity firsthand.

Curtis and Montelius Price made the first ascent of the peak on September 7, 1906, traveling up the southwest side, the upper Sulphide Glacier, and the South Face of the summit pinnacle. They had tried the mountain two days earlier by climbing along Shuksan Arm, but were stymied by the numerous towers and gashes.

Two days later the pair traversed below the Southwest Face and climbed part way up to the Sulphide Glacier. Without a tent, the duo spent a cool night out. They later related, "We had brought extra provisions, and at sunset found a place on the shoulder of the mountain where there was plenty of dry wood. There we built a brush shelter to break the wind."

In the morning, Curtis and Price gained the Sulphide, and several hours later reached the untrodden summit. They built a large cairn, left their names in a bottle and began the descent. The happy climbers glissaded much of the lower snow slopes with the aid of alpenstocks and finally made it back to Table Mountain that night.

Shuksan was climbed again in 1916 and 1920 by a similar route. In 1927 Clarence A. "Happy" Fisher and Dr. Emmons Spearin pioneered the Chimneys

The Fisher Chimneys Route makes a rising traverse on the south side of Shuksan Arm, above the Lower Curtis Glacier

Route. Following a reconnaissance, Esther Buswell, Paul Hugdahl, Lars Loveseth, Winnie Spieseke, and Harriet Taylor joined the two leaders for the climb.

The route went smoothly until they reached Hell's Highway, the broad crevassed chute leading up to the Sulphide Glacier. They wrote, "Here we found our hardest going. By chopping steps in the hard snow and ice we worked our way up, keeping to the base of the rock on the left." After seven hours of climbing from Lake Ann, the entire party reached the top. They could hardly have imagined that in a couple of decades there would be a path worn in the heather slopes from so many climbers.

Although I have climbed the North Face, the Northwest Arête, the Southwest Face, and the Sulphide Glacier routes, Fisher Chimneys is my favorite. It offers an exhilarating blend of firm rock, snow, ice, and glacier travel amid spectacular scenery. I have guided the climb several times and climbed the route in winter. Most memorable was an autumn climb that I did alone.

I left Bellingham at 4 A.M. one morning in late October, hoping to find good conditions on Shuksan and to beat a forthcoming storm. An overcast sky and a breeze signaled a change in the air. At Austin Pass, it was beginning to get light as I shouldered a day-pack with lunch, crampons, and ice tools. It was one of the few trips that I did not carry a camera.

Halfway to Lake Ann a mother black bear and her cubs scrambled up a tree fifteen feet from the trail. She clung to the bark, hissing at me, and without my Nikon there was no reason to tarry. At the start of the Chimneys I changed into boots and cached my sneakers under a boulder. Fire-red patches of huckleberry bushes dotted the talus slopes, while higher up, fresh snow frosted the mountain. It would not be good if the snow obscured the crevasses on the Upper Curtis Glacier. Fall can be the most dangerous time of the year for glacier travel, as snowstorms accompanied by wind can smother the cracks with a layer of fragile snow that holds no weight.

Soon the Chimneys and Winnie's Slide were below me. I picked an easterly route across the Upper Curtis, leading toward the summit pyramid. Although the fall storm had dusted the glacier with a light layer of snow, I could easily make out the crevasses and I skirted around them. Once across the glacier I found excellent cramponing up the left side of the summit's North Face. Leaving the spikes on, I groped around the corner of a rock bulge and hesitated again. A slip would drop me into the deep moat between the glacier and the wall. The solution was obvious—don't fall. Tom Patey's definition of a solo climber came to mind: one man falling alone.

Marianne Hviding traverses the upper Fisher Chimneys in winter

Above the moat, I front-pointed up a patch of hard firn, then took to the rock again. After another hundred feet I was able to remove the crampons and continue up the East Ridge to the summit. The wind had picked up, enveloping Baker's summit in a telltale cloudcap. After a quick snack and a hit of coffee from the thermos, I began the tedious job of downclimbing.

Climbing alone, you are so absorbed with the immediate problems that the passage of time is disrupted. Sections that I thought took hours really only lasted minutes and by mid-afternoon I was back at the car. Aside from nicks in the ice left by my crampons, Shuksan was unchanged. I, on the other hand, felt the rewards of a lone day in the mountains, punctuated by crashing ice, rockfall, the scuffle of boots, and my own breathing.

One year later I was again alone on the mountain when I encountered potentially hidden crevasses on the edge of the Sulphide Glacier above the Southwest Face. I paused, assessing the crevasse danger, and decided to turn back, just as pleased with the day as if I had made the top.

Will Martin and Bobbi Cochran above Hell's Highway

Mount Shuksan: Fisher Chimneys

First ascent: Esther Buswell, Clarence Fisher, Paul Hugdahl, Lars Loveseth, Dr. Emmons Spearin, Winnie Spieseke, and Harriet Taylor; July 3, 1927
Difficulty: Snow, ice, glacier travel, and rock to 5.2 or 5.3
Equipment: A few nuts, slings, and snow and ice pro are useful. An ice ax and crampons.

Access: From Glacier, take Highway 542 24 miles to its end at Austin Pass above the Mount Baker Ski Area. From the pass, hike the Lake Ann Trail 2.5 miles to a junction. Keep left, and hike 1.5 miles more to Lake Ann. From the lake, follow a trail 1.5 miles east to the first large talus slope at 5200 feet. Just past a small gorge, and near the Lower Curtis Glacier, cross talus (in some years a snowpatch) to gain a right-trending gully. (Do not take the right-hand path down to the glacier.) Follow the gully for 300 feet to a knoll, then traverse across talus to the base of the chimneys.

Route: Start up the route next to a large boulder, close to the face. From there, follow a steep right gully-chimney ascent for 600 feet. Near the top of Shuksan Arm the gully forks. The right-hand grassy gully leads over a chockstone and on up to a notch. From the notch you can traverse the south side of a ridge to the top of Winnie's Slide, avoiding the ice pitch. A left-hand gully goes straight up to Shuksan Arm, from where you can traverse above the White Salmon Glacier east to Winnie's Slide and one pitch of ice. Then climb the left side of the Upper Curtis Glacier to below the Hourglass, traverse south and descend to the start of Hell's Highway. Ascend this broad chute up onto the Sulphide Glacier, then climb the glacier to the base of the summit pinnacle. A good finish to the climb is to go up the southeast corner of the summit pyramid. The climbing is enjoyable low 5th class and avoids rockfall from climbers in the gully leading directly to the summit. The Chimneys portion of the route is particularly slippery when wet. Much of the climbing is on exposed paths or compact rock; there are few cracks or horns for anchor placements.

Descent: Downclimb the same route.

Maps: Green Trails: Mount Shuksan No. 14; USGS: Mount Shuksan and Shuksan Arm

Reference: *CAG 3: Rainy Pass to Fraser River*

14 ELDORADO PEAK
Eldorado Glacier

BETWEEN THE CASCADE PASS AREA and Diablo Dam on the Skagit River is a profusion of rugged peaks, including Pinnacle, Backbone Ridge, Austera Towers, Teepah Towers, Dorado Needle, Early Morning Spire, and Eldorado. These mountains are walled off by the brush-filled valleys of Newhalem, McAllister, and Marble Creeks. Climbers setting out to do the Pyramid–Inspiration Traverse will find virtually no paths coupled with hard hiking over difficult terrain. The scenic rewards are great, as a 1937 group of ski mountaineers discovered. They later wrote, "One member of the party (after a winter of skiing in the Alps) thought he was back in the Alps."

"Not the golden Eldorado of the Spaniards of old, but a mountain of snow and ice."

Eldorado is 6.3 miles northwest of Cascade Pass. Its great western wall of banded gneiss rises 2800 feet above the Marble Creek Cirque to a height of 8868 feet. On the backside, the gentle Inspiration Glacier gradually steepens to form a spiny crest of snow leading to the summit.

In August of 1933, Donald Blair, Norval Grigg, Arthur Wilson, and Art Winder made the first ascent, approaching from Sibley Creek and The Triad. The account of the climb tells how the four, from a 3500-foot camp, ". . . headed for their Eldorado. Not the golden Eldorado of the Spaniards of old, but a mountain of snow and ice." They climbed to the summit and returned to camp in a twelve-hour round trip—one more testament that in decades past there were some very fit people.

A group of Mazama climbers in 1956 found the final summit ridge invigorating. As they described it, "The crest proved to be a knife-like ridge of insubstantial, wind driven snow. Great billows of fog blew over the mountain, until the ridge and the leader blended into whiteness." Twenty-six years later I found myself leading three climbers up this same ridge.

It was near the end of a week-long trip in the mountains. We had climbed Dorado Needle the day before, in fog and mist. That night we camped

Eldorado Peak, with the Eldorado Glacier route shown

at the head of the McAllister Creek Glacier, where the clouds dissipated, revealing stars. Enveloped by such beauty in the heart of the mountains, I should have been happy, but dealing with my clients for five days had frayed my nerves. In the evening they would crowd into one tent and gab about relationships, parties, and new cars. They were three thousand miles from home, had paid good money to be guided on the trip, yet had no interest in the adjacent peaks or in learning much from the experience. I kept the lines of communication open for five days, but that was all.

In the morning we broke camp and headed for Eldorado, with the intention of dumping our packs along the way and going to the summit. The weather was flawless, so we carried out our plan and finally crossed the last exposed snowy ridge. "Isn't this great?" I yelled, in a last ditch effort to stimulate those guys. It failed.

On such a day in the mountains it was hard for me to remain glum. The slopes dropped away on every side. I was atop a sparkling world, surrounded by jagged spires and riven icefields. For me, Eldorado was enjoyable, and I spotted many future objectives, including the Southwest Face of Early Morning Spire. There would be other trips and different people to share them with.

Eldorado Peak: Eldorado Glacier

First ascent: Donald Blair, Norval Grigg, Arthur Wilson, and Art Winder; August 27, 1933

Difficulty: Glacier travel and moderate snow

Equipment: Rope and gear for safe glacier travel. Ice ax and crampons

Permit: Permits, required for overnight use in North Cascades National Park, are available from the North Cascades National Park Ranger Station, Skagit District, Marblemount, WA (360-873-4590).

Access: From Burlington, drive 47 miles on Highway 20 to Marblemount. Turn right onto the bridge over the Skagit River to the Cascade River Road. Drive 7.5 miles to the Sibley Creek Road, turn left and follow the latter 4 miles to Hidden Lake Trail. Hike the trail 2 miles. At 5400 feet leave the trail and climb a path (or snow) to a saddle at 6040 feet. Continue following a path left and up, along the ridge crest to just west of The Triad. Cross a snowfield (icy late in the year) on the north to a 6804-foot knoll, then descend a gully to the south side of The Triad. Traverse the southern snow and talus slopes for 2 miles to below the Triad–Eldorado col. From below the col, continue east around a shoulder, then do a long descending traverse to the southwest foot of the Eldorado Glacier (6300 feet). Hike northeast to the nearly-flat plateau of the Inspiration Glacier to begin the actual climb.

Route: From a saddle 7480 feet southeast of the summit on the Inspiration Glacier, travel north, then west, to gain the easy, but exposed, snow ridge to the crest of the summit dome.

Descent: Retrace the ascent and the approach.

Maps: Green Trails: Diablo Dam No. 48; USGS: Eldorado Peak and Forbidden Peak

Reference: *CAG 2: Stevens Pass to Rainy Pass*

15 EARLY MORNING SPIRE
Southwest Face and Upper South Ridge

ONE MILE NORTH NORTHWEST OF ELDORADO is the imposing Early Morning Spire. The 8200-foot peak was not climbed until 1971, when Richard Emerson and Tom Hornbein ascended it via some dozen pitches with difficulty to 5.8, A-1. In July of 1972 Dave Anderson and Bruce Carson put up a grade II on the Southeast Face; Steve Barnett and Mark Weigelt later did a different line on the same face.

"It felt like an alpine peak that narrowed and soared up, with an aesthetic look to it."

In 1981 a fourth route was added to the peak when Mark Bebie, Gary Brill, and Lowell Skoog climbed the right side of the Southwest Face, then finished via the Upper South Ridge. Skoog described the peak's appearance as the three climbers approached it from the snow basin below, "We had this image of the pinnacles in the Alps we had seen photos of. It felt like an alpine peak that narrowed and soared up, with an aesthetic look to it."

The trio were primarily mountaineers who didn't often spend much time rock climbing on lowland crags. Lowell especially, and his brothers Gordy and Carl, focused on skiing and ski mountaineering more than their friends. Carl once admitted to me that if it was so wet in the mountains that any form of alpine activity was out, they would break down and go climbing at the dryer Peshastin Pinnacles. Brill did a bit more rock in his spare time and chose to carry rock shoes for the ascent of Early Morning Spire. As a result of being more nimble without boots, he got more of the tricky pitches.

Low on the route is a short steep corner that even in late season can still seep water from some deep and unseen damp fissure within the mountain. Although this is the technical crux of the route, Northwest climbers are generally more interested in being in the high alpine and having fun than breast-beating over any one hard move. As Skoog describes it, "After we had done that slippery aid pitch [5.9 when freed and dry] we got up to this pedestal

Early Morning Spire on the left. The route begins above the sunlit snow patch

where we had a "singing" belay—we used to make up songs on these trips; Gary and I were having a good time while Mark was leading the next pitch."

Above this point the route climbs several moderate pitches, allowing you to gain elevation quickly. It was here the climbers began to feel the true ambiance of the place that likened it to the greater ranges. "You started in this basin and there wasn't much of a view," he said, "but then as you climbed

Sue Harrington below Early Morning Spire on Dorado Needle

half the height, you got above a ridge and you could look across to Eldorado. It was very scenic."

From a low-angled area that harbors a snowpatch until late in the year, the route diagonals up and right and turns a blind corner. It is here that the route looks improbable, and any direct line to the summit would be extremely difficult and time consuming. Brill, Bebie, and Skoog felt the pull of the unknown even more on that July day. Skoog relates, "Once we made the finger traverse out to the ridge, there was a lot of uncertainty, since it was a new variation. I remember it being super-enjoyable because it was just not hard, it was pretty clean, kind of blocky."

After reaching the summit, they quickly descended the backside and romped over for an ascent of Dorado Needle by the normal route. Back in camp they made plans for an early departure on day three, as Brill was worried about an incoming storm. Skoog's journal from that day reflects the group's ambivalence over the need to hurry. "Five A.M. we munch breakfast," he wrote. "I ignore suggestions to move by falling asleep. 7:45 we decide to stir. Warm morning with clouds obscuring the peaks." The warm front that often presages the real storm had arrived. Even so, they were able to climb The Triad via its south side on the hike out the Triad–Sibley Creek divide.

The trio's climb appeared to be the best line up the 1400-foot face when I traversed beneath it one year later, while leading a group along the Pyramid/Inspiration traverse. The problem, as I saw it, was trying to squeeze the approach and the route into a weekend.

Midsummer of 1989 Sue Harrington and I chose to attempt the route in two days. Going light, we left behind boots and crampons; then, on the approach we encountered a long traverse over frozen snow. The day was perfect, but the slope was far too long to chop steps across. We retreated.

We returned the following summer, armed with crampons and three days to complete the trip. Warm weather turned the snow to mush, making our spikes useless burdens. Once at the Triad–Eldorado Col we pitched our tent and took in the view over dinner. A sea of spires, hanging glaciers, and near-vertical timbered slopes filled the Marble Creek Cirque. Our objective was still a dispiriting four miles away and involved a great deal of up and down scrambling.

Leaving camp at 5:30 A.M., Sue and I descended the Triad Glacier, then crossed snowfields and talus to arrive at the route three hours later. The day was pristine and the rock superb. The climbing included cracks, friction, stemming, and face moves. Sue was down to a tank top and Lycra in the heat, and our pack was full of clothes. The Southwest Face provided nine pitches of climbing to where it joined the South Ridge. Sue led the final clean ramp and undercling that ended on the exposed ridge.

In three more pitches we were on the summit. I started rewinding my film, but it broke inside the camera— the only flaw in the day. I regretted that we had carried heavy leather boots and axes to the summit, while climbing in rock shoes. We could have cut weight by taking plastic shells and one ax.

After a summit snack, we rappelled and downclimbed to an impassable crevasse. A snow bollard allowed our rope to reach the lower glacier, where

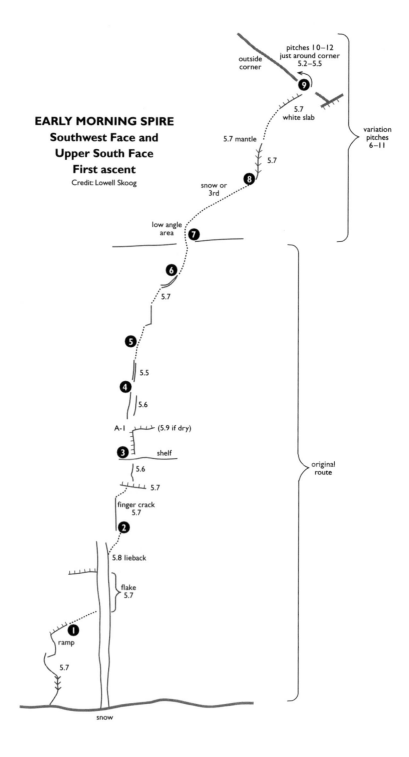

EARLY MORNING SPIRE
Southwest Face and
Upper South Face
First ascent
Credit: Lowell Skoog

outside
corner

pitches 10–12
just around corner
5.2–5.5

9

5.7
white slab

5.7 mantle

variation
pitches
6–11

5.7

8

snow or
3rd

low angle
area

7

6

5.7

5

5.5

4

5.6

A-1 — (5.9 if dry)

3

shelf

5.6

5.7

finger crack
5.7

2

5.8 lieback

flake
5.7

original
route

1

ramp

5.7

snow

we completed the long march back to high camp. As we plodded the last hundred yards to our tent, the sun went down behind Mount Baker, ending a great sixteen-hour day.

Early Morning Spire: Southwest Face and Upper South Ridge

First ascent: Mark Bebie, Gary Brill and Lowell Skoog; July 1981
Difficulty: Grade III, 5.9
Equipment: A standard rack up to a 3-inch cam. Ice ax and crampons.
Permit: A permit is required from the NPS, Skagit District, Marblemount, WA (360-873-4590).
Access: Approach as for Eldorado, described previously. From the south side of the Triad–Eldorado Col climb corners and ramps for one long pitch to the col (5th class). There are many possibilities; take your choice. From the col descend 1100 feet down the glacier to the north, traverse snow and talus below Eldorado, then keep high in the brush and woods next to Early Morning Spire's lowest rock ridge. Once on the other side, an easy snow slope leads up to the Southwest Face.
Route: Begin the climb on the left side of the face, right of a prominent chimney system (1971 Southwest Face Route). **[1]** Climb a shallow corner (5.7) and a right ramp to a belay. **[2]** Cross a chimney, then climb a steep flake (5.7) and a short lieback (5.8) on the right side of the chimney to a belay. **[3]** Jam a thin crack up (5.7), move right, then climb through an overhang (5.7) to a large shelf. **[4]** Climb a right-facing corner (5.9) and a slot to a belay. **[5]** through **[7]** Lead up and right on the face to a low-angle area. **[8]** Traverse right and up on snow or 3rd class rock. **[9]** Ascend a corner (5.7), then a face and a slab beneath a roof lead right to the South Ridge. **[10]** through **[12]** Climb up the right side of the ridge to the summit.
Descent: Downclimb and rappel the north side to the glacier, negotiating crevasses.
Maps: Green Trails: Diablo Dam No. 48; USGS: Eldorado Peak and Forbidden Peak
Reference: *CAG 2: Stevens Pass to Rainy Pass*

16 FORBIDDEN PEAK
West Ridge

AT 8815 FEET, FORBIDDEN'S GNEISSIC TETRAHEDRON is conspicuous from many parts of the Cascades. The Boston, Forbidden, and Taboo Glaciers continue to shape the concave faces of the peak, even though the latter icefield is in its dying stages. A northerly approach to the West Ridge over the Taboo Glacier can be tricky, as massive slabs of melting ice and snow are in constant motion on the slabby rock.

"Heavy snow clinging to the ridge and sides of the peak added an avalanche danger against which we did not choose to pit our energies."

In April of 1940 Lloyd Anderson, Fred Beckey, and Dwight Watson attempted the peak after hiking eleven miles of trail and several more of snow and brush. They climbed the couloir leading to the ridge, finding there, according to their account, "Heavy snow clinging to the ridge and sides of the peak added an avalanche danger against which we did not choose to pit our energies." The group climbed Eldorado on May 19, but ruled out any north side possibilities on Forbidden when they saw it.

On Memorial Day, Beckey, his brother Helmy, Jim Crooks, Dave Lind, and Anderson returned to try the peak they had now dubbed Forbidden, naming it after the peak's unsuccessful attempts and forbidding aspects. From a camp in Boston Basin, they climbed the couloir to within 250 feet of the top, where they encountered a difficult tower. Snow flurries, wind, and chilled fingers persuaded them to retreat and attempt the ridge the following day.

June 1 dawned clear. The five climbers reached their previous high point, where Lind changed into tennis shoes and quickly dealt with the tower. After two hours on the rocky crest the group gained the summit as snow began to fall. Their descent was complicated by fresh sticky snow on the holds; it took as long as the climb up.

▲

Forbidden's West Ridge has become a popular route, as I discovered in 1983. While bivouacked at the North Ridge Col, friends and I watched a

Opposite: *Sue and Rick Harrington on the exposed West Ridge of Forbidden Peak. Mount Torment in the distance*

Forbidden Peak. The West Ridge Route follows the left skyline

procession of headlamps moving slowly down the ridge just after sunset. We counted six different parties bivouacked on the route. Why is the climb included here? After climbing both the North Ridge and the Northwest Face, I did the West Ridge in 1992 and liked it the best. However, it is a matter of taste; I have talked with climbers who prefer the Northwest Face.

If you find many parties are signed up for the ridge, try one of the other routes mentioned here. Although you might climb faster than other groups, it is difficult to get around them on the narrow ridge. There is also the hazard from climber-induced rockfall in the couloir, particularly late in the season.

During August of 1992, Sue Harrington, her brother Rick, and I set out to do the ridge over a Sunday and Monday. Rick was vacationing from New York. The only other climb he had done was the normal route on Liberty Bell in 1987. Based on that experience, we felt we could also guide him up Forbidden. The weather report was not promising, but we hoped it would discourage parties from flocking to the ridge. Rick was apprehensive about the climb, and especially the forecast. "Isn't this the sort of climb you should do when the weather is good?" he asked. "Nah, we'll be fine. The climb's not that hard," I assured him.

Rick hadn't exercised in some time, and part way up the Boston Basin climbers' path he was hurting. Black flies were an unpleasant addition to the upward grind. At the first stream, Rick slipped and doused his cigarettes. Morale was low as we entered Boston Basin. A black cloud coalesced over Boston Peak and jabbed the basin with lightning and rain; it was going to be a fun night in bivy sacs and no tent.

Two British climbers stumbled into camp just at dusk—they had not made the summit that day. Rick wondered how the three of us could do any better. After cous cous and cocoa, we snuggled into our sacs as the first drops from a second storm pelted us. No matter how tight we pulled the draw-strings, some always splattered in.

Morning looked better, with much blue sky to the west and south, the usual direction from which Northwest storms come. We started early and crossed the creaking glacier to the base of the couloir. With no experience on snow, Rick was stumped by the short bergschrund wall. I yelled at him to grab the rope above and Sue gave him a push. Although Rick felt like a sack of flour, he learned quickly and carried out our explicit instructions.

We switched into rock shoes at the col, cached excess gear and started up. The climbing was fun, with exposure in many places. Sue led the tower pitch and yelled down to Rick to watch her progress. He hugged the spine with his eyes directed toward me, the belayer. "I can't look up!" he groaned. To Sue and me, who have shared many peaks, the airiness and the view are often the reasons for climbing an alpine route. "I guess if I did this more often I'd feel more comfortable," Rick confided.

On the summit we smiled for a photo, then began our descent. In minutes a thick fog welled up from below and a thunderstorm that had been lurking to the southeast pounded us with hail. Once in the couloir, lighting exploded on the spires above and reverberated against the rock walls. Strikes within 200 yards convinced me that our existence was about to end. While Sue climbed down to my belay, I got Rick into his raincoat as water streamed out of cracks and corners of the couloir's sides.

We had to recrampon just above the glacier, since Rick was having difficulty crossing a firn slope. Higher up, the snow had been too sticky to justify wearing them. Everyone shivered as the rain and lightning continued. At camp Rick managed to light a damp cigarette while I brewed coffee. It was late, so we finished our coffee on the move, glad for its brief warmth.

Darkness caught us on the hike out and more than once Rick's fatigued legs buckled. Everything was totally soaked. The next morning Rick limped down the stairs at our house and said, "God, am I sore, but that was an incredible experience." He didn't actually say "fun," but perhaps on his third Cascade climb he will.

Forbidden Peak: West Ridge

First ascent: Lloyd Anderson, Fred Beckey, Helmy Beckey, Jim Crooks, and Dave Lind; June 1, 1940

Difficulty: Grade III, 5.4

Equipment: Light rack of gear up to a 3-inch cam and some snow protection. Ice ax and crampons.

Permit: A permit is required from the NPS, Skagit District, Marblemount, WA (360-873-4590).

Access: Approach as for Eldorado, described previously. Drive 14.2 miles farther on the Cascade River Road and park on the left. Hike the old road 1½ miles to its end, then head right, up a steep climbers' path 3 miles into Boston Basin. Follow the path up and left to moraine campsites below the south side of Forbidden. To reach the climb, diagonal up and left across talus and ascend the extreme left side of the Boston Glacier, then diagonal back to the right to reach the couloir. There are no bridges over any of the creeks; crossings are hazardous in high water.

Route: From the top of the couloir, climb mainly the ridge crest. In places, north side traverses ease difficulties around towers. From the lower west summit, drop into a notch and climb up to the east and true summit.

Descent: Downclimb and rappel the ridge.

Maps: Green Trails: Diablo Dam No. 48, Cascade Pass No. 80; USGS: Forbidden Peak

Reference: *CAG 2: Stevens Pass to Rainy Pass*

17 MOUNT BUCKNER
North Face

EAST OF SAHALE ARM THE HUGE BOWL OF HORSESHOE BASIN sweeps up to the 9080-foot summit of Mount Buckner. From the southwest the peak is a scramble, but a view from Forbidden Peak reveals the nature of Buckner's North Wall, a 1200-foot face of steep ice and snow. The mountain was first climbed in 1901 from Horseshoe Basin around the time the Black Warrior Mine began operating. The rusted and weathered remains of tram cables and buckets are the only evidence left after the ore ran out in the early 1950s.

The rusted and weathered remains of tram cables and buckets are the only evidence left after the ore ran out in the early 1950s.

In July of 1938 Calder Bressler, Ralph Clough, Bill Cox, and Tom Meyers climbed over Sahale Peak, traversed the east face of Boston, then crossed the Boston Glacier to Buckner's north face. Armed with tricouni-nail boots and ice axes, the climbers ascended rock adjacent the snow and ice face for 700 feet. At a point 500 feet below the top, they later wrote, "Cox was elected for the lead, and manfully hewed 150 steps up steep ice while we rested and offered sage advice and commentary on his technique and choice of route."

Once on top, they traversed to the higher Southwest Peak, then glissaded snow into Horseshoe Basin. From the basin the group climbed 2000 feet back up to Sahale Arm, then hiked down to Cascade Pass that evening.

During July of 1983 I got a good look at Buckner's ice route while descending the east ledges of Forbidden Peak. Far across the broad Boston Glacier rose the precipitous north wall of Buckner. I was immediately struck with the biggest problem: how to approach it, and how to descend? In August, Tim Boyer and I suggested the North Face to two of our clients, using the same approach as the 1938 party. We felt they could handle the climb in two days and without a mishap. We were wrong.

The first day we hiked 6.2 miles and gained 3600 feet up to Cascade

Tim Boyer and his clients approach Mount Buckner

Pass and beyond to the Sahale Glacier moraine. The campsite was great, the evening was clear. To the south stretched the Ptarmigan Traverse, replete with sharp summits. At 5 A.M. the next day, we climbed over Sahale, then traversed the rotten East Face of Boston Peak.

I find being on loose rock with less-experienced people distinctly nerve-wracking. A climber who spends only a few days a year in the mountains can't be expected to anticipate problems on dangerous slopes. Thus, the client hires experienced professionals to lead them safely up climbs. The 1898 first ascent party correctly called Boston a "heap of low-grade ore." Boulders bounded into space as we traversed ledges and class 3 slabs leading to the Boston Glacier. In 1977 I had been with a park ranger who pulled a huge rock onto his foot and sprained it. I hoped history would not repeat itself!

Crossing the icefield was pleasant. Soon we reached Buckner and put the bergschrund below us. Staying on the ice face offered excellent climbing for 600 feet, where it was necessary to cross a patch of talus and rock rib to reach the final ice slope. As my rope was first, I cautioned my client not to knock any rocks onto the pair below. Tim was leading the rope just behind as my rope companion stepped on a loose, grapefruit-sized stone sending it down the face. Tim screamed "rock!" at his client as we held our breaths. Seconds later Tim yelled to him; he replied he was okay.

Tim came on across the talus and started belaying his client up. The 10.5mm rope came easily and after 100 feet Tim held the chopped end of the rope—but no client! The lower portion of the rock rib obscured our view of the climber below, so we instructed him to keep both tools on the ice and not to move. I downclimbed easy 5th class on the rib to where I could see the client, quickly secured a belay with small Stoppers, and hurled the end of my rope down to him. He clipped into the knotted end of the new rope and I belayed him up.

The North Face Route on Mount Buckner, above the Boston Glacier

Because the remaining sixty feet of his rope still lay on the ice above, he had been completely unaware it was cut by the rock, and was about to resume climbing. Fortunately, there were no further incidents, and the upper ice slope was wonderful climbing on firm water ice. The summit was soon ours, followed by the long drop into Horseshoe Basin and the climb back out. We made our high camp just before sunset, Cascade Pass after dark, and the cars at 2 A.M.

Although both clients had planned to try another ice climb the following day, one took a rest day and one went home. Tim and I came to three conclusions about the adventure: Buckner was a three-day trip for clients, it wasn't a good place for two rope teams and, despite explicit instructions, people still make mistakes.

Mount Buckner: North Face

First ascent: Calder Bressler, Ralph Clough, Bill Cox, and Tom Meyers; July 28, 1938.

Difficulty: Snow and ice to 50 degrees and some rock.

Equipment: Snow and ice anchors, small rock pro, ice ax, and crampons.

Permit: A permit is required from the NPS, Skagit District, Marblemount, WA (360-873-4590).

Access: Approach as for Forbidden, described previously, and drive 0.5 mile beyond the Boston Basin Trail to the end of the Cascade River Road. Hike 3.7 miles up to Cascade Pass, then 2.5 miles up Sahale Arm to a moraine campsite at the foot of the Sahale Glacier. Climb over Sahale Peak, traverse the East Face of Boston, then cross the Boston Glacier to the base of the climb. (To avoid Boston Peak, approach from Boston Basin and Sharkfin Col to gain the Boston Glacier and the North Face of Buckner. With this approach you would have to carry bivy gear up and over, then come down through Horseshoe Basin and over Sahale Arm.)

Route: From the Boston Glacier, ascend the right-hand snow and ice face leading to the southwest peak of Buckner. Near the summit work left across a rock rib, then ascend the final ice sheet to the top.

Descent: Descend the southwest side into Horseshoe Basin, then climb back up a broad talus gully to Sahale Arm.

Maps: Green Trails: Cascade Pass No. 80 and McGregor Mountain No. 81; USGS: Cascade Pass and Goode Mountain

Reference: *CAG 2: Stevens Pass to Rainy Pass*

18 MOUNT TRIUMPH
Northeast Ridge

THE NORTHEAST RIDGE OF TRIUMPH is not a difficult test piece, but rather a basic requirement to establishing oneself as any sort of decent mountaineer. My friends had already climbed it and their comments ranged from, "Oh, yes, a beautiful peak," and, "A classic Cascade ridge climb," to, "You haven't done Triumph yet?"

Driving North Cascades Highway 20 toward Marblemount you catch only glimpses of 7270-foot Mount Triumph between verdant ridges of hemlock and fir. However, from the summit of Mount Baker, and virtually every other major peak in the Cascades, Triumph's pinnacle of Skagit gneiss is clearly visible.

"The goats were one of our greatest hazards, for as we carefully made our way along the bench, they sent down an avalanche of rocks from about 1000 feet above."

In 1938 Lloyd Anderson, Lyman Boyer, Dave Lind, Sig Hall, and Louis Smith made the first ascent, up the southwest side. Ironically, the greatest difficulty the men encountered was not related to the climbing itself, but to the mountain goats they had been following up the mountain. Anderson felt they were lucky; he wrote, "The goats were one of our greatest hazards, for as we carefully made our way along the bench, (on Triumph's southwest side) they sent down an avalanche of rocks from about 1000 feet above. Except for Dave Lind's quick action in flattening himself against the rock wall, letting the rocks fly over his head, they would surely have injured him."

On the opposite side of the mountain, the Northeast Ridge forms a sweeping crest between two glaciers that are still carving away the east and north faces of the peak. In August of 1965, Natalie Cole, Joan and Joe Firey, and Frank Tarver completed the first ascent of this 1300-foot route. The group found the route to be, ". . . a classic alpine ridge offering a fine variety of class 3 and 4 climbing and a few safety pitons."

Mount Triumph. The Northeast Ridge Route ascends the right skyline.

In 1987, Sue Harrington and I set out to climb the Northeast Ridge in one day. After five miles of uphill trail, one mile of winding, brushy climbers path, a long talus slope, and 3000 feet of elevation gain, we reached a notch at 5760 feet. We were now one mile and still a glacier away from the ridge. It was only noon, but we were spent from the approach. Sue and I settled for a scramble up nearby Thornton Peak and promised to return. Who ever named the thing Triumph?

The following summer we organized a second expedition to the elusive crag. When my friends learned of our one-day attempt the season before they scoffed, "Tried it in a day, huh? Kind of a long hike wasn't it?" Now we decided on the conventional weekend strategy, with only a slight twist: Sue and Mike Jacobson would climb as a roped team, while Dave Turner and I would climb the ridge unroped.

Dave and I spent Saturday thrashing ourselves doing hard crack pitches on the Index Town Wall and began the hike into Triumph at 5 P.M. Sue and Mike had sensibly used the day to hike to our previous high point on the notch and bivouac. We reached Thornton Lake at around 7:30 P.M., but the NPS volunteer there informed us that the designated bivy site at the notch was filled to capacity with the allowed six people. Until then I hadn't realized the notch was within North Cascades National Park. We grumbled, ate a dinner snack, and crawled into our bags, along with many mosquitoes.

On Sunday we reached the notch by 7 A.M. to find Mike and Sue still in their sleeping bags. Over their first, and our second, hot drinks, we watched the rosy-orange light of dawn wash over the glacier and the two other climbing parties on it. Soon the four of us were also on the icefield, trudging across it toward the Northeast Ridge.

One of the greatest feelings in the mountains is to move quickly and freely up firm rock with wild exposure and reasonable climbing. Triumph delivered this, and more. As with most ridge climbs of this type, if the climbing looks too hard, you're probably off-route. Investigating the walls to the left or right gets you back on track.

There was only one point of concern, which came from two other climbers on the route unroped and in mountain boots. At the route's crux (which is a 5.7 wide crack if you stay right on the crest) each climber looked shaky. Having the benefit of rock shoes, I edged my way to the extreme left side of a good ledge, trying to get out of their drop zone, and watched with apprehension. They displayed the classic tense moment all climbers have experienced—pause, a long look up, and a long look down. Two more unsteady moves and they heaved over the sheer bit and onto easier climbing.

From the crack to the summit the climbing was enjoyable. Our perfect July day showed no threat of rain or clouds. The top was a jumbled pile of boulders where we enjoyed stunning views of the Southern and Northern

Pickets, Mount Shuksan, Mount Blum, and nearby Mount Despair. The horizon bristled with enough objectives to last a lifetime. In fact, a fair number of Washington climbers have made this state of eight hundred glaciers just that: their life's work.

Off the climb and back in town I felt fairly smug about finally nabbing Triumph. I asked a local, Dave Tucker, about Mount Despair, situated two miles northwest of Triumph. With a twinkle in his eye he looked at me and asked, "You haven't done Despair yet?"

Mount Triumph: Northeast Ridge

First ascent: Natalie Cole, Joan and Joe Firey, and Frank Tarver; August 1965

Difficulty: Grade III, 5.7 (if climbed directly on the crest) and 5.5 if you traverse onto the North Face

Equipment: A light rack of Stoppers and cams. One 3-inch cam is useful for the crack. Ice ax and crampons.

Permit: A permit is required from the NPS, Skagit District, Marblemount, WA (360-873-4590).

Access: Because the heather is fragile, party size is limited. Groups are encouraged to camp only on the rocks, snow, or in existing campsites. From Marblemount drive east on Highway 20 for 12 miles to the Thornton Lakes Road. Turn left and follow the road 5 miles to the Thornton Lakes Trail. Hike 5.3 miles to lower Thornton Lake. From the outlet take a climbers' path that switchbacks up and left, then winds around the west side of the lake. The path crosses just below the outlet of the second, higher lake, then climbs a long talus slope and a gully to the notch at 5760 feet. From the notch it's a gentle glacier walk to the ridge.

Route: Generally, climb the ridge crest. At the high-angle step on the upper third of the ridge you can climb the wide crack in a corner (5.7) or traverse right at the base of the crack onto the North Face (5.5). Once on the north side it's possible to climb to the notch on the ridge again. At the final step, traverse left and up onto a ledge, then ascend steep heather (class 4) to the top. The final heather slopes can be treacherous in wet weather.

Descent: Downclimb and rappel the ridge.

Maps: Green Trails: Marblemount No. 47; USGS: Mount Triumph

Reference: *CAG 3: Rainy Pass to Fraser River*

19 MOUNT DESPAIR
Southeast Route

SEVERAL DECADES BEFORE ABC SPORTS COINED THE TERM, "The thrill of victory and the agony of defeat," Northwest climbers had already named their local peaks in honor of the horrendous approaches, bone-chilling wet weather, and steep, forbidding walls of snow and rock. Success was never assured. Labels like Forbidden, Torment, Stormy, Forgotten, Inspiration, Blizzard, and of course, Triumph and Despair epitomized the range.

Mount Despair isn't close to anything; it lies alone with Mount Blum to the northwest, the Pickets to the northeast, and Mount Triumph to the south. The brush-choked drainages of Triumph Creek on the west and Goodell Creek to the east further guard the summit from any close or easy inspection. Any approach to the peak is primarily an off-trail adventure of no small distance. In fact, in 1939, for Lloyd Anderson, Fred Beckey (age sixteen at the time), and Clinton Kelley it involved a hike of twelve miles up brushy ridges and across steep snow slopes.

A perfect day had dawned, but as a few high cirrus clouds were forming, there was no telling how long it would last.

The young Beckey, having just weaned himself from alpine adventures with the Boy Scouts, climbed twenty-three summits that year. Despair was his initial first ascent. In late June, with Anderson and Kelley, he hiked several miles up what is now the Thornton Lakes Road (at that time it was only a trail), and plunged into the brush. They climbed 3000 feet straight up. Once the three climbers topped out on the high ridge south of Thornton Peak the going got easier and in places the early summer sun had melted away the winter snows, leaving steep bare patches of slippery grass.

Kelley took a tumble on one of these slides, bruising himself badly. The trio decided to make camp near a clump of trees with a spring and allow the injured Kelley to rest up. As it was still early in the afternoon, Beckey and Anderson climbed Mount Triumph while Kelley made the campsite more comfortable. The next morning all three left camp and headed toward Despair

Mount Despair. The route follows the snow slope or, when conditions are bad, the right hand ridge.

with only day-packs. A perfect day had dawned, but as a few high cirrus clouds were forming, there was no telling how long it would last.

Once over Triumph Pass, the climbers glissaded 700 feet to a frozen cirque lake and then traversed northward across rough country toward the peak. More traversing led them up to the south ridge, where they climbed toward the southeast corner of the upper snowfield. Here they found the slope steep and the snow avalanche-prone, persuading them to kick steps straight up, which would cause the least disturbance.

From the top of the snow, the alpinists scrambled to Despair's untrod summit by late morning and built a cairn of stones. For miles around lay unclimbed summits, many more of which Beckey and Anderson would leave their mark on. The following year Beckey would climb eight summits in the Northern and Southern Pickets, as well as others in the Cascades. But from Despair, he could only imagine what ascending those needles of gneiss, granodiorite, and schist would entail. Like Gaston Rebuffat he "preferred ambitions to memories."

------------------------------------ ⋀⋀ ------------------------------------

Despair had been on my list for a long time, ever since getting a good view of it from the summit of Triumph in 1988. Two years later, in mid June, I skied in alone to attempt the peak. Thankfully, the brush was minimal. Much of it was still covered due to the "normal" snowfall the previous winter. On tele skis I reached Triumph Pass late on the first day, but was dismayed at how far away Despair still was. At the time I didn't think I could climb the peak and get back out on the second day, and that's all the time I had.

Eleven years later I returned with a climbing partner and three day's time for the adventure. It was almost 9:30 P.M. at the end of nearly eleven hours of approach when Mike Lee and I finally staggered up to the campsite near Triumph Pass. The hike in had included a traverse across 65-degree brushy cliff bands on the timber rib below Triumph. Secretly, I hoped the weather would be bad the next day, so I could just lay in the tent, eat, and rehydrate. The previous two days, in my "cram-too-much-in" style, I had been rock climbing hard on lower crags, driven 450 miles back home, and then slept only a few hours. My answering machine had Mike's voice on it. "The weather looks good," he announced. "I'll pick you up at 6:30 tomorrow morning." I groaned. Now, here I was lying in the tent with rain pattering down, mist shrouding everything, and no sign of Despair.

The capricious Cascades did their thing as the stars came out, the snow froze hard, and, in the morning, sunlight slanted across the southern slopes of Despair. Mike was motivated and had the stove roaring at 5:30 as we added tape to raw spots on our feet in preparation for grueling day number two. After a mug of cocoa, a dash of instant coffee, and pastries, we were off at 7 A.M.

With the advantage of skis we traversed moderate slopes easily to a pocket lake and up an easy ridge to the slopes below Despair's southeast ridge. Surface conditions were bad, as evidenced by the numerous trails of avalanche debris. The southeast ridge was mostly bare of snow, revealing rock steps,

Mike Lee continues to smile through brush and rain on the approach to Mount Despair

small towers, and patches of heather. At class 3 and 4, we felt it was the best way to stay off the dangerous snow and reach the illusive summit. With the boards stashed at the base of the rock, we started up.

Climbing in Randonne ski boots was not comfortable, and it was not until close to the top that Mike discovered he had his cuffs locked forward. He changed into sneakers and then belayed me up the final two pitches of sound rock. We had brought only a 60-foot piece of 8mm line, some slings and a few biners. We couldn't do any serious climbing, but the gear didn't weigh much either.

Finally, six-and-a-half hours after leaving our camp, we stood on top of Despair. Eastward the southern Pickets knifed the sky with their rock daggers, while just to the south Triumph's profile looked like something out of the Karakoram. The summit register revealed that Despair did not get a lot of traffic, with very few ascents prior to 1995, no ascents between '95 and '99, one ascent in 2000, and ours was the first for 2001, (assuming, of course, that everyone signed in). It was a remote peak, and I wasn't in a big hurry to leave.

The camera clicked and whirred until finally my film ran out. We descended the upper rocks, contemplating the snow slope below. Bombarding it with rocks got much of the unstable surface to slide away. The snow roared over a cliff band 300 feet below—not a good place to attempt a self arrest. But with care, Mike and I downclimbed, belayed each other with buried ice ax anchors, and gingerly traversed past rock outcrops that took slings. For the last anchorless stretch we unroped, not wanting to repeat the macabre scene on the Matterhorn with Whymper and his mates. The snow was weird enough to persuade us to move back over to the southeast ridge for the final downclimb to our skis.

Despite the snow conditions we carved many fabulous turns on our descent to the lake amid the most spectacular scenery in the Northwest. Mike snaked down the slope on the edge of the evening shadows, as Triumph's 1700-foot north wall loomed beyond. The small lake offered up ice water for our bottles as we pasted skins to the bottoms of our skis for the ascent back to camp. With light to spare, we trudged into the pass with tired legs, aching feet, and a gnawing hunger. Several meals later we had decimated our food and were ready for the hike out.

Day three began perfect again. With our boot buckles tight and dry socks on our taped feet we cut many tight turns in an 800-foot descent to the valley bottom. As the snow thinned, the skis went back on the packs. We traversed southward to gain a forested rib that looked a lot easier than our approach in. With only several hundred yards of real brush and two ravines, we scrambled into the woods and climbed up to 4800 feet. Here we put on our skis and skinned our way back up to the 6120-foot saddle on Thornton Ridge. Mount Despair gradually disappeared from view behind peaks, passes, ridges, ribs, valleys, gullies, glaciers, lakes, forests, brush, and clouds. It's there all right, but you will have to work hard and long to see it and climb it!

Mount Despair: Southeast Route

First ascent: Lloyd Anderson, Fred Beckey, and Clinton Kelley; July 1939
Difficulty: Snow to 45 degrees and class 3 and 4 rock. The approach is the difficult part.
Equipment: Depending on your comfort level, perhaps no gear at all. A bit of rope and some slings and biners are useful. The small glacier below Triumph Pass may be crevassed; it was hard to tell in 2001 due to the snow cover.
Permit: A permit is required from the NPS, Skagit District, Marblemount, WA (360-873-4590).
Access: I would recommend using skis no later than May, or wait until July when most of the snow has melted, and hike. The month of June can

provide just the wrong combination of conditions, making the approach horrendous. Approach as for Mount Triumph, described previously, and from the outlet of Thornton Lakes ascend the ridge on the south side of the lakes westward for 2 miles to a 6040-foot saddle just north of point 6200 feet. Traverse the ridge northward for 0.5 mile to the 6120-foot saddle below Thornton Peak. Do a 1.2 mile descent north-northwest to where a stream and timbered rib abuts a rock rampart of Triumph on the southwest side at about 5400 feet. Angle down, cross the stream and descend some 400 feet to where it is possible to finally contour the near-vertical slopes and exit into the valley. (There is no good way to do this part that I have found, except consider the alternate, described following, or show up in May.) Once in the valley, ascend the broad gully to a campsite at Triumph Pass, 5480 feet.

Alternate: From the 6120-foot saddle on Thornton Ridge do a descending traverse north-northwest, switchback southward and continue down westward to about 4800 feet to the edge of a timbered slope (it lies directly below the 6120-foot saddle on the west). Cut left and south into the timber and descend a wooded slope to 4350 feet. Exit timber, cross two small ravines, and diagonal down and northward through brush to 4200 feet. Terrain opens up here; continue traversing to 4000 feet just above valley bottom, then do a rising traverse on up to Triumph Pass. (This route actually worked well in mid-June of 2001, but when the snow is gone at the 4500–5000-foot level, it may be more cliffy and brushy.)

Route: From Triumph Pass descend the glacier (may have ablated away) 700 feet to just above a small lake. Ascend a shoulder about 500 feet to avoid a gully and then traverse the slope northward for 2 miles to a pocket lake at 4960 feet. Traverse around the right side of the cirque, ascend a sparsely wooded ridge to gain the southeast ridge at 6600 feet. If snow conditions are good, you can ascend through a short cliff and then climb directly to the summit up the main snowfield and a bit of rock at the top. Otherwise, the southeast ridge is a good scramble on easy rock.

Descent: Descend the climbing route.

Maps: Green Trails: Marblemount No. 47; USGS: Mount Triumph and Damnation Peak

Reference: *CAG 3: Rainy Pass to Fraser River*

20 INSPIRATION PEAK
South Face

INSPIRATION PEAK WAS FIRST CLIMBED VIA THE WEST RIDGE on August 29, 1940, by Fred and Helmy Beckey. In preparation for the 1200-foot rock route and 7840-foot summit, the teenage brothers changed into tennis shoes once off the glacier. After an hour, they reached the crest of the ridge, where the climbing became exposed and exhilarating. "The rock was firm, with just enough tiny cling holds to get by on," Fred recalled. Higher still, they had to do a shoulder stand. They reached the airy top where, he recounts, "Every side dropped so sheer about us as to give us the feeling of sitting atop the world."

"We didn't really realize how steep it was. It wasn't until we were on that first part, and were looking up at the thing and thinking, 'Oh, shit!'"

In 1958 Beckey returned with Dave Collins and Ed Cooper to scale the unclimbed East Ridge. On June 18, 1969, Mike Heath and Bill Sumner climbed the sheer 1000-foot South Face. Heath felt the route should become a classic, with the combination of excellent rock, continuous exposure, and challenging, but never severe, climbing.

Sumner admitted some of his best climbs were done with Mike Heath. He says, "We had a synergy and compatible abilities, and it was a good match." When planning mountain trips, Heath would go out of his way to save weight. "Mike cut the handle off of his little Sigg billy pot to make it lighter," Bill tells with a laugh. "And then he had this super lightweight pot holder and figured he'd saved some fraction of an ounce. He was that fastidious about all of his equipment." They took a more abrasion-resistant 120-foot Goldline rope because Sumner was worried about the sharp rock of the Pickets. The gear selection was also lightweight, and included some dozen pins, from a knifeblade up to a one-inch angle, and a bunch of slings.

When they made it into Terror Creek Basin they got their first close look at Inspiration Peak. Sumner describes their reaction. "We knew the face on Inspiration hadn't been done," he related. "And I remember first seeing it and thinking, 'Wow, that's a line, that jagged thing up the face!' But looking at it

Paul Sloan approaches the South Face of Inspiration Peak

straight on we didn't really realize how steep it was. It wasn't until we were on that first part [of the climb], and were looking up at the thing and thinking, 'Oh, shit!' We were not sure we wanted to commit ourselves to it, because if something didn't go, up there where we couldn't see, how easy would it be to figure out how to get down?"

But with Heath there was no hesitation about starting up onto new ground. As Sumner philosophized, "If you're paralyzed by the fear of the unknown you'll never do that kind of climbing, because all those climbs are filled with that element of the unknown." The suspense of how the route would turn out stayed with the two climbers all the way. "Once getting into it I remember being really anxious to see what was around the next corner. Is there a route here? If not, we'll have to figure out how to get off of it. That uncertainty carried on right to the very last pitch—the pure joy to just finally break out, and the difficulty ends."

Adventurous players are drawn out by the mystique of alpine climbing. "It's that appeal that sometimes the route's there and sometimes it isn't," says Sumner. "The only thing that you get out of risk, if you look at it that way, is that you risk failure. If there isn't that kind of risk, it's a lesser game." Weather also figures into the equation for reaching summits in the Pickets, or even getting back out. When the crud moves in, believe in your compass.

Sumner related the trial they had exiting the mountains. "We had a bit of an epic coming out 'cause it really socked in. Mike and I decided to go a little higher, and we were in this pea soup shitty weather, and following a compass, and the compass was showing that we were going north instead of south. Of course, the *compass* was wrong, and Mike and I got in this spirited discussion about what had happened. Although it took us a while to figure it out, in this pea-soup fog we were going along the ridge and went right around the ridge, and were going back on the other side the other way. We finally got it sorted out in a couple of hours and dropped down and camped in the pouring rain. We built a fire and Mike tried to dry out his boots."

I remember a dramatic black and white photograph of the South Face that Bill Sumner had pinned on the wall in his small climbing shop, Swallow's Nest. I saw the photo in 1972, the year he started the shop with Mike Heath. I was buying a pair of twenty-one dollar Salewa hinged crampons, but was captivated by the photo that revealed the overhanging face in profile from McMillan Spire. I felt *that* was a peak worth scaling.

Five years later Steve Mitchell and I thrashed into the Southern Pickets over a 4th of July weekend to try the South Face. We lost the Goodell Creek climbers' path at around 4300 feet and traversed devil's club, slide alder, and vine maple along Terror Creek to meadows within sight of the mountain. On day two it rained hard. On day three it was still raining as we waded back out through the brush.

In 1991 Paul Sloan and I made it into a campsite above Azure Lake in a day-and-a-half as rain clouds from the west moved our way. In view of the imminent precipitation and potential runoff, there was a lengthy discussion about where to stake the Westwind tent fly (we hadn't brought the floor or walls). I called it wrong, and the next morning our Thermarests were floating on a two-inch-deep sea of rainwater.

When the weather improved, we traversed the upper Terror Creek basin to the South Face. Soon, Paul and I were swapping leads on the marvelous wall up to the "great gash," where it forked. Paul's pitch was sensational. High above the glacier he led up a vertical ramp and corner that overhung the South Face. Using face holds and a bit of stemming and liebacking, Paul ran the rope out 160 feet to a belay ledge.

Above the ramp we entered a chimney and had one nasty encounter with a large loose block. I led past it, but when following, Paul kicked it into space. The route came out on the West Ridge where, in two pitches, we got to the summit. Although a veil of fog obscured nearby Pyramid, all around us rose the spiny Pickets.

Inspiration Peak: South Face

First ascent: Mike Heath and Bill Sumner; June 1969
Difficulty: Grade III, 5.8
Equipment: A standard rack up to a 3-inch cam. Ice ax and crampons.
Permit: A permit is required from the NPS, Skagit District, Marblemount, WA (360-873-4590).
Access: Two miles past the Thornton Lakes Road on Highway 20 is Newhalem. As you enter the town, cross Goodell Creek and turn left. Follow a gravel road on the east side of the creek for 2 miles, then park on an abandoned road just short of the campground. Hike the overgrown old road for 4 miles or so, crossing several major streams until a climbers' path (marked with a cairn) ascends steeply to the right. Follow the steep well-defined path until about 4300 feet where windfall has obscured the trail. At this point, don't go too far left, but climb straight up, then angle left below cliffs to reach meadows and benches. Do not follow the "brush talus gully" all the way to the 5700-foot notch (per the guidebook descriptions); instead, exit the gully part way and do a gradual north traverse across meadows and heather to the first of

two left-hand ridges. Cross the first ridge at 5700 feet, then traverse north to the second ridge and the higher of two notches at 6200 feet. Drop 400 feet to a moraine and traverse slabby ridges and snow to a 6160-foot saddle above Azure Lake. There are bench campsites 100 feet higher below East McMillan Spire. Traverse west on the glacier below East Mac Spire, drop slightly, then angle up through a talus gully, crossing a rock shoulder below West McMillan Spire. Ascend the Terror Glacier to the base of the South Face.

Route: Continue up and eastward around the lowest rock spur on the glacier to begin the climb. This eliminates two pitches of loose rock. From the glacier, climb to a small notch. Pitch **[1]** and **[2]** scramble up to the start of a long right-slanting ramp. **[3]** Climb a long pitch up the ramp (low 5th). **[4]** Climb another lead up the ramp (mid-5th) to a belay below a fork in the ramp. **[5]** Climb 40 feet up the upper of two ramps and, after the fork, make a couple of face moves back left and into the Great Gash. **[6]** Climb the Gash (a huge left-facing corner) via face holds, cracks, and stemming (5.8) to a belay below a chimney. **[7]** Finish climbing up the gash, then climb the right side of a wide chimney to a belay (5.7–5.8). **[8]** Continue up the chimney and exit onto the West Ridge (5.7–5.8). **[9]** Continue up the West Ridge to the summit (4th and 5th class).

Descent: Rappel and downclimb the West Ridge. From a slab 600 feet above the glacier it is possible to rappel the lower South Face and return to the base of the climb.

Maps: Green Trails: Marblemount No. 47 and Mount Challenger No. 15; USGS: Mount Challenger

Reference: *CAG 3: Rainy Pass to Fraser River*

Paul Sloan leads the spectacular corner pitch on the South Face Route.

21 MOUNT TERROR
North Face

MOUNT TERROR IS THE HIGHEST SUMMIT of the Southern Pickets, at 8151 feet. It is 4.8 miles south-southeast of Mount Challenger and 0.8 miles northwest of Inspiration Peak. The 2500-foot smooth North Face rises from the intimidating McMillan Cirque in a single thrust. McMillan Cirque is not only difficult to get into, but a distressing place to traverse, as ice and rockfall are constant hazards en route to the base of Terror.

"It was only on the fourth attempt that we succeeded, after again resorting to tennis shoes"

The mountain was first climbed up a south-facing gully and the West Ridge in 1932 by William Degenhart, James Martin, and Herb Strandberg. Degenhart and Strandberg had made the first alpine ascent in the range when they scaled Peak 8200 the previous August; after Bill's death, the mountain was renamed Mount Degenhart for him.

With better information on the approach from the year before, the trio set out to climb Mount Terron on August 7th with climbing gear and a two-week supply of food. They hiked Goodell Creek as far as trapper Gasper Petta's cabin, then continued three miles beyond to a creek bottom south of The Chopping Block. Strandberg remembered that Petta, who had trapped in Goodell Creek for years, had not heard of anyone having been in this region before. After 3800 feet of elevation gain, the group reached timberline and made a camp a half mile southeast of The Chopping Block. (The peak still appears as Pinnacle Peak on present-day maps.) It rained the next day as the three climbers took shelter under a lean-to made from boughs. On August 9th they climbed The Chopping Block up class 3 and 4 slabby rock, and then up a 200-foot chimney on the Southeast Face.

From the summit, they named The Barrier—the ridge and wall that descend from Mount Degenhart and separate the Crescent Creek basin from the Terror Creek basin. They dubbed its counterpart in McMillan Cirque The

Opposite: *Mount Terror. The North Face Route follows the shadowed face on the right, above the snowpatch*

Barricade. Both features play an important role when planning approaches to several of the Southern Picket climbs—in soupy bad weather they are difficult to cross, especially if you haven't done so before.

The setting was idyllic. Strandberg described their campsite in Crescent Creek Basin. He reported, "The basin is like a huge rockery, alpine flowers of all kinds growing between rocks and boulders. Within a hundred feet of camp were some twenty varieties of alpine flowers in full bloom, a delightful contrast to the rugged peaks about."

The party climbed the West Peak of The Chopping Block, then the West Twin Needle, before zeroing in on Terror for an August 18th ascent. After scaling the 600-foot gully to the notch, the climbers spent a half day trying to get up the pitch above. Strandberg felt it was the hardest part. "It was only on the fourth attempt that we succeeded, after again resorting to tennis shoes," he related. Nine-hundred feet of scrambling up the West Ridge took them to the summit, where they built a cairn.

In 1961 Charles Bell, Ed Cooper, David Hiser, and Mike Swayne made the first ascent of the North Face. Cooper and his party approached up Stetattle Creek and the south side of Elephant Butte. From a pass, they dropped into McMillan Cirque and traversed below crumbling icefalls and across wet slabby rock to Terror.

The climbers were cut off by a deep crevasse just before reaching the base of the North Face. They rappelled into it, climbed out the other side, and began the ascent of the face in early afternoon. Cooper described the climbing as ". . . enjoyable beyond description. Steep, weathered granite [gneiss actually] offered excellent firm holds and we made rapid progress." Halfway up the route they exhausted the daylight and made a bivouac on a sloping ledge, securing themselves with pitons. The following day the two rope teams gained the top and, failing to locate the West Ridge descent route, rappelled down the east corner of the peak.

Almost thirty years later Chuck Sink and I made it up and down the peak, but had a hard time finding our way back to camp in foul weather. Like Cooper and his friends, we had approached the mountain up Stetattle Creek and in a day-and-a-half reached a camp near the 6280-foot pass. From camp we enjoyed a superb view of the north walls of the Southern Pickets. The weather was perfect the next day as we followed fresh bear tracks down the steep hard snow and into McMillan Cirque. The logistics of Picket climbs are often puzzling. It takes some thought to decide what is the best method for approaching, climbing, and descending the peaks. Because we felt it was impractical to descend the North Face of Terror, we carried bivy gear and food for three days, planning to ascend the north side and descend the West Ridge and south side.

If getting across the cirque wasn't bad enough, the snout of the Degenhart Glacier barred access to Terror. Below the ice was a rock chasm, roaring with water. The glacier snout showed evidence that a sérac had recently collapsed. Chuck and I front-pointed quickly across to the safety of the rock ledges below the North Face. Thirty minutes later a big one swept our path clean—at that point the route seemed more like a means of escape than an obstacle.

After a reasonable night at the bottom, we started up the climb at sunrise. We quickly ran into trouble. The second pitch off the glacier was 5th class rock, with icy water pouring over it from an unstable ice patch

Chuck Sink on the last steep pitch of Mount Terror

above. Anxious to avoid being creamed, I rapidly climbed up, hammered a knifeblade in halfway, and brought Chuck up. He threaded between ice boulders, threw a sling over a horn, and belayed me out of there.

Beyond that, the climbing was great—always interesting, but never desperate. We ascended the shadowed face as the surrounding glaciers and walls rumbled. Far below, we could hear the roar of McMillan Creek. Chuck had been my climbing partner in college, but commercial fishing had taken him away from the sport for some time. Although not as fit as he used to be, he hadn't forgotten how to climb. There was no, "Can you lead this pitch, Al?" He wanted his share of the leads. We climbed steadily and made the summit by late afternoon.

With darkness and fog welling up from Crescent Creek, we picked our way down the south side gully and cleaned off a rock slab for our bivy. It began to drizzle before dawn. Stoked with hot coffee, we traversed talus and slippery heather slopes, searching for the route up and over The Barrier. For two hours Chuck and I wandered back and forth hunting for a break in the wall. Finally, I scrambled up a ramp and slab that ended on easy ground.

The fog thinned enough for us to walk to the other side of The Barrier, where a large cairn marked the descent into Terror Creek basin. Fifty feet down, the exceedingly steep, wet, and grassy gully split. Which way—right or left? The fog became thicker again as Chuck was drawn down the right hand chute. In 200 feet I spotted a rusty pin and a rotted sling, but little evidence of foot traffic. Chuck was reluctant, but I coaxed him back up from the slippery depths.

We found the correct gully and crossed the wet rock slabs of Terror Creek Basin, contoured around the east ledge of McMillan Spire, and were back to our camp at dark. Our plans to climb Inspiration Peak were washed away in the rain. Even so, we were happy lads.

Mount Terror: North Face

First ascent: Charles Bell, Ed Cooper, David Hiser, and Mike Swayne; July 1961

Difficulty: Grade III, 5.7–5.8

Equipment: A light rack up to a 3-inch cam and a few small pins. Ice ax and crampons.

Permit: A permit is required from the NPS, Skagit District, Marblemount, WA (360-873-4590).

Access: Approach as for Inspiration Peak, described previously. From the campsite below East McMillan Spire climb to 7200 feet, then traverse around the east side of the spire on a good ledge overlooking Stetattle Creek. Once across the ledge, you can rappel and downclimb the steep glacier adjacent to McMillan's East Face, or traverse the ridge east between McMillan and Stetattle Creeks to the 6280-foot saddle. Descend

Chuck Sink crosses sketchy ground in the Terror Creek Basin

800 feet, then traverse on slabs below the McMillan Glacier to The Barricade. Traverse snow and a deep gully, then do a rising traverse across easy rock to huckleberries and timber. A faint path climbs steeply up and around The Barricade, through huckleberries, to below the Degenhart Glacier. Cross over the snout to below Terror's North Face, then climb the glacier to the right. Finally, work up and left onto the rock of the North Face.

Route: Climb left, past an unstable ice patch, then mainly continue up the center and right side of the North Face (4th and 5th class with scarce pro). Near the apex of the face work up and left to a notch. Climb a steep-crack pitch (5.7–5.8) up onto the ridge crest. Climb along the crest on the right side, cross part way over to the left side (shattered gray rock overhanging the East Face), then cross back up onto the crest again. Traverse across talus to the West Ridge and follow the ridge to the summit.

Descent: Descend the West Ridge and the south gully of Terror, then traverse the upper Crescent Creek basin south for 2.5 miles. At 6000 feet climb a gully onto the west edge of The Barrier at 6200 feet. Contour due east and descend a steep gully down and left, then take the diagonal sloping ledge down and across to Terror Creek Basin.

Maps: Green Trails: Marblemount No. 47 and Mount Challenger No. 15; USGS: Mount Challenger

Reference: *CAG 3: Rainy Pass to Fraser River; AAJ*: 1987, pp. 62–63

22 LIBERTY BELL
Beckey Route

TWENTY-SIX YEARS BEFORE THE NORTH CASCADES HIGHWAY forever destroyed the pristine wilderness surrounding Washington Pass, Fred Beckey, Jerry O'Neil, and Charles Welsh hiked sixteen miles from the Early Winters Creek Guard Station to the pass. Here, they beheld a cluster of granitic peaks that included 7720-foot Liberty Bell, Concord, Lexington, and North and South Early Winter Spires. The sheer east faces and many of the summits were still untouched, but, unbelievably, a group of California climbers had bagged South Early Winter Spire nine years before.

Beckey wrote, "Today people see the same views from their cars. But do they? The views earned by long hours of toil are more wonderful than those gained in comfort."

On July 20 of 1937 Kenneth Adam, Raffi Bedayn, and W. Kenneth Davis climbed the Southwest Couloir of the South Spire. The remaining summits gradually fell to Northwest climbers: North Early Winter Spire in 1950, Lexington in 1954, and Concord in 1956. When Beckey and his party approached the peak in late September of 1946 the larches on the eastern slopes were beginning to turn gold. There was an autumn chill to the air, with cold nights, and a layer of ice in the breakfast cookpot.

The climbers left their meadow camp at the pass and worked their way around to the west side of Liberty Bell, where they hoped to find a shorter, less difficult route to the top. A deep gully led to a notch between Liberty Bell and Concord; the trio cached their nailed boots and laced up tennis shoes. Fred led the four pitches, which offered varied and solid climbing up flakes, a chimney, a finger traverse, and a smooth slab. Above, a short wall barred access to the summit, but the climbers quickly did a shoulder stand and made the top.

It is difficult for modern climbers to imagine what Washington Pass was like prior to the building of the highway. Beckey was so inspired by the unpeopled wilderness in those years that he later wrote, "Today people see the same views from their cars. But do they? The views earned by long hours of toil are more wonderful than those gained in comfort." When climbing

The Beckey Route on the Southwest Face of Liberty Bell

there, I often try to ignore the noise of diesel trucks grinding up the hill, or the image of the road slicing through forests and meadows. You will not find the solitude of Bear Mountain or Redoubt here. But, on the positive side, there is an abundance of quality alpine rock climbs within an hour or so of the car.

I have climbed the Beckey Route many times, and have always found it an enjoyable adventure. It is often a good way to introduce novices to the alpine game without punishing them on a grueling approach. Sue Harrington took her sister Chari up the climb in 1986. One year later, when her brothers Rick and Bill heard of the ascent, they were eager to try it.

My biggest concern was getting the two brothers decent footwear, as I had no rock shoes that fit their big feet. I suggested they wear sneakers, a better choice for the chimney and slab pitch. Rick complied, but Bill wanted to wear his stiff hiking boots. The brothers had virtually no climbing experience, but Sue and I felt they could do it.

It had rained the day before, and the weather still looked unsettled. Once I was sure none of Rick or Bill's garments were cotton, we started up. At the windy notch we began climbing cracks and flakes to a tree belay. I quickly led the chimney and snuggled into a windless alcove where I could anchor and bring Bill up.

I pulled on the rope but it didn't move. Animal grunts emanated from the deep crack below. "Did Chari climb this chimney?" came the nervous question. "Oh yes!" I assured them. More grunts from the fissure, as I took in a few inches of rope. Each pitch was both a mental and physical barrier for the brothers. As soon as they had reached the belays, another desperate-looking wall would loom above—and Sue constantly reminded them that their younger sister had made every move with both grace and elegance.

The sun appeared when we reached the summit, but the steady breeze persisted. Far below, the gray thread of highway wound off toward the snow-clad peaks bristling on the horizon. Rick and Bill were terrified of the prospect of rappelling, but they survived, and we delivered them, unharmed, to their wives.

Bob Kandiko on the first pitch

I imagine their experience could dissuade other relatives from visiting, knowing what might be in store when they do!

Liberty Bell: Beckey Route

First ascent: Fred Beckey, Jerry O'Neil, and Charles Welsh; September 27, 1946

Difficulty: Grade II, 5.7

Equipment: A light rack up to a 3-inch cam. An ice ax may be needed in early season to reach the col.

Access: Drive Highway 20 beyond Rainy Pass to the Blue Lake Trail, just short of Washington Pass. Hike the trail 1.5 miles to a meadow, then go left up a well-defined path (the main trail continues to Blue Lake), through a little brush, and up a scree gully to the notch between Liberty Bell and Concord.

Route: From just below the notch traverse left to a small tree. **[1]** Climb a rib and flakes (5.2–5.3) up to a belay on a ledge. **[2]** Climb the chimney behind the flake on the right, then continue up a long flaring chimney (5.6) to a belay in the alcove at the top. **[3]** Climb slabs and a shallow corner to a small overhang with a horizontal finger crack (5.6). Finger traverse left, then climb right on the smooth slab beneath overhangs to a belay on the corner (5.6). **[4]** Scramble up and across the right side of the ridge crest, then up a boulder move (5.7) over a short wall. Scramble up to the summit.

Alternate: When the Beckey Route is really crowded (and it often is on weekends) another option is the Overexposure Route, which ascends straight up from the notch. It is also the standard rappel route off the peak. Although a bit harder at 5.8, it has quality climbing up flakes initially, and then perfect corners and cracks. For gear, bring more small- to hand-sized cams and Stoppers. The start looks intimidating, but if you climb up and left, get in some gear with a long runner on it, then work up and right, it goes straight up cracks and corners to the rappel bolts.

Descent: It is best to downclimb a left ramp (when you face south toward Concord) from the top of the third pitch (friction slab), cut back right, then make two 80-foot rappels or one long one into the notch.

Maps: Green Trails: Washington Pass No. 50; USGS: Washington Pass

Reference: *CAG 3: Rainy Pass to Fraser River*

23 NORTH EARLY WINTER SPIRE
West Face

NORTH EARLY WINTER SPIRE, AT 7760 FEET, a quarter-mile south-southwest of Liberty Bell, is part of the Liberty Bell massif. The narrow East Buttress rises nearly 1200 feet from the slabs to the summit, while the West Face is less than half that height. The East Buttress has several grungy and rotten pitches of climbing, but the West Face has none. One party argued that the climb had a rotten first pitch; however, they were off-route.

Wesley Grande, Pete Schoening, and Dick Widrig made the first ascent of the Spire in 1950, climbing up the South-west Couloir and South Face. A snow couloir led to a cleft between the North and South Spires. The halfway point had a cave with an overhang, where Schoening felt the hardest climbing was. As he describes it, "This proved to be the bottleneck of the climb; only after practicing an odd variety of climbing tricks were we able to force a passage up the partially ice-covered rock. We put on tennis shoes to get around some little vertical steps in this gully. You go out onto the rock, then you come back into the gully, and now you're in tennis shoes going up a snow slope. Punching steps in the snow with tennis shoes for a long time was something you didn't want to do."

"Only after practicing an odd variety of climbing tricks were we able to force a passage up the partially ice-covered rock."

Springtime snow is often very wet, and it was hard on the type of gear climbers were using then. Schoening favored manila ropes because they were cheap. He says, "I would buy a couple of manila ropes a summer and generally when the rope got really wet, I would not use it past that point. I didn't have that much confidence in manila ropes. They're just interwoven fibers, and you could loosen something up and then maybe the fibers could slide—it's almost impossible to keep them dry in snow country. Nylon was expensive; manila, you could buy a rope for a couple of dollars."

Opposite: *The West Face of North Early Winter Spire*

Eve Tai works the crux thin crack on the West Face

Although it was late May, wind and driving snow hampered their climb to the top, where they built a cairn. Back at high camp several inches of snow fell overnight. Schoening forgot his crampons, leaving them hanging in a tree by their campsite. Pete laughs, "This guy found a pair of crampons in a tree forty years later and called me up to let me know. The crampons had SCH stamped on them and were pretty close to this little lake. It's easy to do cause you come down and your crampons are all iced up. You kinda hang them up someplace so you can beat 'em out."

Following the first ascent, Tim Kelley, and Richard McGowan put up the lower Southwest Face in 1954, and Fred Beckey and Joe Hieb established the Northeast Face in 1958. Beckey returned with Dave Beckstead in June of 1965 and climbed the West Face using a combination of free moves and aid, including a short pendulum from a bolt.

The total West Face climb is seven pitches in length, and now, as a free route, is outstanding. Dave Turner, an excellent free climber, took a fall off the crux pitch when climbing the route in 1986. Unharmed, he and his partner finished the climb. Four years later I was still intimidated by that information, but having just shed several pounds of body fat in the Pickets with Chuck Sink, I felt ready. Sue Harrington joined us for the climb. We left Bellingham late, hiked to the base and sorted gear for the route. The short September days were upon us and already it was early afternoon. There was a brief discussion about whether to take a headlamp up the climb or not—assuming we had one in the pack. It was probably me that ruled out the six ounces of weight as being too much.

The day was exceptionally cold with a feel of snow in the air. Our fingers didn't respond to thin jams in cold rock. Pitch three went up an unprotected lieback flake, then traversed right around a blind corner. Then an undercling led upward to belay anchors below the crux thin crack. I fidgeted with a hanging belay and wished I'd brought more clothing and some candy bars. The wind sucked the warmth right out of me. I yelled at Sue and Chuck to get moving.

Once everyone was accounted for, I stuffed my fingers between my neck and collar and readied small Stoppers and small cams for the fingertip crack. As it was late in the day and we were all cold, I climbed quickly, slotted Stoppers, and cruised over the hard part. Above, the crack was mostly fun—5.7 to 5.8 and long and continuous. But the light was quickly fading.

Chuck led a short pitch up to where we tagged the summit and beat it back to my belay and a wad of slings indicating the rappel point. We had two ropes, but somehow did not reach a good anchor, and I messed around trying to sling a rotten pillar in the gloom. It was dark as we finally moved into the gully and felt our way down to a chockstone and the last rappel. I went down on one rope and hurried over to our packs in search of headlamps. What I found was one of those dinky flashlights that, with new batteries, last an hour.

Sue and Chuck finished rappelling, and the one tiny flashlight barely illuminated our way down the climbers' path. Because we had pulled off a great climb and nobody had fallen, the bashed shins and scraped hands didn't hurt as much.

North Early Winter Spire: West Face

First ascent: Fred Beckey and Dave Beckstead; June 17, 1965
Difficulty: Grade III, 5.11-
Equipment: A standard rack up to a 4-inch cam. Emphasis on small wires and small cams.
Access: Same as for the Beckey Route on Liberty Bell, described previously. Once above the slabs on the climbers' path, bear right and follow a path to the base of the West Face. On the approach you can see a striking crack worn free of lichen midway up the face.
Route: Begin the route in a left-facing corner and chimney on the left side of the face. **[1]** and **[2]** Climb the corner, flakes, and chimney to a large tree-covered ledge (5.8). **[3]** Climb the chimney on the left side of a cave, and then climb the corner and a crack (5.9) up to a small belay ledge. **[4]** Ascend an offwidth flake up, then drop a little and traverse right around a blind corner (5.10-). Undercling up and right, then move back left to a semi-hanging belay below a crux thin crack. **[5]** Climb the thin crack nearly to its end (5.11-) and move left onto the face. **[6]** Continue up a

finger and hand crack (5.10-) to lower-angled ground and traverse right on a slab and finish climbing up another crack. **[7]** Scramble up to the summit. If aiding, the hard parts use nuts and cams.

Descent: Rappel and downclimb the South Face and the Southwest Couloir.
Maps: Green Trails: Washington Pass No. 50; USGS: Washington Pass
Reference: *CAG 3: Rainy Pass to Fraser River*

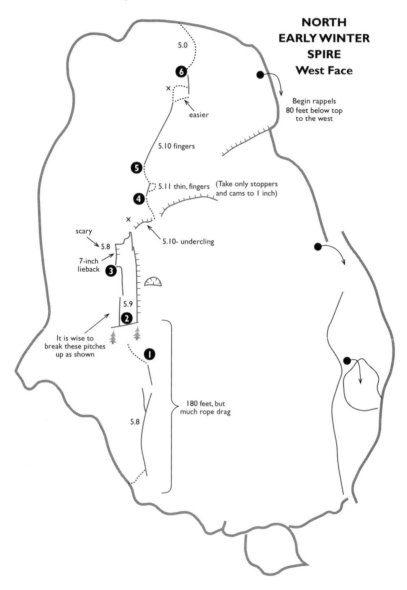

NORTH
EARLY WINTER
SPIRE
West Face

5.0

6

Begin rappels
80 feet below top
to the west

easier

5.10 fingers

5

5.11 thin, fingers   (Take only stoppers
4   and cams to 1 inch)

5.10- undercling

scary
5.8

7-inch
lieback **3**

5.9

2

It is wise to
break these pitches
up as shown   **1**

180 feet, but
much rope drag

5.8

24 LIBERTY BELL
Liberty Crack

LIBERTY BELL'S EAST FACE IS "THE" ELEGANT WALL in the Cascades. On a Yosemite scale, the face is a little over half the height of Half Dome's Northwest Face, but it is the striking lines and position of the peak that are compelling. Some primal urge that demands action is stimulated by the sight of the vertical granite.

By the mid 1960s climbers were making attempts on the face, and there was a rush to bag the good lines. Shortly after Liberty Crack was put up, Fred Beckey climbed a pitch and fixed a rope on what is now known as the Thin Red Line. This should have staked his claim to that route, but there were four younger climbers eager to do the route, and two of them dispensed with Beckey's fixed rope.

Of that first attempt Bertulis said, "The ceiling was so intimidating I decided to put a bolt below the lip, but it took me, like, an hour, just banging away, banging away.

According to Alex Bertulis this was a pivotal move, since Beckey had ropes hanging from various climbs all over the Northwest and climbers were getting annoyed. "For the first time in Fred's career somebody went up and cut it [the rope] off," Bertulis recounts. "I think it was Don McPherson and Ron Burgner. In one of our beer drinking sessions they were not too keen about admitting who did it because, my God, this was Fred Beckey's rope! There was a conspiracy as to who was going to cut. Everybody wanted to do it, and Fred was off in Alaska. And after that Fred never hung another rope."

McPherson's back went out (bad karma perhaps?), and he and Burgner had to hobble out without finishing the route. Jim Madsen and Kim Schmitz were next in line, and they charged in and up the wall. Bertulis had hoped they might stick with the revolution theme he had begun with Liberty Crack and Independence, when christening the route. "He [Madsen] was a rebel at the time," says McPherson, "and he named the route Thin Red Line."

In 1964 Steve Marts and Bertulis hiked in from Twisp, crossing Kangaroo Pass, unaware that the partially-completed North Cascades Highway

Liberty Crack Route from the east. (Photo by Cliff Leight)

existed. Although the road was gravel, climbers had been coaxing their cars up it for climbs in the area, thereby greatly shortening the approach. Marts and Bertulis climbed and fixed two pitches to just above the first prominent roof before time and difficulties forced a retreat. Of that first attempt Bertulis said, "The ceiling was so intimidating I decided to put a bolt below the lip, but it took me, like, an hour, just banging away, banging away. I got totally exhausted, and then I proceeded to do this overhang and I placed a little half-inch angle above the lip. As I stood up the piton went [grating sound] but it didn't pop out, it just rotated 30 degrees. 'Oh shit, Steve, I'm coming off!' I yelled. By then I was so exhausted and spooked I rappelled down to Steve and said, 'Okay Steve, you go.' He said, ' No, I'm not going.' So home we went."

Early in the 1965 season the pair returned, and Bertulis led the pitch over the roof and placed a bolt belay above. The weather turned bad and thwarted further progress. "We rappelled back down and bivouacked right in the schrund below the route," Marts related. "That night some ice came off from way up and hit us." In July Marts returned with Don McPherson and Fred Stanley to complete the line. Bertulis, who had thought to name the route Liberty Crack, from the cracked bell appearance, was unable to join them, as he had made a prior commitment to go to Africa. As Bertulis tells it, "I said, 'Steve, you finish the job,' and he [Marts] recruited Fred and Don. They're both good guys and they had my blessing. They are the ones who named that roof the Lithuanian Lip, because I did the first two ascents of it [Bertulis is Lithuanian by birth]."

The three re-ascended the fixed ropes, from where Marts led a tedious and difficult pitch that took much of the day. In one more lead they hung hammocks for the night. The weather was clear and hot and Marts claimed he'd never gotten so dehydrated. The next day they climbed four more pitches, mostly up a long dihedral, and bivvied on a ledge. Marts felt they climbed slowly; one of the reasons was the time they spent removing gear. As he remembers it, "We were so poor, and iron was so expensive, if we left something it was because we just couldn't get it out."

They reached the top on the morning of the third day, rappelled the Southwest Face and traversed back around to their camp at the base.

I climbed the route in 1974 with Shari Kearney, and again in 1976 with Steve Mitchell. To Steve, a Californian at heart, North Cascades adventures meant more brushy hiking than actual climbing. He was usually right, but I assured him that would not be the case with Liberty Crack.

On a late August morning we carried a haul bag, ropes, and hardware up through a spruce forest to the climb's base. I was alarmed that the mosquitoes were active at such an early hour and that I didn't have any bug dope. The first pitch off the talus was cool and windy, but the sun soon warmed the air. For most of the day we climbed in T-shirts, with the first climber leading and hauling and the second cleaning. Our climbing was mostly aid until the fourth pitch, where we jammed a long crack.

On most wall climbs I have overshot or fallen short of the good bivouac ledges, and Liberty Crack was no exception. After five pitches of climbing there was nothing but the smooth wall. We anchored our hammocks from cracks and squirmed in, along with hundreds of tiny flying demons that had followed us up the climb. As we opened canned fruit for dinner their buzzing rose to a insane pitch. For me it was a sleepless night.

We were moving quickly after a breakfast of canned pudding and fig bars. Climbers eat some bizarre stuff on walls—generally a choice of what tastes good and doesn't make you thirsty. When Dave Dailey and Bryce Simon did Liberty Crack the same year, Simon ate Suzy Q's and drank Cokes the whole way up. Our food was flavored by mosquitoes, a disagreeable spice.

Higher up, the long dihedral pitch had great free climbing, with stemming and jamming all the way. By early afternoon the hard pitches were below us. Fourth class led to the top, where I opened a can of beans, eager to lighten the haul bag. We chugged the remaining water and packed away the gear not needed to descend. Puffy clouds dotted the sky and a steady breeze kept the bugs away for the rappels and hike down. Back at my van a couple of O'Keefe's Canadian brews deadened the aching joints and itching mosquito welts.

Liberty Bell: Liberty Crack

First ascent: Steve Marts, Don McPherson, and Fred Stanley; July 16–19, 1965

Difficulty: Grade V, 5.9, A-3. Pitches 2, 8, and 9 can be done free at 5.11-, 5.10- and 5.10-

Equipment: A standard rack up to a 3½-inch cam with emphasis on wires and small-to-medium cams. The route has been done hammerless since 1974.

Access: From the Blue Lake Trail on Highway 20 drive 1.2 miles to just over Washington Pass. The path to the base starts on the far side of the first pond on the right, after crossing the pass on Highway 20.

Route: The route begins in a solitary crack leading to a prominent roof. **[1]**

Enter from the left on a ramp to gain the base of the crack. **[2]** Climb the crack to below the Lithuanian Lip (A-2 or 5.11-). **[3]** Aid up and over a roof, do a few free moves (5.7), then go up several bolts to a belay (A-1). **[4]** Follow the bolts up and right, then do a possible hook move to gain a crack left of a small roof to a belay ledge (A-3 and 5.10).

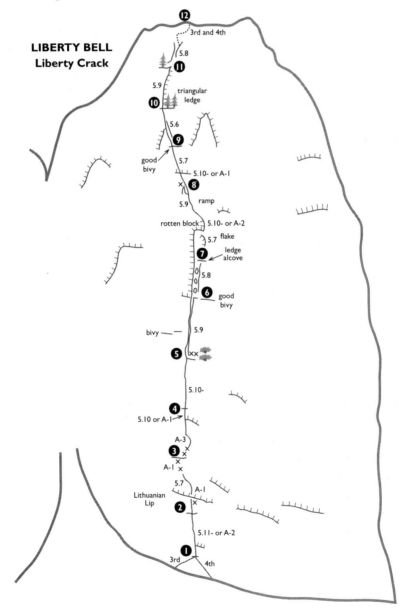

LIBERTY BELL
Liberty Crack

3rd and 4th

5.8

5.9
triangular
ledge

5.6

good
bivy   5.7

5.10- or A-1

5.9   ramp

rotten block   5.10- or A-2

5.7 flake

ledge
alcove

5.8

good
bivy

bivy ——   5.9

5.10-

5.10 or A-1

A-3

A-1

5.7   A-1

Lithuanian
Lip

5.11- or A-2

3rd   4th

Steve Mitchell cleaning a pitch on Liberty Crack

[5] Jam a crack (5.10-) to a ledge with a tree. [6] Climb a chimney to a good ledge (5.9). Bivouac on the left. [7] Continue up a crack past blocks and flakes (5.8). [8] Lieback around a flake (5.7), then climb past a rotten block (A-2 or 5.10-). Continue up to a left-sloping ramp (5.9). [9] Climb past a small roof (5.10-), then up a left-sloping ramp (5.7) to a belay on a ledge. [10] Climb a chimney (5.6) to a ledge with trees. [11] Climb a left-facing corner and crack (5.9) to a belay at a tree. [12] Climb a gully for 40 feet (5.8), then follow 4th and 3rd class leads to the top.

Descent: Downclimb the upper Beckey Route (on the Southwest Face) and descend a ramp eastward and a ledge back westward. A 150-foot rappel from bolts drops you into the Concord–Liberty Bell notch. Descend the gully to the Blue Lake Trail and hike back around to Washington Pass.

Maps: Green Trails: Washington Pass No. 50; USGS: Washington Pass

Reference: *CAG 3: Rainy Pass to Fraser River*

25 LEXINGTON TOWER
East Face

LEXINGTON IS THE SOUTHERNMOST of the two lower spires adjacent to Liberty Bell. As with the other peaks of the massif, the west side is shorter, with gullies leading to within several hundred feet of the 7560-foot summit. The 800-foot East Face is longer, steeper, and characterized by high-quality free climbing up cracks, chimneys, and corners. Tim Kelley and Richard McGowan made the first ascent of the peak on July 5, 1954, climbing up the North Face from the Lexington–Concord notch.

In June of 1966 Steve Marts and Don McPherson climbed the East Face, using some aid on the hard parts. Scott Davis and a partner made the second ascent and the first free ascent of the route shortly thereafter. Steve Marts said of McPherson, "He went to Yosemite for one summer and climbed the Nose of El Cap. He was a fairly gifted climber and had climbed a lot with Jim Madsen." In fact, it was Jim Madsen who influenced McPherson's climbing the most. Marts continues, "Madsen was extremely intense and made a tremendous impact on us. At that time there was no one else around who could climb cracks like he could except Chuck Pratt."

"At the halfway point the climbing became very steep, as they had to traverse beneath an impossible roof, searching for a way up and around it."

Although Madsen wasn't on the Lexington climb, he put up the Thin Red Line with Kim Schmitz on nearby Liberty Bell and left an indelible mark on Washington climbing. On Midnight Rock [in the Leavenworth area], during 1967 and 1968, he freed most of the major crack lines with Ron Burgner and Kim Schmitz, some of them now rated at the upper limit of 5.10. McPherson spoke of Madsen's crack climbing ability and tenacity. "Jim was not at all a natural climber," he states, "but he surpassed us all after a couple of years. He'd get into the cracks, and he was very bright and he could hang on and hang on until he worked it out."

In the 1960s Washington Pass was still inaccessible by road, and there were many routes left to do. Marts and McPherson hiked in from Twisp and

the southeast. McPherson remembers, "We were like blind dogs in a butcher shop. We were sniffing over everything and trying to climb everything." Besides Lexington, McPherson and other partners put up two routes on Liberty Bell, three routes on North and South Early Winter Spires, and one on Concord. Nearly all of the routes were long and committing, in a remote area, with no chance of a rescue. Climbers had to either finish the climbs, or rappel off and leave costly gear behind for anchors.

Once on the climb, the leader had to clean tufts of grass out of cracks to place gear, while the gardening debris rained down on the unfortunate belayer. At the halfway point the climbing became very steep, as they had to traverse beneath an impossible roof searching for a way up and around it. "I remember being disappointed in that big chimney, squeeze crack or whatever it is," says McPherson. "I didn't do it free. I remember putting in a sky hook or something right off the deck—there was nothing between me and Steve." Above that spot the crack turned into a chimney, and, as there appeared to be no anchors for a ways above, he stopped and began placing a belay bolt.

He instructed Marts to begin Jumaring, the only anchor being his body jammed in the narrow slot. Meanwhile Marts' weight on the rope cut into his swami belt as he drilled harder and faster to complete the anchor. "There was no miscommunication," Don recounts. "It was all my taking a chance with both of us. I wanted to get going; I didn't want to slow us down."

After the chimney, a couple more moderate pitches remained to the top, where the climbers began descending. As they were cautiously starting down, McPherson recalled what Marts had said about Fred Beckey on other descents. "The best guy he'd ever seen for downclimbing chimneys and that kinda crap, is Fred Beckey," he says. "He is just amazing to watch going down."

Steve Mascioli and I did the route on a warm September day in 1983. I found it to be a great climb in a fantastic location. Liberty Bell's imposing East Face looms nearby, and the shouts from climbers on Liberty Crack echo off the surrounding walls. Climbers often prefer to repeat really good routes rather than climb new and potentially unpleasant lines. At least I do, so Sue Harrington and I went back to Lexington in September of 1992.

The mountains had been hit with the first snows of the season. The air had turned very cold. As we crossed below Liberty Crack, three pairs of climbers were at the roof or just above it. An autumn wind whipped spindrift snow around in eddies. Sunlight hit the wall momentarily, but the weather looked dubious and I was glad we were attempting a shorter route.

In 1983 Steve and I had gained the climb from the left-hand gully, as Beckey's *Cascade Alpine Guide* indicated. But this time the permanent snowfield at the base was rock hard, which made cutting steps without an ax impossible. We squeezed along the moat, then climbed the right-hand gully to access the East Face. After a left traverse across a brushy ledge, Sue had a hard time pushing a pitch up to intersect the established route. Freezing in the early morning wind, I yelled at her to come down so I could try leading up to the left. Eventually I found some undercling holds that went and our climbing developed a rhythm of swapping leads.

Throughout the day the belayer was never warm and the leader was constantly shoving his or her hands under the sweater collar. I found the airy traverse beneath the large flake just as intimidating as in 1983, and I couldn't be sure the pro-

Sue Harrington below the top of Lexington Tower in a clearing storm

tection at my feet was solid. Often, a cold day on the rock can knock a couple grades off your leading ability, and that was how we felt.

Below the overhanging squeeze chimney Sue and I had a mild argument. If I led the slot I wanted her to bring up the two fanny packs and my camera. She wanted me to lead and carry all my own stuff. I was adamant and, with the aid of a top-rope, Sue struggled up with the gear. With but two pitches remaining, the sky bombarded us with wind-driven wet snow. But the hardest climbing was over. The climbers on Liberty Crack had reached the upper smooth dihedral and, as it quickly became wet with fresh snow, their rope signals got frantic. "More tension!" and "Watch me!" floated across the void.

Just below the top the snowstorm abated, and a silvery fog back-lit by the late afternoon sun crept between the spires. In a few more minutes we descended the west side gully and hiked down the scree. We had made it, and I knew those on Liberty Crack would also. It was one of those special alpine days where weather added uncertainty, but ultimately provided a richer experience.

Lexington: East Face

First ascent: Steve Marts and Don McPherson; June 1966

Difficulty: Grade IV, 5.10-

Equipment: A standard rack that includes a 4-inch cam. An ice ax.

Access: Same as for Liberty Crack, described previously. The permanent snowfield at the base of Lexington can make reaching the rock tricky. I've always been able to get to the rock without an ice ax either from either the left or right gully, but it's better to have one.

Route: Climb 100 feet up the left-hand gully on the East Face. **[1]** Scramble right to a crack and chimney system in the middle of the face. **[2]** Climb cracks and the face to a tree (5.5). **[3]** Climb a left-facing corner up to a ledge (5.8). **[4]** Continue up this corner (5.7) to a belay beneath a roof. **[5]** Climb up, traverse right on a horizontal crack to beneath a flake, then jam a flaring crack (5.10-) up and left to a belay in an alcove. **[6]** Climb an overhanging chimney/offwidth (5.9) past a bolt. Continue on up the chimney, cracks, and a higher chimney (5.8–5.9) to a bolt and chockstone belay in the chimney. **[7]** Climb a flaring chimney a short way, then move left and up the face and cracks (5.7) to easier ground on the ridge crest. **[8]** Climb the ridge crest up and around the right side of a gendarme to a notch below the summit (4th class).

Descent: Most parties do not go to the actual summit from the top of the East Face route. It is quite difficult, with poor rock and poor pro. Descend the gully on the west via downclimbing and rappels. In recent years parties have been rappelling the East Face, which solves any problem of retrieving gear from the base.

Maps: Green Trails: Washington Pass No. 50; USGS: Washington Pass

Reference: *CAG 3: Rainy Pass to Fraser River*

26 SOUTH EARLY WINTER SPIRE
East Buttress

LAST IN THE LINE OF LIBERTY BELL'S GREAT PINNACLES is South Early Winter Spire. Although I have included the East Buttress in this collection of climbs, the South Arête, first climbed in 1942 by Fred and Helmy Beckey, is also a popular line up the 7807-foot peak. The arête is within many climbers' abilities, at 5.5, and there's plenty of scrambling. Between 1964 and 1967 the spire saw a tremendous amount of new route activity, with lines established on the Southwest Rib, West Face, Southeast Face, East Face, and Northeast Corner. Climbers involved in these ascents included Donald Anderson, Fred Beckey, Jim Madsen, Steve Marts, Don McPherson, Paul Myhre, Jim Richardson, Larry Scott, Fred Stanley, and Margaret Young.

Leen lowered him from the partially completed bolt ladder, where the tired climbers settled in for a second bivouac on the wall.

During June of 1968, Fred Beckey and Doug Leen climbed six pitches up the 1100-foot East Buttress and placed the first of twenty-six bolts. They rappelled off, leaving one rope anchored over the hardest pitch, and returned in six weeks to complete the buttress. Leen was first up the fixed line and, to his horror, discovered that most of the mantle had been chewed through. As on Slesse, it was probably the work of bushy-tailed woodrats.

The pair spent the first day getting their haulbag and packs up to their June high point, where they bivouacked. The next day Leen nailed a flake, placed three bolts, and hooked his way to a small ledge. Beckey led a crack that ended on an ample ledge where Leen joined him with the gear. Beckey then spent the remaining daylight bolting to the top of a crescent crack, where it finally accepted pitons. Leen lowered him from the partially completed bolt ladder, where the tired climbers settled in for a second bivouac on the wall.

In the morning, Leen took over the lead, placing two more bolts before

Opposite: *The East Buttress of South Early Winter Spire*

moving onto hooks, then onto two shaky pins. The remaining pitch went free, with tricky mantles up to a belay stance. Beckey climbed two moderate pitches to where Leen led the exposed traverse to just beneath the summit. Dumping their gear, the pair bouldered up the summit rock, ending a fine climb amid flawless weather.

The East Buttress route had been on my list for a long time. I finally persuaded Kitty Calhoun to try it in June of 1985. Kitty, with her Carolina drawl and stubborn nature, would later succeed in climbing many fine alpine routes, including Makalu and Dhaulagiri, in Nepal. But in 1985 she was still in the middle of the learning curve.

Although I had climbed a bit in Tennessee in early May, most of that fitness had evaporated by late June, due to many successive rainy Northwest weekends. We got an early start and climbed the snow-filled gully between the North and South Spire to the start of the buttress. The first steep lead up flakes was mine. I was rattled, not having led anything for some time. From my belay, Kitty jammed the long fist crack methodically as the sun warmed the rock. Once at the belay she hollered down, "Alan I'm off. Y'all can come on up now."

The next pitch was partly free, then followed a line of bolts onto the buttress crest. I was

Alison Palmer and Kathy Zaiser on the East Buttress

starting to feel better about climbing when I tried to clip a carabiner into the homemade bolt hangers. It wouldn't go. Modern biners with fatter gates didn't work on the old hangers. I threaded $9/16$-inch quick-draws through the bolts and clipped in the rope. This method was okay for a little fall but anything long would cut the sling. Confidence had been short-lived.

Above, a moderate crack and face moves led to the last long bolt ladder, where the angle relented. The top pitches were enjoyable free climbing right up to the summit. Once down the west side, we traversed around to the south and to the broad talus slope and the gully leading to the road hairpin. As we began the descent a startled mountain goat bounded across the rock slabs below the spire.

At the car I chugged a beer and offered one to Kitty, but she turned it down on the grounds that she was in training.

South Early Winter Spire: East Buttress

First ascent: Fred Beckey and Doug Leen; July 27–29, 1968

Difficulty: Grade IV, 5.9–5.10- or 5.11- (If done all free, the clips are awkward, since the bolt ladder was done on aid and the bolts are ratty)

Equipment: A standard rack up to a 4-inch cam. The old homemade bolt hangers require old-style or small carabiners to clip them. An ice ax may be needed in early season to reach the climb.

Access: From the road hairpin 0.8 miles beyond Washington Pass on Highway 20 you can climb the gully between the spires in early season when it's filled with snow. Later on, it's better to go up the broad gully above and west of the hairpin, then make a right-rising traverse up talus and small cliffs to the base of the buttress.

Route: [1] Climb slabby rock on the buttress crest (easy 5th class) [2] Climb cracks and flakes (5.8) to a tree belay. [3] Jam a large crack in a left-facing corner (5.9) past a small overhang to a ledge and a tree. [4] Continue up the big crack, move left past a bolt to gain a low-angle dihedral that leads to a triangular ledge (5.9). [5] Climb friction up and right to gain a long bolt ladder (5.8 A-1 or 5.11-) to a vertical crack past a hole, then go up and right to a small ledge. [6] Climb right on a fading crack, then execute face moves (5.10-) to a ledge. [7] Ascend a bolt ladder (A-0 or 5.11-) to an arcing crack and more bolts to a belay. [8] Climb 60 feet to a ledge (5.6). [9] Climb right and up a long pitch to a ledge (5.4). [10]

From the right edge of the ledge, climb 30 feet left to a step around, then 40 feet to the summit (5.4).

Descent: Scramble and rappel the South Arête.

Maps: Green Trails: Washington Pass No. 50; USGS: Washington Pass

Reference: *CAG 3: Rainy Pass to Fraser River*

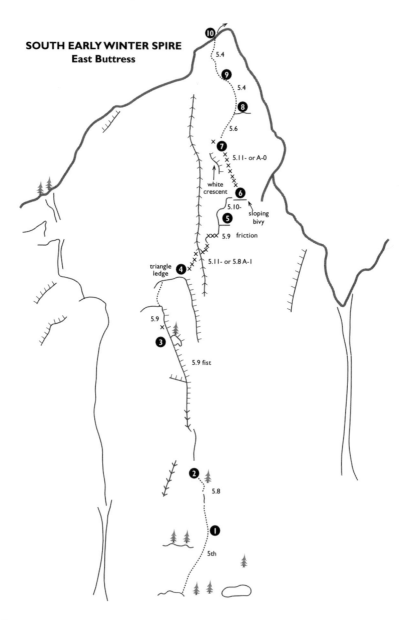

SOUTH EARLY WINTER SPIRE
East Buttress

10
5.4

9
5.4

8
5.6

7
5.11- or A-0

white crescent
6

5.10-
sloping bivy

5
5.9 friction

5.11- or 5.8 A-1

triangle ledge
4

5.9

3

5.9 fist

2
5.8

1
5th

27 BIG KANGAROO
South Face Right

IN THE 1943 MOUNTAINEER ANNUAL WALT VARNEY told how Kangaroo Ridge was named. He wrote, "Long ago, in the days of Babe, the Blue Ox, there must also have been a legendary Blue Kangaroo. Some old prospector looked at a long ridge of granite towers southeast of Washington Pass and visualized the course the Blue Kangaroo might have taken through the air on a series of running bounces."

The highest summit of the ridge is Big Kangaroo, at 8280 feet. It was first climbed by Varney and Fred and Helmy Beckey in June of *The light began to fade as I climbed with demon speed to just under a small roof, where Jeff aided quickly left to a belay below good hand cracks.*

1942. On the 21st the trio plodded up a long talus and snow slope to scale the final summit pyramid. Low 5th class climbing led to within ten feet of the top, where Beckey belayed Varney from a small stance. Varney straddled the ridge to the top, then built a cairn, using rocks carried up in a rucksack for just that purpose.

Fred returned to the South Face in 1967 with Dan Tate to climb a diagonal line up the center of the 900-foot cliff. This wall is not visible from Washington Pass or Silver Star Mountain, but an intrepid climber can spot it from Half Moon or Wallaby, two peaks farther south along Kangaroo Ridge. I was treated to such a view in July of 1984.

In August of 1984 I persuaded Jeff Thomas and his father Bill to join me on a two-day trip to Big Kangaroo. We spent most of the first day hiking talus slopes and wading through krummholz to reach meadows below the face. I was feeling tired, and expected to crash out in the meadow, as it was already 4 P.M. Jeff had other ideas, and pointed out that we had time to do one new route before dark and another one the following day.

Jeff's Dad scowled and said he would join us the next day, and that we had better not get ourselves stuck in the dark. Jeff had pointed out a line of

The South Face of Big Kangaroo

cracks and corners he thought would go, so we started up. We didn't take any extra clothing, food, water, or a headlamp, but I put a butane lighter and bug dope in my pocket. Because the mosquitoes were bad and the nights cool, I considered these items essential for survival. The idea was to climb quickly and make it back to camp before dark.

We scrambled up ramps and ledges to where the wall turned vertical and was split by long beautiful cracks. I quickly climbed the second pitch, a wide crack that accepted almost no pro due to the limited contents of our rack. Jeff's lead took him around a corner, then up a thin crack to a belay ledge. Above, a crack went part way, then ended beneath small overhangs. Constantly aware of the time, I grabbed the gear and stemmed up a flaring slot, jammed a crack, then moved left out onto the face. Meanwhile, back at the belays, Jeff hurled off poised boulders and flakes, hoping to make the route safer for the next party. I struggled getting a Stopper in and finally pulled over the small roofs.

Jeff now confronted a left-facing corner with an 1-inch crack in it—too wide for fingers, and not big enough for good hand jams. He freed a bit of it, then started slamming small cams in and yanking on them. It just wasn't the time or place to dally with the moves. With a very tight top rope, I just barely made the moves when following the crack. The light began to fade as I climbed with demon speed to just under a small roof, where Jeff aided quickly left to a belay below good hand cracks.

One more reasonable pitch led to the top, shortly after sunset. We rapidly descended a talus gully on the west, then groped our way south in the inky dark. Moonlight would have been helpful. Every so often I fingered the lighter and bug dope in my pocket, just to make sure I still had them in case of an unplanned bivouac. Another talus gully led down and east to our meadow camp, where we made a noisy entrance at 11 P.M. and woke Bill.

I had serious doubts about the adventure succeeding when we began the climb that afternoon, but I hadn't voiced them aloud. Now I was glad I had kept quiet. Throughout the climb we never once discussed retreating. I realized tremendous things were possible if one focused completely on summiting. Three months later, in Patagonia, I would find this attitude invaluable.

Big Kangaroo: South Face Right

First ascent: Alan Kearney and Jeff Thomas; August 1984

Difficulty: Grade III, 5.10- A-l

Equipment: A standard rack up to a 5-inch cam, with emphasis on small to medium cams (¾-inch–2-inch).

Access: From the road hairpin on Highway 20, 0.8 miles beyond Washington Pass, hike nearly to the head of Early Winters Creek, below Kangaroo Pass. From the basin head up talus to a 7500-foot notch 0.2 miles north of Half Moon. Cross over, then descend a snow couloir (in early summer) and traverse north to meadows below the South Face.

Route: A major feature of the climb is a large left-facing dihedral between the 1967 South Face route and the Southeast Buttress. **[1]** Climb the face up onto a crescent-shaped ramp and up into the big corner (5.7–5.8). **[2]** Climb a chimney (5.7) at the start of a huge left-facing corner. **[3]** Climb the corner and an offwidth (5.10-) then ascend a fist crack on the right which leads out of the corner (5.8). **[4]** Climb a left-facing corner and then a steep face on the left (5.10-) and work back right to a belay on the ramp. **[5]** Continue up the ramp (5.7) and climb a crack in the corner up to a left-facing corner. Continue up a 1¼-inch crack (5.10- and A-1), (it possibly will go free at mid- 5.11). **[6]** Climb lower-angled pitch leads to beneath a roof (5.6). **[7]** Undercling and aid left to exit the roof, then gain a large slot higher (5.10- and A-l), (possibly free at 5.11). **[8]** Climb hand cracks (5.8) up to where you can scramble to the top.

Descent: Descend gullies on the west, then traverse back south and drop into a meadow below the South Face.

Maps: Green Trails: Washington Pass No. 50; USGS: Washington Pass and Silver Star Mountain

Reference: *CAG 3: Rainy Pass to Fraser River. AAJ*: 1985, p.189

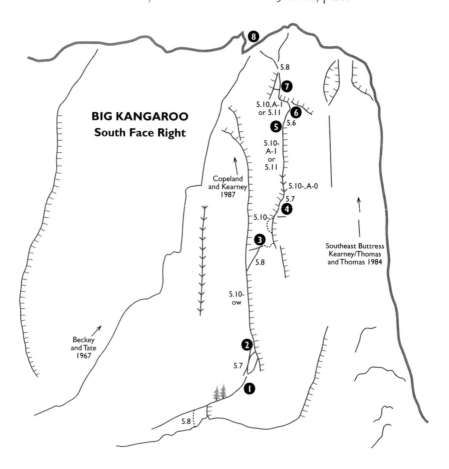

BIG KANGAROO
South Face Right

Copeland and Kearney 1987

Southeast Buttress
Kearney/Thomas
and Thomas 1984

Beckey
and Tate
1967

28 BURGUNDY SPIRE
North Face

LESS THAN FOUR MILES NORTHEAST OF WASHINGTON PASS are the jagged gray granite teeth of the Wine Spires: Burgundy, Chianti, Pernod, and Chablis. These Chamonix-like pinnacles can be reached in four to six hours via light brush and a climbers' path north of Willow Creek. All the summits were climbed during 1952 and 1953 from approaches up Silver Star and Cedar Creeks.

In August of 1953 Fred Beckey, Michael Hane, and John Parrott camped on a rock outcrop of the Silver Star Glacier, prepared to siege the North Face of 8400-foot Burgundy Spire. On the first day they

It had taken an exhausting three days to scale Burgundy; the spire would remain the "technically most difficult" summit in the Cascades for many years.

climbed a snow couloir on the northeast side to a sandy bench, where they picked up a cache from the year before. From the bench, the climbing was up slabs and flakes, where intricate route finding consumed the day. Beckey anchored his rope to a granite sliver, then the team descended to camp. In the morning, the climbers prusiked their fixed ropes, then went to work on the 200-foot sheer wall above their high point.

Hane led the first pitch of free climbing and aid to a tiny stance, where he secured the belay with a single angle piton. Parrott followed, then climbed a second tedious pitch that ended on a ramp and ledge system that cut across the upper Northwest Face. From a stance on the north edge, the climbers surveyed the rock walls that barred access to the summit ridge before rappelling for the day.

Once up their lines the next day, they climbed using aid, then lassoed a block. In another hour of climbing along a sharp arête they reached the summit block and placed a bolt to get up the final overhang. It had taken an exhausting three days to scale Burgundy; the spire would remain the "technically most difficult" summit in the Cascades for many years.

Five years later Donald Anderson and Jim Richardson climbed a route directly above Burgundy Col, crossed the North Face route, then continued

to the summit via the upper Northwest Face. Modern ascents of Burgundy incorporate the lower Northwest Face, mid North Face and upper Northwest Face, thus retaining the best climbing from both lines. In September of 1971 Carla Firey and Jim McCarthy climbed the West Buttress of Paisano Pinnacle, a granite spire adjoining the lower walls of Burgundy. Combining Paisano Pinnacle with the North Face of Burgundy creates a thirteen-pitch, 5.9 route that is highly recommended.

⛰

In August of 1984 Linda Givler and I left our camp in the basin below Burgundy's west side and hiked the talus gully to Burgundy Col. The weather was marginal; to the west dark clouds obliterated the Liberty Bell peaks. Snowflakes dusted us, but to the east there was blue sky. Confident the weather was on the mend, we started up the Northwest Face and North Face. Linda had a topo from Seattle friends, which showed we could climb six pitches up the North Face, traverse way right on ramps and ledges, then climb a corner and a short offwidth to the summit ridge.

I had just finished leading a steep flake pitch to a ledge belay when I heard strange voices around the wall to the west. As I belayed Linda up, I leaned over to see a man hanging by his fingers from a thin overhanging crack and, with his other hand, scrubbing lichen with a wire brush. I soon learned he was Bryan Burdo—he was climbing a new route on sight and cleaning it. I was impressed!

Linda led a great pitch up a clean corner just below a ridge crest on the North Face Route. At that point we traversed a long pitch right, then climbed a full lead up a perfect dihedral. From a belay stance I stuffed a big cam into a wide crack, then squirmed up onto the summit ridge. Moments later we stood on top of the spire under clear skies and ate snacks. I don't know what we missed by not climbing the original upper North Face, but by going right instead we found some of the finest and most varied climbing in the area.

Burgundy Spire: North Face

First ascent: Fred Beckey, Michael Hane, and John Parrott; August 15–17, 1953

Difficulty: North Face: Grade III, 5.8; Paisano West Buttress and North Face Burgundy combined: Grade IV, 5.9

Opposite: *The North Face of Burgundy Spire. Paisano Pinnacle is on the lower left*

Equipment: A standard rack up to a 4-inch cam. An ice ax may be needed in early season to reach Burgundy Col.

Access: Approach as for Liberty Bell and Big Kangaroo, described previously. From the road hairpin on Highway 20 drive 2.8 miles farther to a wide paved shoulder and a small "Silver Star Mtn." sign. Park here and hike down talus, through woods, and across Early Winters Creek. Go 0.3 miles in an easterly direction until you cross the abandoned Early Winters Trail. Go right on the old trail and watch for a cairn. Pick up a climbers' path that follows a dry creek drainage and then parallels a stream higher up. A good path continues up the wooded rib and crosses through larch forest. As the path fades, continue toward Burgundy, aiming for the left-hand gully. Follow this gully to Burgundy Col and the base of the Northwest Face and North Face. If climbing Paisano, take the right hand gully where the main gully forks and follow it up to Paisano.

Route: [1] and [2] From Burgundy Col scramble up to the sandy bench area. [3] Angle up and left on the North Face (class 3) to ledges below a steep wall. [4] Climb cracks and flakes (5.8) to a good ledge. [5] Climb a book nearly to the ridge crest (5.5), then move right to the beginning of a long traverse. [6] Traverse way right on a ramp and ledges to a long clean corner. [7] Climb the long corner and a short face pitch to a belay (5.7) [8] Move left, then climb a short wide crack (5.8) to the summit ridge. [9] Continue up the ridge to the summit. For the Paisano start, traverse right when the top of the right-hand gully ends below slabs. The climb begins at a small notch and mostly follows the buttress crest. From the top of Paisano descend a short way, cross a sandy bench, then continue up the North Face of Burgundy.

Descent: Rappel directly down to pitch 6, traverse back to the top of pitch 5 and continue rappelling the route.

Maps: Green Trails: Washington Pass No. 50; USGS: Washington Pass and Silver Star Mountain

Reference: *CAG 3: Rainy Pass to Fraser River*

29 JUNO TOWER
Clean Break

NORTH OF THE WINE SPIRES LIES PINNACLE-STUDDED Vasiliki Ridge, its shorter west sides facing Highway 20, and large eastern walls overlooking Silver Star Creek. Although the summits were climbed in May of 1952 by Fred Beckey, Joe Hieb, Herb Staley, and Donald Wilde, the more difficult faces remained untouched for another thirty years.

In 1984, when Bryan Burdo and his partner finished their route on Burgundy Spire they made an attempt on the 1400-foot Northeast Buttress of 7920-foot Juno Tower. They climbed two pitches up the route before retreating in the face of sustained difficulties and lack of time. Eager to return, Burdo asked various partners to join him, knowing such an obvious line *Merrand was leading when the incipient crack he followed ended, and protection became scarce.* would not remain unclimbed for long. His partner on the first attempt returned with another climber (without telling Burdo), and climbed three pitches up the buttress before leaving a red retreat sling on a tree.

The following summer Burdo and Yann Merrand hiked up Silver Star Creek. They made a camp below the face and fixed two pitches on the route that day. Burdo's heart sank when he looked up and saw the red sling. "I was sure someone had done the route," he said, "but I thought, what the hell, the second ascent will be just as good." In the morning Burdo and Merrand went up the fixed ropes and began climbing cracks toward the sling.

Merrand was leading when the incipient crack he followed ended, and protection became scarce. He wanted to fix a pin at the top of the crack before climbing left on thin face holds and blank rock. However, Burdo wanted the route to go clean, with only nuts and camming devices. The two climbers had a shouting match 400 feet above the ground. Merrand yelled down that he was the one leading and he was putting in a pin. Burdo laughed as he later told the story—after following the pitch he realized the piton was necessary.

All day long the climbers jammed up cracks, smeared across smooth slabs and stemmed up corners. With each pitch they looked for further

Juno Tower from the east, showing the Clean Break Route

evidence of the other party, but there were no more slings, pitons, or nuts. As they slotted hands in the final steep handcrack leading to the summit they felt confident that no other climbers had done the route. Burdo and Merrand named the climb Clean Break, for the light rock scar on the face, and because they had put up a long route in good style.

Over the third weekend in June of 1992 the weather forecast was bleak. Satellite pictures showed clouds clear across the state. Sue Harrington and I felt that climbing was out. We drove to Seattle on Saturday to visit vacationing friends from the East Coast, and we met Peter Kelemen at Mark Blatter's house. The moment we stepped in the door Peter said, "The storm is moving counterclockwise and it will clear off on the east side first. We should go do this great climb I heard about on Vasiliki Ridge."

Several cups of coffee later Peter had reached Bryan Burdo by phone and was drawing a route topo by dictation. Sue and I winced at the ratings Peter was writing down, and wished we'd spent a few extra spring weekends preparing on the Crags. But I love spur-of-the-moment adventures, where urgency keeps everyone moving. The big issue was whether we could hike in on Sunday, do the climb on Monday, and hike out. No one had to work on Monday, but Peter had to catch a plane to California early Tuesday morning.

I had been up Silver Star Creek once before, but my memory of the approach was bad, and we crossed several patches of slide alder unnecessarily before gaining snow-covered talus slopes. A brief shower cut loose as we put up tents a few hundred yards from the base of the route. The weather looked rotten, but Peter insisted we fix at least one rope up the first 5.10 pitch. Actually, Peter led the damp, thin hand crack, Mark belayed, and I took photos. Sue thought the whole adventure a bit mad and stayed in the tent.

At dark the three of us scooted down the snow slope to camp and brewed up hot drinks and dinner. The rain returned; no one discussed the wake-up hour or set watch alarms. Most of us felt there was little chance of climbing anything in the morning. But the Cascades are unpredictable, and I poked my head out of the tent at 7 A.M. to see sunshine illuminating the features of the buttress. "Hey get up! The weather's great, let's get on the climb!" I shouted.

Few people are cheerful before their morning coffee, and our soggy crew was no exception. By 8 A.M. we were moving up the snow and, after Mark and Peter Jumared their fixed rope and pulled it up, I attacked the thin crack. For ninety feet I torqued fingers and toes into flaring jams, all the while slotting Stoppers and stuffing small cams in for protection. Feeling no sensation left in my fingertips, my eyes searched desperately for good footholds and a better rest. I moved six feet right, paused to shake out, then moved back into the crack and climbed up to a belay ledge. The sun was warm, and I felt great.

Above, another outstanding pitch went through a series of roofs, then moved left to a ledge with small pines. Sue struggled up with our one daypack that contained water, snacks, trail shoes, and raingear. She led the next moderate pitch to beneath a corner. In two more pitches I got the thin crack

Peter Keleman jamming the first pitch of the Clean Break Route

and face traverse by Yann Merrand's fixed piton. I was glad he had placed it, for without the pin the leader would face a really long fall.

We kept close behind Peter and Mark, and at every belay chatted with one of them while the other pushed the route higher. By afternoon a grim buildup of dark clouds to the east started moving toward us. Anxious to reach the summit and get down, I climbed quickly up and left, and then the rain hit. Peter was working on the last hard crack around to the right, but he abandoned it when water started pouring out. Soon, we all made the top as rain lashed the spires and a thick fog obscured the view.

The descent north to a saddle, then back south to our camp, lasted until 9:30 P.M. I suggested to Sue that we hike out in the early morning to where she could call work, but Peter and Mark were determined to make it to the car that night. The following morning we saw fresh boot prints on the climbers' path. "How did they find this trail in the dark?" I asked Sue. Later we learned the hikers had just gone down the trail a couple hours before us, after a forced bivy in the wet brush.

Mark and Sue missed work, Peter missed his plane, and I (self-employed) fired myself. But we all felt it was worth it.

Juno Tower: Clean Break

First ascent: Bryan Burdo and Yann Merrand; August 1985
Difficulty: Grade IV, 5.10-
Equipment: A standard rack up to a 4-inch cam with emphasis on small to

medium cams, plus steel nuts. An ice ax may be needed to reach the base in early season.

Access: Continue on Highway 20 for 8.5 miles beyond Washington Pass to Silver Star Creek. Pick up a path on the east bank of the creek, then climb through open forest, paralleling the creek and crossing several talus fields to where the valley levels (4900 feet) near the end of meadows. Cross the stream to a talus slope and rock slabs on the west side of the valley. Keep left of slabs and do a rising traverse toward the

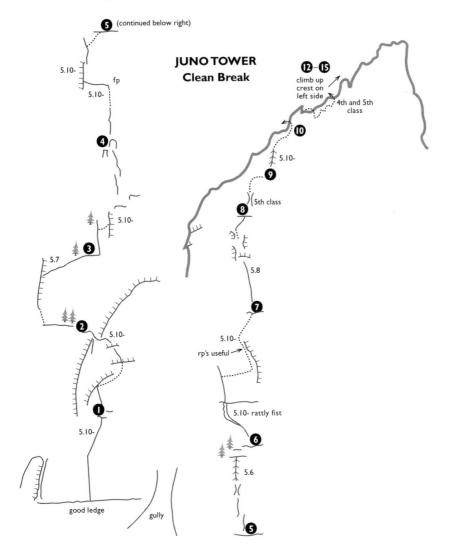

basin to below the northeast wall of Vasiliki Ridge (open timber and talus slopes). There are campsites at 6400 feet and bivy sites at 6600 feet close to the base of the route.

Route: The climb follows the Northeast Buttress and ridge of Juno Tower, and begins in an obvious 90-foot thin hand crack on a smooth wall. **[1]** Climb a crack 90 feet to a belay (5.10-). **[2]** Work up and through three overlaps (crack and face 5.10-), then move left to a ledge with a bushy tree. **[3]** Work left, then climb a left-facing corner and traverse back right across a finger crack (5.7). **[4]** Climb a short way up a left-hand corner, then step across (5.10-) and pull up onto ledges. Climb cracks and blocks to a belay in loose blocks and flakes. **[5]** Face climb to a fixed pin and traverse left on thin holds (5.10-) to the edge. Jam a thin crack up and right to a ledge belay. **[6]** Climb cracks and a short chimney, then climb the buttress crest to a belay at a tree below a short vertical wall (5.6). **[7]** Jam a hand and fist crack (5.10-) up onto a clean slab. From the top of the crack, traverse right and climb the face adjacent to a left-facing corner (5.10-) to a belay. **[8]** Ascend a hand crack (5.8), then flakes and a face to the ridge crest. This pitch leaves the buttress and moves onto the ridge. **[9]** Climb a short pitch up a chimney to a belay below a short vertical arête. **[10]** Work up a thin crack onto the arête (5.10-), then continue up cracks to a huge ledge on the ridge. **[11]** Climb through a hole between blocks on the left side of the ridge, then climb to the ridge crest again. Go up cracks on the crest to a belay. **[12]** through **[15]** Climb the ridge crest mainly on the left side until reaching a platform below the summit. The original route went around to the right and up a hand crack. We climbed cracks and blocks leading toward the south notch, then scrambled to the top.

Descent: Drop into gullies on the west side of Juno and Jupiter Towers until it's possible to traverse beneath their West Faces. Continue traversing the west side of Vasiliki Ridge (do not be tempted to descend the many gullies on the east) to 7200 feet, then climb down the ridge crest to a saddle at 6800 feet. From this saddle, talus and snow lead back southeast to camp. Some parties have carried all their gear up and over the climb, then descended south to the Burgundy Spire climbers' path, and hitched back to their car.

Maps: Green Trails: Washington Pass No. 50; USGS: Silver Star Mountain
Reference: Bryan Burdo 1992

30 CATHEDRAL PEAK
Southeast Buttress

IN THE FAR NORTH END OF WASHINGTON'S Pasayten Wilderness is a small group of granitic peaks that include Apex Mountain, Amphitheatre Mountain, and Cathedral Peak. The latter, rising to 8601 feet, lies 0.6 miles south of the Canadian border. The Pasayten is like a little slice of Wyoming—rolling open meadows and pine forests characterize the dry region, and lightning storms are common in summer months. All three of the peaks have sheer walls on one side and gentle slopes on the other; descents are easy. When it's pouring rain in the Cascades, the long hike (eighteen miles one way) into Cathedral Lakes can pay off. In July of 1983 I climbed for five sunny days in the area while rain came down in buckets elsewhere.

They compared the beautifully colored, 1500-foot Southeast Face to an enormous stained glass window.

Cathedral was first climbed on August 3, 1901 by Carl William Smith and George Otis Smith. In the summers of 1963 and 1964 Donna Hawkins accompanied her husband while he did a petrologic study in the area. During that time the pair scrambled up Cathedral. A rope was needed for the last few feet. They thought the peak probably had never been climbed by any other route, and compared the beautifully colored, 1500-foot Southeast Face to an enormous stained glass window. Four years later in September, Fred Beckey, John Brottem, Doug Leen, and Dave Wagner climbed the face in seven pitches.

In June of 1973 Dave Anderson, Steve Barnett, Julie Brugger, and Pete Doorish attempted the Southeast Buttress to a point halfway up the route before a snowstorm forced them off. Doorish returned in July with Glenn Wilson and did the buttress. It was during a time when climbers were trying out nuts for protection, and Doorish admitted being nervous about their use. "1973 was the year everybody switched to nuts," he said. "Before that people climbed with pitons. We were just trying them out to see what they were like." Doorish was busy that summer—he established eight more routes on Cathedral and the nearby peaks, ranging from easy 5th class to 5.9.

The Southeast Buttress of Cathedral Peak

During September of 1980 Bobby Knight and I hiked into Cathedral Peak via the Chewack River and Tungsten Creek Trails. We wanted to do a reasonable climb, then hike out and try Bear Mountain. I was also nursing a bad knee and wasn't eager to carry an ultra-heavy pack just yet.

Having worked as an Outward Bound instructor in Washington, Bobby was aware that the Canadian OB school often took students up the peak on various routes. We wanted to check the place out, and brought in several days of food and climbing gear. It took us a day-and-a-half to reach a meadow camp below Cathedral; although the trail was easy, the distances in the Pasayten were impressive.

The weather looked good on the third day. We began the Southeast Buttress up a gully behind the adjacent Monk. Excellent cracks comprised most of the route; belays ended on spacious ledges with tufts of grass and tiny clumps of flowers. Bobby got the one sustained hard pitch up high, which he dealt with efficiently. The only sour note to an otherwise perfect climb was finding the word "Keremeos," a name of a town in B.C., indelibly etched in the dark lichen on top of a huge ledge. With slow-growing lichen it will be many years before the light granite is once again covered and the ugly graffiti obliterated.

We made the top by mid-afternoon and hiked back down to camp. With time remaining, we decided to start hiking out that afternoon and begin work on our next project.

Cathedral Peak: Southeast Buttress

First ascent: Pete Doorish and Glenn Wilson; July 1973
Difficulty: Grade III, 5.9
Equipment: A standard rack up to a 4-inch cam.
Access: From the town of Winthrop (30 miles east of Washington Pass on Highway 20) take the Chewack River Road 23.5 miles to the Andrews Creek Trail. Hike this gentle trail 15 miles to Spanish Camp, in 15.6 miles reach the Boundary Trail and in 18 miles Cathedral Lakes. From Upper Cathedral Lake you can hike 0.5 miles over Cathedral Pass to reach the Southeast Buttress. It has been reported that the Boundary Trail from the Canadian side is a scenic approach to Cathedral Peak.
Route: The climb begins on the left corner of the Buttress, behind the lower feature called the Monk. Climb several pitches up the left corner via cracks, ledges, and a left-facing corner to the base of the upper headwall. Climb the headwall in two pitches (5.9); follow a long finger crack and an offwidth crack to the ledge. Two more pitches up the buttress crest lead to the summit (5.7).
Descent: Scramble down the western side of the peak via the West Ridge Route.
Maps: Green Trails: Coleman Peak No. 20; USGS: Remmel Mountain; CFM: 92 H/2 Manning Park
Reference: *CAG 3: Rainy Pass to Fraser River. CHGSWBC*

31 GLACIER PEAK
Frostbite Ridge

IN 1965 MY PARENTS AND I JOINED A GROUP OF MAZAMAS for a week-long climbing outing to Buck Creek Pass. Just fourteen, I stormed up the last mile of trail with a fully loaded new Cruiser pack, anxious for a view of surrounding peaks. What I saw was a huge snow- and ice-mantled mountain, thirteen miles to the west, rising to over 10,000 feet—Glacier Peak. To my disappointment, our schedule did not include an ascent of the mountain. I had to settle on climbing the smaller nameless peaks near High Pass. Five more years would pass before I could climb the massif the Indians called DaKobed (Great Parent).

They named Disappointment Peak when the fog cleared and they saw the true summit a half mile away and 800 feet higher.

Although the craggy summits of the Northwest offer more-challenging climbing, it is the volcanoes that capture everyone's imagination. Early explorers saw these mountains from great distances. Newcomers to our region become fascinated as the snowy giants appear through airplane windows.

Glacier Peak was first climbed in 1897 by a U.S. Geological Survey crew that included Darcy Bard, A.H. Dubor, Thomas Gerdine, and Sam Strom. They followed what is now called the Disappointment Peak Cleaver Route. They named Disappointment Peak when the fog cleared and they saw the true summit a half mile away and 800 feet higher. In 1906 A.L. Cool and Claude E. Rusk climbed the Cool Glacier, and in 1910 L.A. Nelson and companions did the Chocolate–Cool Cleaver.

By the mid 1930s a number of groups had made ascents of the Kennedy Glacier, the Milk Creek Route, and the Dusty Glacier. Early records are unclear, but it is presumed that O. Phillip Dickert, Perry Dodson, and Bob Dwyer made the first ascent of Frostbite Ridge. This aesthetic cleaver rises for 1300 feet, separating the Kennedy and Dusty Glaciers.

I first reached the summit of Glacier Peak in 1970 (also with a Mazama group) via the Sitkum Glacier. I climbed several more routes between 1979

Glacier Peak. Frostbite Ridge follows the left skyline above the Kennedy Glacier

and 1989, including a climb and ski descent of the Cool Glacier in 1987 with Sue Harrington. Over the years people talked highly of Frostbite Ridge, prompting Sue and me to carry skis for a Memorial Day 1992 ascent.

As often happens when one person comes up with a good weekend plan, others want to join in. Our party consisted of Sue, Julie Hirsch, Debbie Martin, and Doreen Richmond. There were lots of cars at the White Chuck trailhead on Saturday morning as we strapped skis onto our heavy packs.

It was a long grind up to a snowy campsite overlooking the edge of the Kennedy Glacier. My pack, the first overnight one of the season, felt brutal. A few scattered clouds moved lazily across the sky as we melted snow for dinner and drinks. There was even enough late afternoon sun left to melt snow in a black garbage bag basin and save some stove fuel. As the sun finally set behind White Chuck Mountain, the northwest side of the peak turned rosy orange in the wash of evening light.

At 4 A.M. we made a quick breakfast, traversed snow-covered talus and pasted on our skins. The night hadn't been very cold; it was easier going in the soft snow with skis than without. Higher on the Kennedy Glacier the surface became hard, and we stashed our boards and hiked up, snow crunching beneath plastic boots. At the 8800-foot saddle between the Kennedy and Ermine Glaciers we stopped for water and snacks as the crisp dome of Mount Baker rose far to the north.

Above, the slope gradually steepened, and halfway up we put on the spikes for the climb to the eroded lava pinnacles called the Rabbit Ears. A few tricky moves across frozen snow got us through the portal, then we dropped 100 feet into a col for another water break. From the notch, steep soft snow led up to Point 10,307, where we cached our day-packs for the hike to the summit. A light breeze barely kept the heat at bay. As I stepped out of the track for a photo, I went thigh deep into a hidden crevasse. Glad for the rope, I decided to follow the leader's tracks up the final sastrugi slope. It was those windblown snow formations that so neatly hid the glacier cracks.

The top was a busy place, with parties converging from various routes and exchanging summit small talk. We hurried down in hopes of catching some good skiing low on the Kennedy, but a bottleneck of ascending climbers in the col below the Rabbit Ears slowed our descent. I suggested to the group that to save time we could traverse low on the west side of the pinnacles and parallel the Kennedy Glacier. This worked well; I recommend it as an early-season maneuver.

Soon, we were at the skis, but the sun had turned the snow to oatmeal. The skiing was purely of the combat variety, with every turn becoming a physical workout. Once at camp, Sue, Debbie, and I crashed, knowing we still had Monday to hike out. Julie and Doreen were determined to go out that night to attend a folk music festival in Seattle the next day. We wished them well and settled back to enjoy another beautiful night in the high alpine country.

Glacier Peak: Frostbite Ridge

First ascent: Phillip Dickert, Perry Dodson, and Bob Dwyer; July 5, 1935
Difficulty: Moderate snow (water ice in late season) and easy rock
Equipment: Snow and ice anchors and a few slings for rock horns are useful. Ice ax and crampons.
Access: For the latest conditions contact USFS, Darrington Ranger District, 1405 Emmens Street, Darrington, WA 98241 (360-436-1155). From Interstate 5 take Highway 530 for 32 miles to Darrington. Take the Mountain Loop Highway for 9.2 miles to the White Chuck River Road (No. 23). Follow the White Chuck Road 10.4 miles to the White Chuck trailhead. Hike the White Chuck Trail 4.9 miles to trail No. 639. Go left on No. 639, then hike 1.7 miles to the Pacific Crest Trail. Go left on the Crest Trail, then continue just over 2 miles to where the trail crosses

Sue Harrington, Julie Hirsch, Doreen Richmond, and Debby Martin above the Rabbit Ears

Glacier Creek below the snout of the Kennedy Glacier. Leave the trail just before it crosses the creek and hike up and right to campsites on the ridge. A good early season approach to Frostbite Ridge is to climb along the left edge of the Kennedy glacier to the Kennedy–Dusty Glacier saddle at 8800 feet.

Route: From the saddle climb the ridge directly, climbing through the Rabbit Ears, down to a saddle, then back up to traverse just below point 10,307. Drop into the crater, then continue on up the final slope to the summit.

Descent: Downclimb the ridge. In early season it is possible to traverse beneath the Rabbit Ears on the west. To do this, from the col at 10,000 feet drop 300–400 feet and contour northward above Kennedy Glacier to regain the ridge lower down.

Maps: Green Trails: Glacier Peak No. 112; USGS: Glacier Peak West, Glacier Peak East, Gamma Peak, and Lime Mountain

Reference: *CAG 2: Stevens Pass to Rainy Pass*

32 SPIRE POINT
Northeast Route

THE PTARMIGAN TRAVERSE, WHICH WAS FIRST COMPLETED IN 1938, is the most popular of the high alpine routes in the Cascades. It starts at Cascade Pass, wends southward through spectacular terrain, and ends at Downey Creek, just north of Glacier Peak. At the southern end of the Ptarmigan Traverse is a small glaciated granitic peak that rises 450 feet above Spire Col and 800 feet above the Spire Glacier on the northwest. The peak is flanked on the east by the Dana Glacier, and on the north by the jagged needles of Northeast Spire Point. Rising to 8264 feet, Spire is one of many peaks that lie within striking range of climbers doing the Traverse. Climbs of Formidable, Spider, and Le Conte tend to be crumbly adventures on gneiss or schist, and it is only farther south that you encounter solid rock.

Rising to 8264 feet, Spire is one of many peaks that lie within striking range of climbers doing the Ptarmigan Traverse.

In May of 1938, Phillip Dickert, Dave Lind, and George McGowan approached Spire Point up Sulphur Creek and another creek leading up to Itswoot and Cub Lakes. They camped at 5500 feet, where Dickert described the view. "Two beautiful lakes glimmered through the fog," he later wrote, "their water source being the south glacier of Spire Point." On the 29th the group left camp and headed up in a northeasterly direction toward the glacier. After traversing the west side of the icefield, they started up the south face of the west ridge. The climbing involved a series of gullies and snow patches to the ridge crest, where they continued east to a high point.

From the point they were forced to descend into a gap, then climb to the actual summit and the junction of the north and west ridges. After a traverse on the north side, they climbed to the top from the northeast and built a cairn. Modern parties can access the northeast corner (where the first ascent team finished their climb) by climbing across the east face from Spire Col. Although this makes for a short climb, it is the obvious route, and is interesting climbing on good rock.

The author on the summit of Spire Point

On several guided trips of the Ptarmigan Traverse in the early 1980s, I would take clients up Spire Point at the end of the trip. I had found a challenging variation on the last pitch that involved climbing a short overhanging hand crack to the top. I would offer the harder crack to people wanting to try it, and I could still belay others up the easy 5th class twenty feet farther north. Not wanting to carry a lot of hardware along the Ptarmigan for this one short pitch, I would bring only several slings and a half-dozen carabiners.

At the base of the steeper climbing, I would scan the ledges for an assortment of rocks ranging in size from ¾-inch to 2-inch. Using several of these natural chocks, I would lead the crack, loop a sling around a rock and slot it into the fissure. It was great fun, and it illustrated what you could do with very little gear. On a later Traverse I brought along a couple of cams to stuff into the crack. I was disappointed at how easy the short steep wall was with the high tech pro.

It is a long approach to reach Spire Col just to climb Spire Point. I feel most parties would either do it as part of the Ptarmigan Traverse, or as an outing to climb several peaks such as Marmot Head, Elephant Head, and Dome Peak. Many fun climbs abound in the area that require no or little hardware, but plenty of mountaineering sense.

Spire Point: Northeast Route

First ascent: Phillip Dickert, Dave Lind, and George McGowan; May 29, 1938

Difficulty: Grade I, 5.1–5.2 or 5.8 via the handcrack

Equipment: Some protection up to 2 inches for the crack variation. Ice ax and crampons.

Access: From Darrington, drive Highway 530 north 6.4 miles to the Suiattle River Road No. 26. Turn right onto the Suiattle Road and drive 20.5 miles to Downey Creek. Hike the Downey Creek Trail 6.6 miles to Bachelor Creek, then follow the unmaintained and overgrown trail for 5.5 miles to Cub Lake Pass, 5880 feet. From the pass drop down and follow a path around Cub Lake, then ascend in an easterly direction to gain Itswoot Ridge. Follow the ridge and the southwest slope up to Spire Col; Cub Lake to Spire Col is 2500 feet elevation.

Spire Point from Spire Col. The route ascends the right side of the face

Route: From Spire Col do a long, easy, right traverse onto a ledge, then climb a class 4 trough on the right side to just below the summit. Climb around a corner right (low 5th) to the summit; or jam the overhanging hand crack past a small roof on the left (5.8).

Descent: Downclimb the ascent route.

Maps: Green Trails: Cascade Pass No. 80 and McGregor Mountain No. 81; USGS: Downey Mountain, Dome Peak, and Agnes Mountain

Reference: *CAG 2: Stevens Pass to Rainy Pass*

33 DOME PEAK
Dome Glacier Route

JUST UNDER 9000 FEET IS THE ICE-CLAD MASSIF OF DOME PEAK, with its quartz diorite summit. On the northeast side, the one- by three-mile-long Chickamin Glacier forms a blanket of ice visible from far north along the Ptarmigan Traverse. The much smaller Dome Glacier lies on the southwest side. *The final climb was up steep snow and a knife edge rock ridge to the top.* The peak is studded with ridges of gendarmes such as Dynaflow Tower and Hydramatic Spire. Difficult access, as Norval Grigg pointed out in the 1936 Mountaineer, was Dome's protection. He wrote, "After enjoying many years of splendid isolation, both summits of Dome Peak were finally climbed during the past summer."

Grigg and Forest Farr chose May of 1935 for their attack on the peak, hiking up Sulphur and Bath Creeks to a camp where they watched it rain for four days. They returned on July 4th via the same route, only to again be hit with rain. As they were leaving, the clouds parted. They made a stab at the peak, but were forced back by snow-plastered rock at 8500 feet. Grigg was now thoroughly familiar with the hike in, claiming, "We felt we knew enough about Sulphur Creek and that approach to Dome, that we could climb it backwards through a thick fog."

In July of 1936 Grigg returned again, this time with Farr, Don Blair, and Bob Hayes and, although clouds swarmed in, there was no rain. Blair, Farr, and Grigg made the rocky summit with the help of tennis shoes at 4:30 P.M. on July 5th. They felt the Southwest Peak was the highest and true summit. The next month Erik Larson and George Freed climbed the Northeast Peak from an approach up Agnes Creek. The final climb was up steep snow and a knife edge rock ridge to the top. They believed their 8920-foot summit to be higher, and it is—by 40 feet.

Opposite: *A climber pauses in Dome Peak's cannon hole*

Dome Peak from the west in winter. (Photo by Cliff Leight)

In August of 1982 I had led a weary group the length of the Ptarmigan Traverse and camped at Spire Col. After a climb of Northeast Spire Point one member remained enthusiastic for more summits, so we headed for Dome. The early morning snow was still firm on the lower Dana Glacier, and Elephant Head cast a great shadow across the icefield. As the sun cleared the summit of the spire, we began a long rising traverse toward the Dome Glacier and the final slopes of the peak.

Passing the 10- by 20-foot cannon hole between Hydramatic Spire and the Northeast Peak we were amazed at its size and position, as though some geological mortar blast had ripped through the wall of rock. I insisted my client climb into the aperture for a photo, which later was used on the cover of a book. Shortly thereafter we reached the summit arête and traversed carefully to the highest point. It was a cloudless day, the perfect culmination of our week in the high mountains. That evening we enjoyed a big dinner and intense sunset from our 7760-foot camp at Spire Col.

Dome Peak: Dome Glacier Route

First ascent: George Freed and Erik Larson; August 1, 1936
Difficulty: Grade I, snow and class 3 rock
Equipment: Gear for glacier travel. Ice ax and crampons.
Access: Approach as for Spire Point, described previously. Instead of climbing all the way to the Spire Col, make a rising traverse from Itswoot Ridge across a south-facing slope and below toes of rock ridges to the Dome Glacier. If approaching from the Ptarmigan Traverse, camp at 6600 feet on the Dana Glacier, then do a rising traverse south-southeast and cross over to the Dome Glacier at 7600 feet.
Alternate: A long brush-free, high, and scenic way to approach Dome is via Image Lake, Canyon Lake, around the west side of Bannock Mountain, north to Ross Pass, and then to the Chickamin Glacier near the South Peak of Gunsight. You can then traverse the Chickamin Glacier west to the 8560-foot col on Dome Peak.
Route: Once on the Dome Glacier, continue up to a 8560-foot col just north of the Northeast Peak. From the col, ascend a snow ridge southeast for 300 feet, then climb the arête to the final summit ridge.
Descent: Descend the same route.
Maps: Green Trails: Cascade Pass No. 80 and McGregor Mountain No. 81; USGS: Downey Mountain, Dome Peak, and Agnes Mountain
Reference: *CAG 2: Stevens Pass to Rainy Pass*

34 BIG FOUR MOUNTAIN
North Face in Winter

BOASTING A 4000-FOOT NORTH FACE, the crenelated peak of Big Four Mountain rises to 6135 feet. It lies twelve air miles due east of Mount Pilchuck, above the Stillaguamish River. At the southern end of the Mountain Loop Highway, Big Four is one of the most accessible peaks in an area that contains Whitehorse Mountain, Three Fingers, Pugh Mountain, Mount Dickerman, Sloan Peak, and the dagger-like spires of the Monte Cristo peaks. On Big Four, the rock ridges and buttresses are composed of phyllites, slates, sandstones, and conglomerates, and as such do not lend themselves to quality alpine rock climbing. What the peak does offer is one of the finest winter ascents in the Northwest, when in condition.

Throughout the day the temperature never got above freezing, and just below the summit they began wonder how to finish, as the summit blob was overhanging with icicles.

That in mind, we need to define what "in condition" means in this land of maritime influence. I have completed a number of excellent winter ascents of Mount Baker, Mount Shuksan, and North Twin Sister, and climbs in the Stuart Range, all after a settled spell of good weather. Once the snow stops falling, an alpine face gradually stabilizes with a combination of snow sliding off, warm days, and cold nights. The result is often a well-bonded surface of white concrete. And, if you're lucky, the snow will contain a lot of moisture throughout, thereby freezing deep. The unpleasant alternative is sometimes a firm crust on the surface that collapses, revealing unconsolidated fluff beneath, and creating extreme avalanche hazards.

The monolithic peak of Big Four was first climbed in 1931 by Forest Farr and Art Winder, going up the Northwest Ridge. In 1942 a complete ascent of the North Face was made by Montgomery Johnson, Ken Prestrud, and Charles Welsh. These two ascents were done in the summer, and the first winter ascent of the peak was not until February of 1963, when Kenn Carpenter, Bob Marcy, and Ron Miller climbed the Southwest Buttress. Eight years later in July, Miller teamed up with Ben Guydelkon to put up the Tower Route on

The North Face of Big Four. (Photo by Joe Catellani)

the North Face of the peak. Miller admitted the rock was of average quality, but what made the route special was the exposure and spectacular scenery. "I absolutely loved the bivouac site," he raved. "It was totally classic. On the very top of the second tower there was a snowpatch and a level patch of heather with running water."

Climbers kept an eye on the North Face as a possible winter climb, and in January of 1974 an arctic air mass dropped the temperatures in Seattle down into the 10- to 15-degree range for a good spell. (I was on Colchuck Peak that month and the temperatures were 15–20 degrees below zero.) Cal Folsom and Rich Carlstad literally canceled all other commitments and blasted up to Big Four in the middle of the night, hoping to scale the face before the weather

Gregg Cronn leads an ice pitch on the North Face of Big Four Mountain

pendulum swung back. The pair were armed with tools that Folsom had modified. "I had an REI ax," he said. "Chouinard tools were out of our price range. I drooped everybody's picks. I had a torch, and I filed teeth on them. They worked great, and never broke." He also was using REI ten-point crampons that he had welded front points onto; "I brazed them on and used stainless steel that wouldn't bend; nothing I welded ever broke."

The pair started climbing at midnight, hiking up to where the ice caves were to begin the ascent. Folsom remembers it being very cold. "It was so clear, the air was so clear the starlight just . . . we didn't use headlamps," he raved. "I don't think we owned headlamps (I don't think we could *afford* headlamps). We had flashlights; we were ill prepared." For footwear the two young climbers (Folsom was nineteen at the time) had Galibier leather boots that fit snugly for summer alpine routes, but were not well suited for a winter ascent and zero-degree temperatures. As a result, Carlstad damaged his feet on the climb from a combination of cold feet and having his toes jammed in small boots.

"We climbed roped together up the couloir with basically a running belay," relates Folsom. "The conditions were just so good—the nicest consistency of aerated icy snow." It had been a heavy snow year and the rock at the bottom, which is sometimes bare, was plastered heavily from avalanches and was in good shape for cramponing. "I remember one prominent narrow section we got to just after the sun came up, and two Whidbey Island jets came flying up the valley below us. Rich screamed at the top of his lungs, 'We are dead!' We thought it was an avalanche."

Throughout the day the temperature never got above freezing, and just below the summit they began wonder how to finish, as the summit blob was overhanging with icicles. As Folsom describes it, "Just around the right side, to the west of the icicles there was a little ramp that went right up the rock. That's how we finished, and we got to the top just as the sun was setting." Alpenglow washed over the summit ridge, painting everything with that indescribable mix of mandarin orange and plum hues as the shadows turned a cold blue. To his chagrin, Folsom's camera froze up, robbing him of a celluloid image, but he was left with crisp memories.

On the descent west and then down the north side the climbers waded through chest-deep powder snow that was sliding under their feet. Folsom closes his account of the climb with, "We're probably lucky that we're alive."

Several of my friends had climbed Big Four in the winter and praised it as a steep alpine winter climb with a short approach. Finally, during January of 1994, conditions had firmed up enough to justify an ascent of the austere and huge face. Gregg Cronn and I left Bellingham the night before, planning to sleep in the Ice Caves parking lot and get an early start. Originally from Spokane, Gregg had done a lot of climbing in the Canadian Rockies during all seasons. I met him in the mid 1980s while we were both guiding and teaching on Mount Baker. Raising a family had cut into his time spent in the mountains, but as far as I could tell, had not diminished his skill.

I had just come from the beaches of Thailand, with nothing more under my belt for conditioning but a few bolted rock climbs—not exactly the best training for a 4000-foot icy face. An hour or so before light we arose in the cold air, gulped down some cocoa, and began hiking to the face. Keeping up with Gregg is always hard, especially now, since he does triathlons—and wins in his age group. That day was no exception. We climbed unroped for a long ways until I finally insisted we tie in and place some gear. Greg was adamant about the need for the rope, and it was at this point I felt somewhat like a client. But we can't be in top form on every trip, and it was just going to be "one of those days."

Scottish climber Tom Patey referred to this state of mind and body as the "off-form ploy." He stated that a climber who was on form during the morning can be feeling off form by early afternoon. If an interval of forty-eight hours or so has elapsed between climbs, a climber might talk of being out of condition. If the interval is a month or longer, he or she may justifiably consider himself to be out of training. I felt as if I were in a vise somewhere between those warm sandy beaches and the cold wall that loomed above.

It was lucky for me that, for the most part, the snow was hard and crampon points and ax picks bit deeply and securely. Add to that the stunning winterscape of frosted peaks in every direction, which soon mollified my anxiety. My luck also held when Gregg got the hardest pitch, a near vertical slot of rotten ice and snow that was completely unprotected. Hanging from one shaky screw at the belay, I was not amused by the prospect of a 3500-foot ride to the bottom. Far scarier big alpine routes had honed Gregg for this pitch, and he methodically moved upwards, testing each shaft and foot placement with care.

We popped onto the summit ridge with light to spare, and without hesitation began the long traverse east and south to locate the East Face descent route. I had a few more tense moments downclimbing a short vertical gully while Gregg chided me for being slow. From there we continued down snow slopes, did a couple of rappels over cliff bands in the dark, and then crashed through swamps and brushy woods to the Stillaguamish River.

By then it was 10:30 at night and even my indomitable partner was showing signs of fatigue. It was very dark, and in front us was a quiet expanse of icy water. With no idea of its depth and no sign of a log jam to cross over on, we looked at each other with a shrug and plunged in, boots on and all. The water was shallow, and soon we were across and clawing upwards through brush to the highway. As we squished back to the car under starlit skies, I had that slightly euphoric feeling that comes over oneself after a fine ascent. Pulling off a winter ascent is also satisfying, especially in the Cascades.

Big Four Mountain: North Face in Winter

First ascent: Rich Carlstad and Cal Folsom; January 4, 1974
Difficulty: Grade III or IV with alpine ice and snow mostly in the 50-degree range and steeper
Equipment: A longer rope in the 200 foot (60m) range is helpful, as are screws

and pickets. Some rock gear is useful if the face is showing more rock in drier seasons.

Access: Take Highway 92 (east of Marysville) to the town of Granite Falls. From Granite Falls drive the Mountain Loop Highway for 19 miles to the turnoff to the Big Four Ice Caves, 1.4 miles east of Big Four campground. Follow the ice caves trail for 1 mile to the base of the face. In heavier snow years you can climb directly up toward the gully left and east of the North Rib Route. In 1994 we were forced to traverse way to the right, climb through some brush to gain the broad snowfield that spans the lower face, and then traverse back left to gain the gully.

Route: Many lines are possible on Big Four, depending on conditions. Gullies on either side of the various ribs have been climbed; some are more difficult than others. We chose the gully left of the North Rib, as it looked the most straightforward at that time. From the left side of the broad snowfield it is possible to climb up and slightly right, past icy sections and one near-vertical slot, and from there onto the steep slopes leading to the summit.

Descent: From the summit, traverse east 0.2 mile until it's possible to descend 300 feet, then go in a southerly direction to gain a saddle at 5800 feet. Downclimb snow slopes to a large gully that leads down into a basin. Traverse northwest across the basin to avoid cliff bands below, and then switchback right and down a gully adjacent the cliffbands. From there continue to the base of the peak and traverse in a northwest direction back to the Ice Caves Trail. As the going was rough in the swampy bottomlands, we chose to forge due north for the river and the highway—not necessarily the smartest plan. Other parties have also descended the northwest ridge to the 4520-foot saddle between Big Four and Hall Peak. On Big Four it is easy to find yourself cut off by cliffbands in the dark (especially in winter), and we found the East Face route to work well.

Maps: Green Trails: Silverton No. 110; USGS: Silverton
Reference: *CAG 2: Stevens Pass to Rainy Pass*

35 PRUSIK PEAK
West Ridge

PRUSIK PEAK RISES EAST OF MOUNT STUART, on the west end of Temple Ridge and has come to epitomize the Cascades version of a Chamonix spire. Gleaming white granite and perfect crack systems characterize this enchanting pinnacle. Fred Beckey made the first ascent of the 8000-foot peak via the East Route in 1948 with Art Holben, Pete Schoening, and Ralph Widrig. The group chose Memorial Day weekend for their adventure, and while hiking up the hot trail coined the name for the area— the Cashmere Crags—

Holben made several throws with their spare ³⁄₈-inch-line and managed to lasso the summit block. From there it was short work to prusik to the top, accomplishing the first ascent and naming the peak as well.

which sticks today. Their primary mission was the ascent of as many rock spires as possible on Temple Ridge. After tackling The Monument, they worked up the east ridge of Prusik late in the day.

According to Pete Schoening, Cascade climbers would climb on the rocks of the Icicle and Tumwater Canyons during March, April, and into May. By mid or late May access into the Cashmere Crags became feasible. They would then plod up snow slopes to the base of the rock spires in boots, and change into tennis shoes. Says Schoening, "Any canvas shoe was called a tennis shoe. I generally found that the cheaper the tennis shoe, the thinner and flimsier it was, which was an advantage, because then you could get something that was tight to your foot. What I'd do before each climb was take a saw and curve the bottom and chew up the shoe a little bit—just enough to make the rubber so it wasn't smooth. You didn't want those big thick-soled things."

Schoening and his friends were also innovative when it came to making their own hardware for wide cracks. Craig Lubben, the Colorado inventor of the Big Bro, would have been amazed to learn what was used in 1948.

Opposite: *Prusik Peak. The West Ridge Route follows the left skyline*

Schoening continues, "I remember using 'plumber's helpers.' Where you would have a gap, you can have two pieces of pipe and add a little piece of pipe, and you could screw it on one end and the other end. We used it in reverse and would put it into a crack and then screw it out, so it compressed against the other side of the crack. It was like putting a coat rack inside of a crack." I asked Pete if he took along a wrench to tighten it. "Oh yeah," he replied. "You had to take along a monkey wrench!"

On the East Ridge of Prusik Peak the climbers would have been decked out in war surplus clothing, wearing flimsy tennis shoes, tied together with manila rope, and carrying all sorts of gadgets, including pitons, hammer, carabiners, "plumbers helpers" (if there were big cracks), and a monkey wrench.

Climbing some on aid and traversing when necessary, Schoening, Holben, and Widrig gained 180 feet to within sight of the overhanging summit pinnacle. In the spirit of the day, Holben made several throws with their spare ⅜-inch-line and managed to lasso the summit block. From there it was short work to prusik to the top, accomplishing the first ascent and naming the peak as well.

Michelle Potter on the West Ridge of Prusik Peak

Beckey was also present on the first ascent of the West Ridge in 1957 with Fred Ayres, John Rupley, and Don (Claunch) Gordon. He referred to it in his *Cascade Alpine Guide* as a route of purity on marvelous granite. A climber tackling the ridge encounters a variety of moves, airy exposure,. and a lofty summit overlooking sparkling lakes.

Even though nearly three decades have passed since I first climbed the West Ridge, the memories remain crisp. That summer I had been scrambling alone in the Cashmere Crags, an area abundant with granite spires and outcrops, in hopes of finding a partner for the peak. The August weather was clear and warm, but my packets of instant oatmeal and cocoa were running out.

Not a climber was about, and the clean granite ridge, bristling with gendarmes, beckoned in the afternoon light. I had a rudimentary knowledge of rope soloing but I was considering doing it without a rope. My upper limit then was 5.8; the only climb I had finished at that level removed several layers of tissue from my hands and a respectable amount of blood. On second thought, I brought the rope.

From Prusik Pass I climbed quickly up class 4 rock on the ridge's north side and gained the crest. Hopping along it, I began to feel that soloing wasn't all that tough. My new blue rock shoes with red laces were the ticket. When I reached the 5.7 unprotected slab pitch I was fairly puffed up about my abilities. "This appears to be a simple problem," I thought. But, upon closer inspection, the slab looked almost sterile—no cracks, no holds, no anything. Fear infiltrated my brain.

After fidgeting, and finally anchoring the rope at the slab's base, I climbed cautiously, feeding the line through a Jumar attached to my swami. There was a point of hesitation where I eyed the sharp boulders twenty feet below and good handholds six feet above. I reached for a rounded nubbin of white granite, pulled up and stood on the hold with a sigh of relief.

Traversing along the south side of the ridge was also frightening, but at least there were good grips. Several ample ledges brought me to the lieback crack where I conceded the rope would again be useful. I even placed a small brass nut as intermediate protection part way up, but to my horror it fell out and slid down the rope.

Although my earlier confidence had vanished, I felt that now was the moment to restore it. With forearms burning, I pushed hard with my feet and kept them close to my hands. Watching for the most minute sign of slippage, I inched up, heaved myself onto a ledge, and gulped air greedily. Soloing was a demon in disguise.

From the ledge, a good hundred feet of steep climbing remained on some of the finest rock in the Northwest. The jugs were big, the exposure wild, and an afternoon breeze whipped my hair about. I made the summit and sat in the sun, thinking. It was quiet except for the occasional whoosh of a swallow. I had climbed the peak alone and felt very satisfied. But I had not forgotten those moments of fear that had shoved my heart into hyper-speed. It was something to remember—that juxtaposition of ecstasy and elevated terror.

Prusik Peak: West Ridge

First ascent: Fred Ayres, Fred Beckey, Don (Claunch) Gordon, and John Rupley; May 25, 1957

Difficulty: Grade II, 5.7

Equipment: A light rack that includes a 3-inch cam.

Permit: Permits, which are required for camping in the Enchantment Lakes between June 15th and October 15th each year, can be obtained from the USFS Ranger Station, Leavenworth, WA 98826 (509-782-1413). Write for permits after February 25th. The Enchantments are popular, so write in early. The ranger station also issues two walk-in permits a day. For these permits, the group size can be from one to eight, for a total of two to sixteen people. They are on a first-come, first-served basis, so call ahead for the ranger station hours.

Access: Drive Highway 2 east 100 miles to Leavenworth. Just as you enter Leavenworth from the west, turn right on the Icicle River Road. Go nearly 5 miles to the Snow Creek Trail parking lot on the left. Hike the Snow Creek Trail 10+ miles to Prusik Pass, climbing 5000 feet past Nada and Snow Lakes.

Route: From Prusik Pass ascend to where the ridge steepens, then climb nearly to the crest. Traverse up on the north side for one pitch to the crest. Continue along the crest to an unprotected slab pitch (5.7) and climb it to the top. Cross over to the south side of the ridge, then traverse an exposed catwalk to the belay. Scramble left on ledges to the base of the lieback corner. Climb the corner (5.7), then ascend a lieback flake and a chimney to the summit.

Descent: Rappel and downclimb the ridge, or rappel the North Face and traverse back to Prusik Pass. In early season the north side can be treacherous with steep snow.

Maps: Green Trails: Enchantments No. 209; USGS: Blewett and Enchantment Lakes

Reference: *CAG 1: Columbia River to Stevens Pass*

36 PRUSIK PEAK
South Face

PRUSIK PEAK'S VARIOUS FACETS BECKON the adventurous climber like a giant white crystal. In 1962, Fred Beckey returned to the peak with Les McDonald and two Frenchmen, Guido Magnone and Jean Coure, in hopes of establishing a route on the 900-foot South Face. The four had pushed the line part way up the wall, but 200 feet from the summit Magnone and Coure chose to retreat, due to lack of time. Beckey and Dan Davis returned several days later and went back up to work on the face.

"Then Mike had the crux pitch and there was a 5.9-ish kinda thing that worked out left and it was difficult getting a pin in. That was the hardest part on the climb.

They climbed quickly over familiar ground up chimneys, ramps, ledges, and cracks to the high point. From there Beckey felt the climbing was not that bad. "There were only two pitches requiring just three pitons for aid and several more for safety," he reported. At a notch in the East Ridge, Beckey and Davis aided up a short crack that led to the summit. Seven years later Mike Heath and Bill Sumner climbed the route all free by moving slightly right on the pitch above Snafflehound Ledges.

Sumner remembered getting off-route in 1969 and having to find another way. "I had the lead that was getting up under this chockstone [now known as the Burgner/Stanley Route]," he relates, "and there looked like there was a crack out around the chockstone. I tentatively tried it, but I ended up dropping down and climbing some cracks looking for a way to get up. Then Mike had the crux pitch and there was a 5.9-ish kinda thing that worked out left and it was difficult getting a pin in. That was the hardest part on the climb."

In its entirety, the South Face provides eight pitches of superb climbing on excellent rock. Although some guidebooks tout the Burgner/Stanley Route as the "one to do," I have always preferred the original line up the face. I have climbed it many times, including once in the winter of 1976 with Les Nugent.

Chuck Sink and I routinely made forays to the Cashmere Crags from

Steve Mitchell below the South Face of Prusik Peak

Washington State University, even though it was 225 miles from Pullman to Leavenworth. On a Friday afternoon, in late September of 1973, we began the awful drive. Jay Foster had joined us reluctantly, after weeks of my badgering him to go. He was concerned that he might miss an 8 A.M. mammalogy exam Monday morning, being a far more dedicated student than either of us. Exchanging sly winks, Chuck and I assured Jay this was only a two day trip and we would deliver him, with brain and body intact, to Dr. Johnson on Monday.

Chuck's 1957 Ford Fairlane roared across the Palouse wheat country at terrifying speeds. By listening to the sound of the engine, Chuck would inform

Jay or me when we exceeded safe velocities. Besides the car having bald tires, the speedometer was broken. We stopped in Leavenworth Friday night and slept five hours or so.

All day Saturday we plodded up the Snow Creek Trail, reaching Lake Viviane in the Enchantments, by late afternoon. Peg and Bill Stark greeted us at their Marmot Boulder camp and told stories of nearly two decades of trips into the lakes. Bill said the larches were not as brilliant gold as the year before, but to us they were stunning. We studied the South Face that evening, then crawled into our bags after dinner and mugs of tea.

Up early on Sunday, I squeezed my feet into a pair of size five brown Galibier RD's (my normal size being six). I got them on sale for twenty-five bucks, but they were a touch too small and they really hurt. Once up the heather slopes, I took the first lead and squirmed up a narrow chimney to a belay. An autumn breeze quickly cooled my blood, and I stamped about at the stance while Chuck and Jay followed the big crack. Chuck led a reasonable pitch, then I took over again and immediately got us lost. I was too far to the west, probably on the Burgner/Stanley Route.

That wretched mistake cost us a lot of time, but once back on track we climbed diagonally upwards toward Snafflehound Ledges and the final vertical pitches. Jay had been reluctant to lead, but Chuck and I insisted he take the crux pitch. It looked like outrageous face and crack climbing, and Jay was our small holds expert. He methodically moved up, tinkered with Stoppers and hexes, got in solid pro, and slowly disappeared above us.

When we reached his belay he was raving about how neat the pitch had been, which only proves that, although harder, leading is much more rewarding. The sun was starting to drop when Chuck climbed quickly up cracks to the summit ridge. "I'm not going to make it to the mammalogy test am I, Al?" Jay asked. "Uh? It doesn't look like it Jay," was the reply. By this time Jay realized we had fibbed to him about the approach and length of the climb, but he was smiling.

We paused on the summit for a quick photo, then began rappelling. On the first rap the ropes became hopelessly stuck, so I prusiked back up to free them. By the time I got back down it was pitch black. Had we brought spare batteries for our headlamps we might have made it down the West Ridge in an hour or so. Instead, it took several hours of crawling down and feeling for cracks and holds. Jay insisted we leave plenty of gear behind on the rappels that had become necessary in the darkness.

From Prusik Pass it was still a long, shin-bashing way down to our camp at the lake, where we crawled into sacks at midnight. We awoke late on Monday morning as Peg Stark brought us hot tea in bed. Jay sighed, "Well I might as well just drop the mammalogy class and take it again next semester." We all laughed as we packed up for the leisurely hike out.

Prusik Peak: South Face

First ascent: Fred Beckey and Dan Davis; June 26, 1962

Difficulty: Grade III, 5.9

Equipment: A standard rack up to a 3-inch cam.

Permit: A permit is required from the USFS Ranger Station, Leavenworth, WA 98826 (509-782-1413).

Access: Same as for the West Ridge of Prusik Peak, described previously. Do not hike to Prusik Pass, but ascend heather and talus directly above Lake Viviane to the South Face.

Route: The climb begins in a deep chimney left of the V features. **[1]** Squirm up a chimney (5.7) and after 120 feet exit left up cracks to a tree (chimney protects with small Stoppers). Belay at the tree or continue up and right to a higher belay (the latter will enable you to reach Snafflehound Ledges in two long leads). **[2]** Continue up and right past a broad bushy pine, then climb slabs and cracks to a belay (5.6). **[3]** Climb a short chimney, then follow cracks and corners to major ledges (5.9). Pitches 2 and 3 are two crack systems right of the deep chimney on the Burgner/Stanley route. **[4]** Traverse rightward and up on ledges to the start of a crack system leading to the summit notch. **[5]** Do a short pitch up to a small tree on a ledge. **[6]** Climb a hand and fist crack (5.9) and then a slot with cracks, to a ledge belay on the left. **[7]** Climb the right-hand of two cracks to the cleft east of the summit (5.8). **[8]** Climb onto the north side, then descend a bit and move right onto a ramp. Then do a friction traverse (5.7–5.8) to a corner and climb a crack to the summit. From the cleft, you can also jam a short, perfect, thin hand crack directly to the summit (5.10-).

Descent: Same as for the West Ridge, described previously.

Maps: Green Trails: Enchantments No. 209 S; USGS: Blewett and Enchantment Lakes

Reference: *CAG 1: Columbia River to Stevens Pass*

37 COLCHUCK PEAK
Northeast Buttress

DWARFED BY THE MASSIVE BULK OF NEARBY DRAGONTAIL, Colchuck Peak is often overlooked by alpinists as a climbing objective. Climbers venturing into the east side of the Stuart Range frequently opt to do one of Dragontail's eighteen routes. Although Colchuck, at 8705 feet, is 135 feet lower than Dragontail, in many ways it is the more striking peak. When viewed from Colchuck Lake a mile to the northeast, the mountain presents two sharp buttresses of granite rising above a small glacier and icefall. Why then has Colchuck seen less activity, especially on such a pleasing line as the Northeast Buttress? It might be that Colchuck lacks the charismatic name of its ominous neighbor, or it could be that its Northeast Buttress has earned a bad reputation due to its rotten start and route-finding riddles. A thick wad of retreat slings atop the first pitch testifies to the disappointment climbers have shown in the line.

A thick wad of retreat slings atop the first pitch testifies to the disappointment climbers have shown in the line.

Julie Brugger and Mark Weigelt did the first ascent of the buttress in 1970, beginning in the shallow chimney which has repulsed many parties. Brugger had taken a University of Washington climbing class taught by Weigelt and after only several sessions, decided she wanted to be a climber. "I was struggling to find people to go climbing with," she relates. "Mark was basically a climbing bum and went climbing all the time. That's what I wanted to do, so I had found this perfect person." For the next two years they were nearly inseparable. "Mark had this red Volkswagen. We used to load it up with a box of peanut butter, honey, and wheatberry bread and leave to go rock climbing, or to climb this or that."

In June of 1970 Brugger and Weigelt started into Colchuck with the idea of being back at the car that night. They carried no ice ax or crampons, as Weigelt had a penchant for going light that was ahead of its time. He claimed you should be able to go anywhere without crampons. On the Northeast Buttress they each led their share of the pitches. Brugger relates, "Although he

was a macho guy, Mark and I would alternate leads, but at the same time he would give me a hard time for not being fast enough. But then you go climb with these guys who don't think you (a woman) should lead anything, so on a spectrum he was on the better end."

On Colchuck, if the climbing looked improbable, Brugger would relinquish the lead. "If I got to the bottom of some crack," says Brugger, "and it looked like it was going to be really hard, I could say, 'You do it.'" Primarily, she did her share in an era when it was typical for male climbers to lead everything.

───────────────────── ▲▲▲ ─────────────────────

That was essentially the way Shari Kearney and I did all our routes. The object was to swing leads unless one person was particularly adapted or more fit to lead a certain pitch. The summer of 1978, Shari and I climbed a half-dozen pitches up the granite prow keeping a sharp eye out for the twin cracks described in *CAG*. We never found them, and ended up climbing a very thin shallow corner in mountain boots before retreating. It was frustrating to leave behind a lot of runners and nuts, because we had failed to bring a haul line, and had to do short raps.

In August of 1990 Sue Harrington and I marched into Colchuck Lake for an attempt on the Northeast Buttress and a try at a route on Dragontail. Clear skies the first night gave way to gray mist creeping down the walls the following morning. We hiked up the moraine and cached climbing gear under a boulder as a few raindrops spattered the ground. Back in the tent, we read books and slept.

Day three dawned perfect as we hiked to the route's base before the sun hit. Determined to find a better start to the buttress, we climbed up the glacier 150 feet left of the shallow chimney mentioned in *CAG*. Starting in a small dihedral and crack system, I led up a full pitch on sound rock to almost the level of the boxcar ledge. Typical of early morning starts, my fingers went numb as I fumbled to place small cams in a shallow crack. Sue led a long right traverse to the ledge, then we followed the guidebook description for five pitches up onto the left-trending ramp in search of the twin cracks.

As the cracks still did not materialize, we continued traversing the ramp left and up until it ended near the base of a huge right-facing corner. Sue did

Opposite: *The Northeast Buttress Route on Colchuck Peak, showing the direct start from the toe*

Sue Harrington climbing the Northeast Buttress

an excellent pitch up a small left-facing corner and crack system that stopped just shy of the buttress crest. Six more pitches, mostly on the crest, led to the summit plateau, where we dumped the pack and strolled to the top.

Although a thin haze had blotted out the blue sky, there was no wind, and best of all, no rain. We followed a gentle south slope down to the Colchuck–Dragontail Col, then started down the Colchuck Glacier. We soon encountered water ice and cleverly (I thought) donned our four-ounce instep crampons, my latest weapon for saving weight on alpine routes. I hadn't tested them before, and I was alarmed to discover how insecure they really were. I vowed to dump them in the recycle bin at home as I chopped bollards for two full-length rappels down the slippery ice.

Back at the tent, we were happy to have cracked the puzzle of the buttress that had provided a fine fifteen-pitch route up sound rock.

Colchuck Peak: Northeast Buttress

First ascent: Julie Brugger and Mark Weigelt; June 1970
Difficulty: Grade III or IV, 5.9
Equipment: A standard rack up to a 3-inch cam. Ice ax and crampons.
Permit: Although it is not in the Enchantment Lakes, permits for overnight

use of Colchuck Lake are required from the USFS Ranger Station, Leavenworth, WA 98826 (509-782-1413).

Access: Approach as for Prusik Peak, described previously, but drive 3.5 miles farther up the Icicle Road to Bridge Creek Campground. Turn left and follow the Eightmile Road 4 miles to the Stuart Lake Trail. Hike the

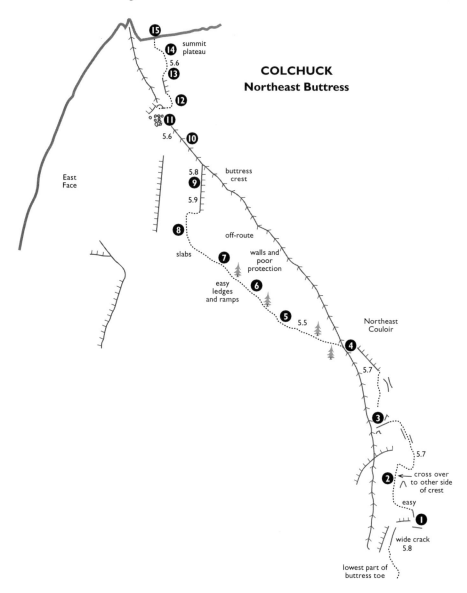

COLCHUCK
Northeast Buttress

summit plateau

5.6

buttress crest

5.8

5.9

East Face

off-route

slabs

walls and poor protection

easy ledges and ramps

5.5

Northeast Couloir

5.7

5.7

cross over to other side of crest

easy

wide crack 5.8

lowest part of buttress toe

trail for 2.5 miles, then exit left to Colchuck Lake. Reach the lake in 2 miles, follow a path around the lake's west side, then angle up and right toward the Colchuck–Dragontail Col on talus. At the top of the moraine, traverse to the right across the glacier to the buttress.

Route: Begin the climb at the lowest part of the buttress toe. **[1]** Scramble up to a wide crack (5.8), then traverse right to a belay on a ledge. **[2]** Meander up easy rock to a notch. **[3]** Descend from the notch, traverse right and climb cracks and the face up to a ledge. **[4]** Climb up and right past a short chimney and up a left-facing corner (5.7). **[5]** Scramble to the other side of the crest to gain a long left-slanting ledge system (5.5). **[6]** through **[8]** Diagonal up and left on a ledge/ramp to gain a left-facing corner and crack leading to the buttress crest (4th and 5th). **[9]** Climb the left-facing corner almost to the crest (5.8–5.9). **[10]** Continue up a corner (5.8), then on up the buttress crest. **[11]** and **[12]** Climb the buttress crest to below the final headwall (easy 5th). **[13]** Traverse right on ledges and ramps onto the north side. **[14]** Climb a crack behind the flake, then climb on up to the top of the buttress and traverse off right (5.5–5.6).

Descent: Descend the south slope of Colchuck to the Colchuck–Dragontail Col, then go down the Colchuck Glacier to the lake.

Maps: Green Trails: Mount Stuart No. 209 and Chiwaukum Mountains No. 177; USGS: USGS: Blewett and Enchantment Lakes

Reference: *CAG 1: Columbia River to Stevens Pass*

38 DRAGONTAIL PEAK
Backbone Ridge

RISING 2800 FEET ABOVE COLCHUCK LAKE in a massive, 0.8 mile-wide wall is the North Face of Dragontail Peak. The 8840-foot summit is 0.7 miles due east of Colchuck Peak, and can be easily climbed up the east side from the higher Enchantment Lakes. Dudley Kelley and William A. Long followed this route during the first ascent of the peak in 1937. Much of the North Face has class 3 and 4 terrain, with a number of routes containing harder pitches.

Backbone Ridge is unique as Cascade climbs go because it has a very sustained crack pitch instead of an odd hard move here and there.

The peak had several routes established between 1962 and 1970 on the north and east sides. Fred Beckey and Dan Davis climbed the Northwest Face (adjacent Backbone Ridge) in June of 1962; the same month they put up the East Face of the Northeast Towers. In July of 1970 Dave Beckstead and Paul Myhre climbed the Northeast Couloir, and in August John Bonneville and Mark Weigelt scaled Backbone Ridge.

During the early 1970s Chuck Sink and Dave Neff (my college mates) and I repeatedly heard of Al Givler, Mead Hargis, Del Young, and Mark Weigelt. This seasoned group of alpinists could be expected to put up new high-caliber routes every year. Two years after Weigelt completed Backbone, his passion for first ascents was forever terminated when he died from rockfall on Mount Stuart's Ice Cliff Glacier.

Backbone Ridge is unique as Cascade climbs go because it has a very sustained crack pitch instead of an odd hard move here and there. At the time Weigelt climbed it he was living on 17th Street in Seattle's University District in a house full of climbers and "itinerants." John Bonneville lived there as well, and although he had done very little climbing, Weigelt would drag whoever he could get to go out into the mountains. Julie Brugger tells why he did so many new routes in the Cascades. "He really liked exploring," she relates. "Even when he went climbing he was always looking for new stuff to do. He didn't mind hiking and thrashing to get to these new places."

To support their habits, Weigelt and Brugger picked fruit in the Wenatchee Valley in the fall. "The orchard owners used to love us because we worked so hard," says Julie, "But other than that Mark didn't work. I did my first trip to Yosemite because I had saved some money from another job. Mark couldn't go because he was picking fruit." Also to save money, instead of buying every new piece of climbing gear that came out, he made his own. It helped that his dad was a machinist, and that he learned a lot from him, but Mark never wanted to embrace his dad's profession full time.

He eventually did get to Yosemite Valley and learned how to climb wide cracks, essential training for Backbone Ridge. As Brugger describes him, "Weigelt was a high school gymnast. He was a short, stocky guy and he was an awesome climber in mountain boots. He would work on boulder problems in boots where other climbers were using their rock shoes."

Back from an adventure on Dragontail, Weigelt wouldn't say much about the route, but immediately began planning another trip to an unexplored area. When I asked Julie where he got his many ideas for new routes she said, "Phil Leatherman was a good friend of his and he took really good black and white photos of peaks everywhere. He would show the prints to Mark, and that would be the seed that would sprout into another mountain journey."

In 1978 I climbed the route with Shari Kearney. We reached the summit in a lightning storm, and the resulting photo showed my long hair standing straight up. We made a rapid descent with tingling scalp! I returned to Backbone eight years later with Chuck Sink. During summers, while in college, Chuck worked for the forest service in Leavenworth; with Eric Gerber, he put up several new routes in the range, including a line on Dragontail. But Backbone had escaped him, and I wanted to climb it again.

Chuck was just down from fishing in Alaska and it was my job to provide him with all gear, including a pack. Somehow I blew it; when we arrived at the trailhead there was no pack. From inside my car we rustled up a huge canvas bag with thin unpadded shoulder straps and no waistband. I loaded Chuck up with all the sleeping bags and pads while I carried the heavy stuff. We recorded the scene on film, roared with laughter, then started up the trail.

That day we made it to a camp high on the moraine above Colchuck

Opposite: *Dragontail Peak's Backbone Ridge and the moraine spur (middle right) used for the approach*

Shari Kearney leading on Backbone Ridge

Lake where we snuggled between boulders for the night. The next morning we started up the route with minimal gear. I hadn't climbed with Chuck in three years and we had a blast. Backbone proved to be as good a climb as I remembered. The 5.9 six-inch crack was just as runout as before—by a full forty feet above the last piece. Just above the crack a brief hard rainstorm nailed us. I thought we'd been had, as the black lichen is incredibly slippery when wet. But the storm passed on while we were munching snacks, and a light breeze quickly dried out the rock.

The climbing eased as we moved quickly up low-angle cracks and ledges to the small spiny ridge leading toward the upper wall. We finished by climbing up and across the "fin," then hiked out the same day after a great climb. On the drive back we vowed to keep alive our old climbing partnership and made tentative plans for the following summer—with the proper packs.

Dragontail Peak: Backbone Ridge

First ascent: John Bonneville and Mark Weigelt; August 5, 1970

Difficulty: Grade IV, 5.9

Equipment: A standard rack that includes one big camming device in the 5- to 6-inch range. Ice ax and crampons.

Permit: A permit is required from the USFS Ranger Station, Leavenworth, WA 98826 (509-782-1413).

Access: Approach as for Colchuck, described previously. You can access the route from near the top of the moraine ridge.

Chuck Sink climbing The Fin of Backbone Ridge

Route: Traverse from moraine ridge across to a wide gully between Serpen-
tine Arête and Backbone Ridge. You can start Backbone Ridge from the
left edge of the gully by climbing class 3 and 4 to gain the right side of
the ridge. (*CAG* describes starting the climb from the very toe, although
I've never done it.) Continue up on the right side of the ridge to gain a
right-facing corner and a large crack. Jam the 6-inch crack (large pro
useful) to its end (5.9), then step left to a belay stance. Six to seven
pitches lead on up the broad ridge crest (easier climbing with a few
hard moves) to the bottom of The Fin. Climb a narrow crest (5.8) up
onto The Fin, then diagonal up and right across the face of The Fin
(5.6–5.7) to the far right side. One more pitch climbs a left-facing corner and flakes (5.7) to easy ground below the summit.

Descent: Descend a gully on the northwest past Rooster Finch and Bull
Durham Towers to the Colchuck–Dragontail Col. From the col, snow
or ice in late season drops you down to the lake again. If you choose
not to carry an ax or crampons, it is possible to descend from the summit south to the top of the upper Snow Creek Glacier. Do two long
rappels on rock just north of the final steep slope of ice, then descend
to Mist Pond, Aasgard Pass, and continue down to Colchuck Lake.

Maps: Green Trails: Mount Stuart No. 209 and Chiwaukum Mountains No.
177; USGS: USGS: Blewett and Enchantment Lakes

Reference: *CAG 1: Columbia River to Stevens Pass*

39 MOUNT STUART
Complete North Ridge

THE GREAT ROCK AND ICE BASTION OF MOUNT STUART rises to 9415 feet, making it the highest point in the Stuart Range. Its fortress-like profile is visible from Interstate 90, Mount Rainier, and many points in the North Cascades. Stuart boasts some thirty-six routes and variations, which vary from easy scrambles to 5.11+ grade V walls. Although the peak contains several ice routes, recent low snowfall years and glacial recession have made their mark. The Ice Cliff Glacier is in a state of slid-

A sudden hail and rainstorm convinced them [Rupley and Gordon] to rappel 75 feet to a catwalk, where they exited onto easier climbing. Even so, the wet slabs were tricky.

ing away, and the Stuart Glacier Coulior completely melts out earlier every year.

Are Northwest alpinists destined to take up sport climbing on their glacier-clad peaks? If so, Mount Stuart has the quality rock for this, and still has a lot of potential for more good lines.

Pioneer climber Claude Ewing Rusk felt Angus McPherson might have first climbed Stuart in 1873, going up the Southeast Route. For fifty years parties scaled the peak, using this same route, until July of 1933 when Lex Maxwell, Louis Ulrich, and Joe Werner climbed what came to be known as Ulrich's Couloir. Two years later Maxwell, Fred Llewellyn, and John Vertrees put up the popular and circuitous West Ridge Route. The first north side climb was done in 1937, when Ulrich, Edward Rankin, and Joe Riley ascended the Northwest Buttress.

In June of 1944, during World War II, Helmy Beckey and Larry Strathdee cramponed up the Stuart Glacier Coulior. In June of 1956 ice and snow specialists Bill and Gene Prater, along with Don and Nelson Torrey, climbed the Sherpa Glacier, naming it after their Sherpa climbing club. That same year, in September, Don (Claunch) Gordon and John Rupley established the North Ridge (about the upper two-thirds, or 1800 feet of climbing).

Opposite: Mount Stuart. The Complete North Ridge Route ascends the ridge crest from the lower right toe

Gordon, Rupley, and Fred Beckey approached Stuart's north side via Ingalls Creek, Ingalls Pass, Goat Pass, and the Stuart Glacier. They had planned to try the complete ridge, but decided it would take longer, so they settled for an attack on the upper ridge. They hoped to do the route as a threesome, but Beckey felt ill and returned to their camp in Ingalls Creek.

Rupley and Gordon climbed steadily up moderate terrain, placing an occasional piton for safety on the various short steep walls. Gordon admitted the ridge had its tedious sections. The arête was so very narrow and exposed on both sides that they often had to straddle it. By early afternoon the pair reached a stance below the Great Gendarme, where they contemplated its ascent. A sudden hail and rainstorm convinced them to rappel 75 feet to a catwalk, where they exited onto easier climbing. Even so, the wet slabs were tricky. They finally made the summit at 4 P.M.

The first continuous climb of the North Ridge occurred in July of 1963 when Fred Beckey and Steve Marts did the Lower North Ridge West Side. In July of 1970, Mead Hargis and Jay Ossiander created what was to become the preferred long alpine climb on the peak by climbing the Lower North Ridge East Side. In conjunction with the upper ridge, this route offers 3000 feet of interesting and enjoyable climbing.

My first experience with the North Ridge came in 1974 when Chuck Sink, Shari Kearney, and I did the upper ridge, descended the Sherpa Glacier and thrashed out Mountaineer Creek. That was not the best way to descend and hike out, as the glacier was steeper than we had anticipated, and the brush along the creek was laced with windfalls. Shari and I returned in 1978 to retrieve gear from an accident, and to climb the complete ridge. Earlier in the season an Oregon climber had fallen and broken his hip while trying to climb an off-route seam on the lower ridge. Shari and I hiked in with Paul Smythe, climbed to the gear, tossed it down to Paul and the two of us continued up the ridge. I returned three years later, in 1981, to climb the route alone, and nearly got myself into trouble.

For me that year had been turbulent, fraught with relationship problems and not much climbing. In fact, I had done very little rock climbing when I set out to do the complete North Ridge during early September. I chose that month knowing the Stuart Glacier would be bare ice and thus safer for unroped travel.

From a camp at Ingalls Lake I rose just before dawn and loaded a day-pack with ax, crampons, rock shoes, water, snacks, a headlamp, and a 7mm line. I was surprised at how quickly I reached the toe of the ridge, where I laced up rock shoes. The ax, boots, and crampons went inside the pack, to be hauled up the harder spots. All went well for the first two pitches. I climbed up, reached a stance, brought the pack up, and set it on a ledge.

From the top of a four-inch crack the wall seemed to go blank, but leftward there appeared some scant holds. I had no memory of any previous hard climbing at that place, and I began moving left with uncertainty. The holds became smaller. As my arms began to tire I realized I had made an irreversible move. I had to either keep going or pancake 250 feet onto the glacier below. Gripped as hell, and with legs shaking, I pulled up on a sloping hold . . . and sunk my hands into a perfect crack!

Shari Kearney on the lower ridge

It was the turning point. For over a year my personal problems had completely eroded my self confidence and had delivered me to the shaking, near-death predicament on that ridge. Of course, it had been foolish to attempt the climb in my mental condition, but then I might as easily have stepped in front of a moving car on the freeway without realizing it. Once my heart rate slowed I felt better than ever. I knew I could finish the climb, and in much better style—I was now back in control.

On up the ridge the climbing was pure fun. I climbed with the pack on for a long way, finally uncoiling the 7mm line again at the Great Gendarme.

Two other climbers were negotiating the slab pitch as I rappelled down to the traverse. "Where did you guys come from?" they shouted across. "There's just me," I responded. "Oh!" floated back to me. I passed them carefully, trying not to knock any rocks down from the class 3 ground leading to the summit.

Although I don't recommend that climbers go off alone when they're mentally and physically down, it did work to restore my self esteem; however, I was lucky not to have fallen off. The experience for me became a valuable mountaineering tool—acquiring judgment. From then on, I examined my personal state more closely before attempting either maneuvers or entire climbs near my limit and without a belay. Retreat took on a new meaning.

Mount Stuart: Complete North Ridge

First ascent: Upper North Ridge; Don (Claunch) Gordon and John Rupley, September 9, 1956. Lower North Ridge, East Side; Mead Hargis and Jay Ossiander; July, 1970

Difficulty: Grade IV, 5.8

Equipment: A standard rack that includes a 4-inch cam. Ice ax and crampons.

Permit: A permit is required from the USFS Ranger Station, Leavenworth, WA 98826 (509-782-1413).

Access: Approach as for Colchuck–Dragontail, described previously, and continue up the Stuart Lake Trail for 2.1 miles past the turnoff to Colchuck Lake. Continue around the north side of Stuart Lake, then go through forest and meadows to gain a prominent gully leading up to the Stuart Glacier. Traverse the glacier east, then drop 800 feet to the toe of the ridge.

Route: Begin climbing at the very toe on the east side, near the edge of the Ice Cliff Glacier. Scramble across to a ledge with trees. **[1]** From the left side of the ledge, climb a lieback (5.7) to a right-slanting slot with a short offwidth (5.8) at the top. (From the top of the first pitch you will notice a beautiful, but discontinuous, thin crack up and left on a clean face. Do not be tempted to go that way, as it is quite hard, the pro fades, and it has been the scene of several long falls and one serious accident). **[2]** From a belay stance, climb right and up to gain a 40-foot 4-inch crack (5.8) above a ledge. Climb the crack to its end and belay. **[3]** Climb left across a face (5.8), then climb a second crack leading to a good ledge. **[4]** Climb a face pitch (5.7) to a belay. **[5]** Continue up this rock face (5.7) to easier ground. **[6]** through **[8]** Continue up to a notch in the ridge (5.0), from where six more pitches lead to a notch on the Upper North Ridge. For the upper ridge, you can climb right on the crest all the way (maximum 5.7) to the rappel below the Great Gendarme. Rappel 75 feet, traverse a catwalk and slabs around a gully, then climb slabs (5.5) up to gain 3rd class terrain leading to the summit.

Descent: Descend the West Ridge nearly 400 feet and 0.4 mile westward to where it's possible to drop over the north side and descend the Northwest Buttress (1958 variation) down to Goat Pass and the Stuart Glacier. Keep peering over the north side until you can see the way down is not too steep. This is mostly class 3 and 4, with snow patches in early season. If you're not familiar with the mountain, it's best to descend the Southeast Route (Cascadian Couloir) into Ingalls Creek. Hike the trail up to Ingalls Pass, then traverse talus back over to Goat Pass.

Climbers on the gendarme pitch of the upper ridge

Maps: Green Trails: Mount Stuart No. 209 and Chiwaukum Mountains No. 177; USGS: USGS: Blewett, Enchantment Lakes, and Mount Stuart

Reference: *CAG 1: Columbia River to Stevens Pass*

40 MOUNT STUART
Direct Northwest Face

BELOW STUART'S SUMMIT stretches a smooth, rounded, 1500-foot face of quality granite. The Northwest Face is bordered by the Stuart Glacier Coulior to the west and the North Ridge to the east. This aesthetic rib was first climbed on July 20, 1970 by Dave Beckstead and Paul Myhre with the help of a dozen aid pitons. Dave Neff, Chuck Sink, and I heard about the route and set out to climb it in August of 1972.

It was my first night out on a mountain. We split an orange and shared candies as the northern lights danced across the sky.

Dave and Chuck had considerably more mountaineering experience than I, and, although skeptical of my abilities, they agreed to let me join them on the climb. I had been hiking and climbing alone in the Enchantment Lakes and met my two friends at Stuart Lake on a Friday evening. They had just gotten off work and had stormed up the trail with full packs in an hour and forty-five minutes. Chuck gloated about their speed, and informed me we would try to climb Valhalla (the other name given the Northwest Face). Yes, I did have a 165-foot rope. But, did they have extra food? Mine was gone. With the logistics settled, we fought the mosquitoes through the meadows and up the talus gully to a bivy on a rock island next to Stuart Glacier.

In the morning we loaded day-packs with pitons, nuts, water, food, and down jackets and set off across the glacier. Immediately left of the Stuart Glacier Coulior the climbing began. I got the second pitch studded with several fixed pins, and instead of clipping etriers into them just stood on the pins and climbed quickly up. Later Chuck wrote about my climbing on that pitch in our college climbing club journal. "It was like sticking a quarter into a climbing machine," he said. I climbed fast because I was scared. Dave and Chuck couldn't see me leading the last bit, and when they reached my belay they wondered how I had climbed the pitch. "Oh, I just stood on the pins," I informed them. This relieved them, and I got a nod of approval from Chuck.

For most of the day we ascended clean corners and slabs, sometimes wandering too far right or left and losing precious time. I had never done a

Mount Stuart. The Direct Northwest Face Route begins left of the Stuart Glacier couloir

climb with so many pitches, and often needed directional guidance from my belayers. Dave and Chuck had a harder time on the steep slabs in their stiff Super Guide boots. I was wearing an oversize pair of floppy Raichles and could friction up the slabs with less effort. Chuck was impressed again after I ran up an improbable looking crack. "When I got to that crack and saw Al grinning up there in his belay seat I couldn't figure out how he led up that goddamned thing, let alone with his pack on," he marveled.

Dave struggled to lead a long thin seam in the early evening but finally ran out of light. We were only one pitch from the class 3 rock leading to the top, but had to bivouac.

It was my first night out on a mountain, and the most memorable in two decades of climbing since. We hung our feet over the edge and, once the boots were off, wiggled our aching toes in space. The water was nearly gone, but we split an orange and shared candies as the Northern Lights danced across the sky.

During the night Chuck and Dave got to huddle together for warmth on their portion of the ledge, but my situation was more exposed. By morning I was ready to get moving, and Chuck rubbed life back into my numb toes. After an hour of climbing up across a steep granite slab we unroped and scrambled to the summit.

Once on top we lounged in the sun a bit and then began the long descent of the West Ridge. Completely out of water, we were anxious to find a snowpatch; I wondered if my partners really knew where they were going. After many gendarmes, walls, and gullies we made it down to the slopes leading to Ingalls Pass. A tiny drip from a snowpatch satisfied a fraction of our thirst, but we had to keep moving.

Finally, we made the glacier, meadows, and Stuart Lake where we took a quick dip just before dark. On out the trail I had a rough time staying awake, and when we sat down at the last bridge I leaned against a stump, fell asleep, and tumbled into the creek. Dave and Chuck rushed in and grabbed me—without which my alpine career would have come to an abrupt end. For two more miles to the car my boots squished, but I was awake. As a result of that first long alpine route on Stuart, I was hooked on climbing, and knew I belonged in the mountains. The ascent had also erased any doubts about my climbing ability. I was one of the boys.

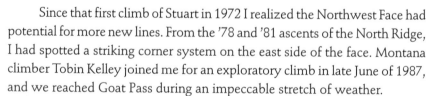

Since that first climb of Stuart in 1972 I realized the Northwest Face had potential for more new lines. From the '78 and '81 ascents of the North Ridge, I had spotted a striking corner system on the east side of the face. Montana climber Tobin Kelley joined me for an exploratory climb in late June of 1987, and we reached Goat Pass during an impeccable stretch of weather.

We camped at the pass where the mischievous mammal *Neotoma cinerea* again wreaked havoc. My watch disappeared and undoubtedly was added to a subterranean storehouse of items that included eyeglasses. My friend Paul

Tobin Kelley liebacks the perfect corner on the Direct Northwest Face

Sloan lost his only pair to the woodrats in 1986, causing him to abort their climb of the North Ridge.

Tobin still had his timepiece, and we rose early and brewed hot drinks. The glacier was firm snow, and trail shoes and ice axes helped us reach the climb without crampons. Right out of the moat the climbing was hard, and I led up a thin arching finger crack to a semi-hanging belay. Tobin got a chossy pitch that needed garden tools, and then we scrambled up easy ground on clean rock.

The sun finally hit the wall, and all was silent but for the lone rock bounding down a nearby gully. A flaring narrow chimney led upwards and again it was Tobin's lead. He complained mildly that I was getting all the good pitches and, like most climbers, he did not like squeeze chimneys. The year before in Yosemite he showed his disgust for large difficult cracks when we climbed Twinkie on the Cookie Cliff.

"Just do it! You've got knee pads on," I assured him. From his belay I started up the long perfect corner feeling a bit guilty. My pitch was incredibly fun, and a rest would materialize every time I needed to place pro. Tobin nearly finished the corner and then moved off left onto the face. We had brought a 7mm line to haul our one pack on the hard pitches, and had hammers and a few pins for

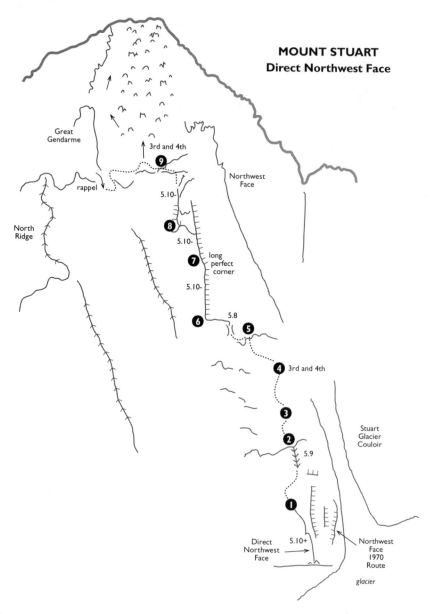

MOUNT STUART
Direct Northwest Face

tiny cracks. On the last difficult pitch the protection was scarce and I hammered in a knifeblade and tied it off. In several more friction moves I gained a small ledge and looked westward to my bivy ledge of 1972.

A lot had transpired in fifteen years; it was a great feeling to embrace the same mountain that had been so influential toward my climbing. It is often satisfying to return to old places, climbing harder and faster than before in that race with time, life, and good health. There is a point where improvement finally ceases due to age or ailing health. But Tobin and I were not there yet, and it was a joy to experience the high mountains.

Mount Stuart: Direct Northwest Face

First ascent: Alan Kearney and Tobin Kelley; June 27, 1987

Difficulty: Grade IV, 5.10+

Equipment: A standard rack up to a 4-inch cam with emphasis on small to medium Stoppers and cams. Several small pins are useful. Ice ax and crampons. (We did manage to get to the base by cutting a few steps, saving the weight of crampons).

Permit: A permit is required from the USFS Ranger Station, Leavenworth, WA 98826 (509-782-1413).

Access: Same as for the upper North Ridge, described previously. Traverse the Stuart Glacier eastward to just past the Stuart Glacier Couloir.

Route: Immediately left of the original Northwest Face route is a bulge and left-facing corner; 20–30 feet farther, left of the corner, is a small left-facing corner and crack. Begin the climb in a thin, arching, finger crack. **[1]** Climb the thin crack to a semi-hanging belay (5.10+). **[2]** Climb cracks and a mossy corner to a large ledge (5.9). **[3]** through **[5]** Scramble up on easy, but good, rock. **[6]** Climb a flaring chimney and a corner up and left to the base of a long left-facing perfect corner (5.8). **[7]** Lieback and stem the corner to a small stance (5.10-). **[8]** Continue up the corner partway and exit left onto the face and slab (5.10-). **[9]** One more pitch up slabs and a flaring seam end at class 3 below the summit and the junction of the North Ridge route (5.10-).

Descent: Same as for Complete North Ridge, described previously.

Maps: Green Trails: Mount Stuart No. 209, Chiwaukum Mountains No. 177; USGS: Blewett, Enchantment Lakes, and Mount Stuart

Reference: *AAJ* 1988, p. 128

41 MOUNT MAUDE
North Face

NEARLY FIFTY MILES NORTH OF MOUNT STUART, the Entiat Mountains lie on the dry side of the Cascade Range. Mount Fernow, Seven-Fingered Jack and Mount Maude are bordered on the east by forty-four mile-long Lake Chelan, a deep trench cut by glacial action. According to Fred Beckey, 9082-foot Mount Maude was named for a General Frederick Stanley Maude of British Mesopotamian troops in World War I, not for a famous feminine heroine.

"The clouds obligingly moved and disclosed a painfully easy route up the South Ridge, one apparently much in favor with goats."

Maude's rock is unstable and slabby, but if you choose the North Face the climbing is primarily ice and snow. The North Face has become a popular ice climb due to its classic and uniform nature. There are no looming séracs, as on glaciated volcanoes, but late season ascents may be prone to rockfall as the annual snow melts away. The broad north side rises 2000 feet to the summit where the gentle south slope drops down to Ice Lakes, providing the easiest descent in the range. Like Cathedral Peak, Maude sometimes offers an escape from west side precipitation, along with the chance to experience open country, dotted with larch trees.

John Burnett and Hermann Ulrichs first climbed the peak in July of 1932, ascending the Northwest Couloir. Once on top, Ulrichs noted they had not climbed the easiest route. "We were congratulating ourselves on a good climb," he reported, "when the clouds obligingly moved and disclosed a painfully easy route up the South Ridge, one apparently much in favor with goats."

In 1957 Fred Beckey, Don Gordon, John Rupley and Herb Staley hiked fifteen miles up the Entiat River and Ice Creek to a camp at Ice Lakes. From the lakes the four scrambled over a col between Spectacle Buttes and Maude, then descended onto the Entiat Glacier and traversed the glacier west to the North Face. Once at the bergschrund, Beckey took the lead, climbing directly

Opposite: *The North Face of Mount Maude in late season, during a dry year*

Mike Mrachek and Dave Neff on the North Face of Mount Maude

up an ice groove and onto a smooth face. The climbing was mainly up firm snow of a moderate angle, and the group climbed quickly but carefully. They gained the summit by early afternoon, descended the south side, and hiked back to their car the same day.

My relationship with Maude began in 1972, when Dave Neff and I hiked in from Leroy Creek on the west, only to be rained out. Since I had only worn-out ski boots and a lousy ice ax for gear, I wasn't terribly disappointed in failing. A year later Dave and I returned with Mike Mrachek for a second attempt. When Mike discovered he had forgotten his crampons, he became apprehensive about the climb and felt an easy "out" was assured. Dave and

I wouldn't settle for that excuse, so we stopped in Leavenworth to borrow a pair from Chuck Sink.

Now Mike was really worried. His eyes darted back and forth as he tried to think of another ploy. But, with soothing words we told him the climb wouldn't be too hard and marched him into Ice Lakes. We all crashed early and tried to sleep, but I didn't get much. Up at 2 A.M., I downed a can of mandarin oranges, followed by cocoa, then we were off. From their lofty perch, a herd of mountain goats watched us stumble across the talus. Soon we were on the Entiat Glacier, threading crevasses and climbing in and out of shallow ones where no other route existed.

One short ice wall gave Mike trouble. "Cheap ice axes in certain situations don't hold too well and tend to pull out and hit people. I got it right between the eyes," he commented. Dave and I patched him up, took a photo of his face and marched on. He looked awful.

The ice climbing up the face was great, with a bit of verglassed rock, hard snow/ice and, at the top, a section of perfect water ice. Screws went in well and at times I was able to slot Stoppers in the adjacent rocks. A few pieces of rock pro on ice climbs are very useful, and go in much more quickly than tubes.

I was nearly out of gear at the top of the face and tried twisting in my last piece, a Charlet Moser non-tubular screw. It went in a couple of inches and fractured the surrounding ice into huge plates. I tied it off and sank my ax pick in six feet away, then brought the others up. Mike was overjoyed to have completed his first ice climb and, like so many climbers before, he realized what was possible for him. We lounged in the September sun, snacking on candy bars and picking out future objectives on the distant peaks.

It was a long hike down the south side and out the Leroy Creek Trail to Dave's van. Twenty-six miles of dusty road led to Leavenworth, and the first of many Coke machines that would sustain us through the night on our drive back to college.

Mount Maude: North Face

First ascent: Fred Beckey, Don Gordon, John Rupley, and Herb Staley; June 16, 1957
Difficulty: Grade III, snow and ice to 50 degrees
Equipment: Ice screws, fluke, picket, and a few small pins and Stoppers. Ice ax and crampons.

Access: From the town of Leavenworth drive Highway 2 east 20 miles almost to Wenatchee. Turn left on Highway 97 and go 17 miles to the Entiat River Road. Turn left and follow the road for 38 miles to Cottonwood Campground. Hike the Entiat River Trail 8.5 miles to the Pomas Creek Trail. Go left, cross the river and go left again. Follow the Pomas Creek Trail for 1.2 miles and turn right on the Ice Creek Trail. Follow this trail for 4.6 miles to a camp between the Ice Lakes. From the lakes, you can ascend northwesterly to the 5600-foot col below the East Ridge of Maude. From the col, descend north 400 feet onto the Entiat Glacier and traverse the glacier to the far west side and the start of the North Face.

Route: Ascend the right-hand slope of snow and ice to the summit. A bergschrund and two slabby rock bands are encountered low down, then a uniform smooth face leads to the top. In recent years the climb has melted out by late summer and fall. June and July are recommended months for an ascent.

Descent: Descend the south slope to Ice Lakes.

Maps: Green Trails: Holden No. 113 and Lucerne No. 114; USGS: Holden and Trinity

Reference: *CAG 2: Stevens Pass to Rainy Pass*

42 MOUNT GOODE
Northeast Buttress

THE IMPOSING NORTH WALL OF MOUNT GOODE is well concealed by scores of jagged peaks. Climbers in the 1930s had difficulty assessing potential routes on the face hidden deep in the heart of the North Cascades. Oregonians Joe Luethold and Everett Darr attempted the 9200-foot summit in 1935 from the southwest. Darr later described the north side. "The great Goode Glacier has scooped out a vast cirque with a vertical drop from the summit of close to 4000 feet, making this side practically, if not absolutely, impossible," he wrote.

"Here we had steep and exciting climbing, but an abundance of sound holds kept the difficulty moderate."

Seattle alpinists Wolf Bauer, Joe Halwax, Jack Hossack, George MacGowan, and Phil Dickert climbed the peak in 1936, going up the Southwest Chimney. Four more routes graced the mountain between 1937 and 1954 as climbers from Washington, Oregon, and California established the Bedayn Couloir, Southwest Couloir, Northwest Buttress, and Northeast Face. In 1966, Fred Beckey and Tom Stewart climbed the elegant Northeast Buttress during August.

Beckey had already been up the peak twice. He knew of the mountain's east side potential. "For years I've had a secret plot to be the first up the magnificent East Buttress of Mount Goode," Beckey confided. He and Stewart approached from Lake Chelan, the Stehekin River, and Bridge Creek, which led to a bivouac site below the face late on the first day.

The next day they cramponed up the glacier and climbed the buttress rapidly to within 500 feet of the summit, where the narrow crest slowed their progress. Beckey relates, "Here we had steep and exciting climbing, but an abundance of sound holds kept the difficulty moderate." They made the summit that day, then descended to Park Creek. Twelve years later Jim Price and Dave Seman completed the second ascent of the route.

Goode's remoteness and off-trail approach thwarted climbers for years. In 1980, when I stood on the summit with Dave Dailey, the buttress had been

Mount Goode and the Northeast Buttress from the east

climbed only a half-dozen times. Dave and I chose August for our ascent. On the first day we soaked up sun and scenery on the boat ride up Lake Chelan. At Stehekin we obtained backcountry permits, then got a ride on the park service shuttle to Bridge Creek. Soon, we were eating dust on the trail toward Mount Goode.

We pitched a tarp that evening by the North Fork of Bridge Creek, below the peak. Without a stove, dinner was cold fare of bagels and salami, but we felt we could climb faster with less gear. Uncertain about the eventual descent, Dave fretted constantly throughout the brushy approach and the climb of the buttress. As if to hasten the inevitable, he climbed at a feverish rate and hogged all the leads except the last one. Although Dave didn't look fit, I could barely keep up with him.

Gasping for breath, he reached the summit and tore into the register (a scrap of paper stuffed into a sardine can). He began reading how other climbers planned to descend. We both cracked up at the final entry, which said, "How the hell do you get down off this thing? Scotty, beam me down."

In reality, some downclimbing and a couple of rappels led into the Southwest Couloir, where we slid down snow to talus fields below. Goode's loose, sharp rocks chopped my new rope on the last rappel. That night we reached a campsite in Park Creek, then caught the shuttle back to Stehekin the next morning. Except for the untimely death of my rope, it was a perfect adventure.

Mount Goode: Northeast Buttress

First ascent: Fred Beckey and Tom Stewart; August 1966

Difficulty: Grade III or IV, 5.5

Equipment: A light rack up to a 2-inch cam. Ice ax and crampons.

Permit: At Stehekin, get a permit for overnight use from the NPS (North Cascades National Park, Stehekin, WA 98852), or contact the Chelan District Office at 509-682-2548 before departing.

Access: Approach as for Mount Maude, described previously. From Entiat, continue on Highway 97 for 21 miles to Chelan. Take the ferry up Lake Chelan to Stehekin; it runs daily between April 15 and October 15 and leaves Chelan at 8:30 A.M. The costlier express boat gets to Stehekin more quickly, permitting more time for the approach. The boat service is *Lady of the Lake*, phone 509-682-2224. Catch the NPS shuttle to the Bridge Creek Trail. Hike the trail 3 miles, then go left up the North Fork of Bridge Creek. Cross Grizzly Creek at 3.2 miles. Then hike another 0.8 miles to just below the mountain. Crossing the North Fork can be treacherous; in 1991 we found a large log across the stream beyond the meadows at 3400 feet, where the trail begins to climb steeply. This is about where the timber rib reaches the valley. Wade upward through brush to a dry stream and, as it steepens, traverse right to the right-hand watercourse. Ascend a rock ridge to the immediate left of the watercourse, then bear left to the only stand of conifers. Ascend to beneath a cliff, then climb left up talus and slabs to the glacier.

Route: The climb can be approached by ascending up and left on the glacier to gain the buttress crest above the toe. Climb mainly on the crest, switching to either side when there are difficulties. Much of the route is class 3 and 4, with 5th class on the upper third of the buttress.

A climber leads the final pitch to the summit of Mount Goode

Descent: Descend the Northeast Buttress past two notches, then traverse a ledge south to the Black Tooth Notch. Rappel and downclimb the west side into the Southwest Couloir. Continue down into Park Creek, hike the trail to the road and take the shuttle back to Stehekin.

Maps: Green Trails: McGregor Mountain No. 81; USGS: Goode Mountain, Mount Logan, and McGregor Mountain

Reference: *CAG 2: Stevens Pass to Rainy Pass*

43 MOUNT CONSTANCE
West Arête

ACROSS PUGET SOUND FROM WASHINGTON'S NORTH CASCADES
on the Olympic Peninsula are the Olympic Mountains. This compact range
of peaks is the wettest in the Lower Forty-eight, with Mount Olympus receiv-
ing 200 inches of precipitation (mostly
snow) annually. As the weather systems   *"Finally, a good piton gave me a chance*
move east toward 7743-foot Mount Con-   *of surviving, should the whole vein peel*
stance, the moisture decreases dramati-   *away from the face."*
cally, with the town of Sequim (to the
northeast of Olympus) getting only seventeen inches per year.

Although the range tops out below 8000 feet, incredible relief, unique
vegetation, abundant animal life, and dramatic scenery provide an enticing
alpine realm. Arduous approaches lead to mountains with alpine lakes nestled
beneath steep rock walls and hosting numerous mountain goats. Mount
Constance, in particular, is reached by a nearly-vertical trail that gains 3200
feet in two miles. Olympic peaks are composed primarily of sedimentary and
metamorphic rocks, and in general are friable. The West Arête of Constance
is an exception, and it provides a remarkably solid route with exhilarating and
exposed climbing.

Robert Schellin and A.E. "Bremerton" Smith first climbed the peak in
June of 1922 via the South Spur and Northeast Ridge. The pair approached
the mountain from the Dosewallips River and Tunnel Creek Divide, carrying a lot of food and blankets. On the 26th the two climbers rose at 5:30 A.M.
and started for the summit, taking snack food and extra clothing.

They climbed up snow slopes, then followed along a ridge where they
encountered a vein of rotten red rock. Smith later wrote, "One side broke sheer
away with no possible footing; the other was a steep slope 50 or 60 degrees,
ending with a cliff. A rope would have been a great help here." Once across the
obstacle, Schellin and Smith reached the top in another 1000 feet of climbing.

The following year L. Chute and W. Thompson established the Finger
Traverse, which ascends the South Chute and the upper South Ridge. In 1932

J. Kiley, Robert Pollock, and B. Winiecki climbed the southeast side. In 1957 Don Anderson, R. Knight, and Jim Richardson put up the West Arête. Climbing on steep Olympic rock is tricky, as Anderson, Richardson, and Richard Hebble discovered again two years later on the Northwest Face. As Anderson describes it, "The first pitch yielded no piton cracks, and Dick negotiated a bulge about 100 feet up on small holds. Finally, a good piton gave me a chance of surviving, should the whole vein peel away from the face."

The West Arête, which Anderson, Richardson, and Hebble climbed, is firmer than the nearby Northwest Face, as I found in 1992. I first attempted the climb in July with Sue Harrington. Hiking the steep trail up to Lake Constance I didn't want to look at my altimeter watch. Sue had hers on and asked, "Want to know how high we've come?" "No!" I replied. "The news is better than you think," was her response. I gave in, and learned we had gained 1200 feet, but instruments more often than not are frustrating. On that trip we failed to reach the summit, as we were rained out on the crucial ascent day.

I returned alone in August to try again, in one day from the car. The weather was perfect. Carrying only a small pack with ice ax, food, clothes, and rock shoes, I reached Crystal Pass, 5000 feet above the trailhead, in slightly over three hours. As I laced my rock shoes and drank some water, a lone mountain goat ventured close by. Half an hour later I was several hundred feet up the route as the goat watched my movements from the pass.

The climbing demanded every bit of my attention; it was steep with an occasional wiggly handhold. The small vertical walls had few cracks that lured me up, then blanked out. In forty minutes I found myself at the base of a large, sheer wall where the route traversed up and right, then straight up. It was airy, where a misstep would have sent me some 800 feet to the talus below.

After an hour and ten minutes of climbing I topped out on the ridge south of the summit, and scrambled to the top in another forty-five minutes. Far to the west I could make out Mount Olympus between intermittent puffy clouds. After a quick snack I was on my way down, trying to puzzle out the descent. Having never before climbed the peak, I worked out the standard route in reverse. Part way down I noticed some white paint on the rocks that marked the route. Once through a small notch it was a long scree slide down the southeast side, then a descent of the South Chute to Avalanche Canyon.

Mount Constance. The West Arête Route follows the left skyline

I made it back to the car at 3 P.M., ending a fantastic solitary day in the mountains. The needle-like summits of the Olympics intrigued me and would require further exploration.

Mount Constance: West Arête

First ascent: Don Anderson, R. Knight, and Jim Richardson; 1957
Difficulty: Grade III, 5.4

Equipment: A light rack up to a 3-inch cam and large slings. Ice ax for early season ascents.

Permit: A permit is required for overnight use; obtain it at the Dosewallips Ranger Station. For further information contact Olympic National Park, 600 East Park Avenue, Port Angeles, WA 98362, (360-452-4501).

Access: Turn off Highway 101 just north of Brinnon and drive west on the Dosewallips Road. Keep right at 11 miles. The Lake Constance Trail is at 13.8 miles; the Dosewallips Campground and ranger station are at 15.2 miles. Lake Constance and the peak are in the national park; camping at the lake is limited between mid-June and early September. Drive to the Dosewallips Ranger Station to obtain a permit and drive back down the road 1.4 miles to the trailhead and parking. The 2-mile trail up to the lake is straightforward except at 4000 feet, where it's best to keep right and near the stream. From the lake ascend Avalanche Canyon north to Crystal Pass and the start of the climb.

Route: Climb the right side of the buttress for several pitches. Near the top, move left onto the arête instead of climbing a chimney. Once on the arête, climb mainly on the crest or just below it. Climb a wide chimney left of the crest, then drop and traverse into a saddle below a large steep wall. Ascend the right side of the wall via a steep slanting ledge. Climb the ledge up and right (5.4), then diagonal up and left to easier ground. Higher, a short wide crack leads up to a left-facing corner. Climb the wall left of the corner, then diagonal up and left to easy ground. From the top of the arête you can drop 300 feet onto the normal route and continue to the summit pinnacle, which is climbed around the north and west sides.

Descent: From the summit, go down the southeast slope, rock outcrops, and a descending ledge system. Continue down gullies in a steep cirque and contour south a quarter-mile across heather and snow slopes to a ledge. Ascend to a notch, cross over and traverse ledges, and then drop down a broad scree gully to a saddle at 6500 feet near the Cat's Ears. From here, descend the west slopes down to Lake Constance.

Maps: Green Trails: The Brothers No. 168 and Tyler Peak No. 136; USGS: The Brothers and Mount Deception

Reference: *CGOM*

44 MOUNT OLYMPUS
Blue Glacier

TWENTY-EIGHT MILES WEST OF MOUNT CONSTANCE, in the very heart of the Olympic Range, lies glacier-clad Mount Olympus. Rising to 7965 feet, triple-summited Olympus is usually accessed from the lush Hoh River Valley. The temperate rain forest of the Hoh is filled with moss-blanketed Sitka spruce, western hemlock, and a variety of maples. As you gain elevation, the forest types continue to change from lowland to montane, and finally to subalpine where Alaska cedar, mountain hemlock and subalpine fir are found.

"With a mighty cheer, and then a song, we started our task of cairn building, record writing, and picture taking."

In 1907 a group of ten Mountaineers led by L.A. Nelson approached Olympus from the Queets River. They established a camp east of the peak, near the Humes Glacier. On August 13 the party set out at 5:30 A.M. in hopes of reaching the summit. They crossed the Humes Glacier and climbed a thirty-five-degree slope to Blizzard Pass, where their objective was finally visible. After a 700-foot drop, they ascended the Hoh Glacier and made the top of the Middle Peak shortly after lunch.

Thick clouds rolled in as they were crossing the upper Blue Glacier, obscuring everything. They mistakenly climbed a pinnacle north of the true summit, but discovered their error when the clouds parted. In another quarter-mile they gained the proper peak, climbing to the top from the north side. There was no evidence of previous visitors on the summit. The account of the climb relates, "With a mighty cheer, and then a song, we started our task of cairn building, record writing, and picture taking."

Since the extension of the Hoh River Trail to Glacier Meadows, the Blue Glacier Route has become the most popular way to climb Olympus. Although lengthy, the rain forest approach is both worthwhile and memorable. In July of 1978, over a three-day weekend, I approached the peak via this route, along with Shari Kearney.

Mount Olympus and the Blue Glacier from High Divide. (Photo by Brett Baunton)

Prior to the Olympus climb we had always hiked in our mountain boots, but the map revealed it was going to be a very long walk. We made two great discoveries on that trip—sneakers and aspirin. Both items helped immensely, but our feet still took a pounding. I also carried a 200mm lens with my camera in hopes of photographing animals. With the boots, equipment, and a three-day supply of food inside, my pack was heavier than I had expected.

Saturday was a long day, but the hike through the rain forest was pleasant. That evening we made camp at Glacier Meadows, within sight of Olympus. Around 5:00 the next morning we hiked onto the Blue Glacier and gradually ascended the bare ice for several miles. We chose to detour off the normal route to climb two near-vertical pitches in the icefall. It was much too warm to be climbing séracs; water poured into my clothing and I watched my hanging belay screws melt down two inches. Above the sérac we topped out on smooth glacier, convinced that was where we should have been all along. From there we hiked on firn, then steep seasonal snow, to the summit pinnacle, where a scramble ended on top.

On the return to high camp the sun was hot; a few wispy clouds had appeared in the sky. With the remaining light that evening we packed up and hiked part way out. As we still faced a long drive back to Portland on Monday night, we wanted to eliminate some of the hiking. Halfway to the car my feet were in agony, and Shari suggested aspirin for the pain. It seemed to take the edge off. Once at the road we drained a couple of cold Cokes from the cooler.

From that trip I learned that soft light shoes were preferable for hiking. As for heavy packs, I still haven't figured out how to weed out the weight. In some cases it's better to attempt climbs in a single long day, needing less gear and food, and not spend the night out. However, that was impractical on Olympus.

Mount Olympus: Blue Glacier

First ascent: A.W. Archer, J.B. Flett, T.C. Frye, Anna Hubert, Charles Landes, Henry Landes, Lorenz A. Nelson, W. Montelius Price, E.E. Richards, and Professor Weaver; August 13, 1907

Difficulty: Glacier travel and class 4 rock

Equipment: Ice ax, crampons, and some snow and ice protection.

Permit: Get a permit for overnight use in Olympic National Park. Permits are available from the Hoh Rain Forest Ranger Station, or from the main office in Port Angeles.

Access: From Port Angeles, drive Highway 101 nearly 70 miles to the Hoh River Road. Drive this road 19 miles to the Hoh Rain Forest Ranger Station. Hike the Hoh River Trail 17.4 miles to Glacier Meadows and campsites.

Route: Continue up the valley from the meadows to the top of a lateral moraine at 5100 feet on the east side of the Blue Glacier. Descend 150 feet onto the glacier. Ascend the glacier, cross to the west side, then climb northwest over rock and snow to the Snow Dome at 6600 feet.

Shari Kearney in the Blue Glacier icefall

Continue south and up to a 7200-foot pass, then turn right and climb to the top of the Upper Blue Glacier. From a saddle between Five Fingers Peak and the West Peak, climb steep snow to the northeast side of the rock summit, which is climbed by ledges and cracks on the east side.

Descent: Descend via the same route.

Maps: Green Trails: Mount Tom No. 133 and Mount Olympus No. 134; USGS: Mount Olympus and Mount Tom

Reference: *CGOM*

45 MOUNT RAINIER
Liberty Ridge

AT A HEIGHT OF 14,410 FEET, MOUNT RAINIER'S HUGE MASS is a Northwest landmark of grand proportions. Rising as it does from 3000- to 4000-foot countryside, the peak's relief is formidable. Many climbers have underestimated the size of the mountain and discovered a single weekend inadequate for scaling one of its glaciers, ridges, or walls. At present, Rainier has over sixty climbing routes and variations, primarily on snow and ice.

"As I left one set of foot and hand holds and went on to another, everything that I had been standing on gave way and went tumbling down the mountain."

Hazard Stevens and Philemon B. Van Trump made the first ascent of the mountain on August 17, 1870, reaching the summit via the Gibraltar Ledges. This route became popular with large groups until near the turn of the century, when an unknown party established the Ingraham Glacier–Disappointment Cleaver Route. The latter route was found to be less hazardous than the ledges and became the normal route. Rev. J. Warner Forbes, George James, and Richard O. Wells climbed the Emmons–Winthrop Glacier in August of 1884. In the summer of 1891 Van Trump, Alfred Drewery, and Dr. Warren Riley climbed the Tahoma Glacier and in 1905 Ernest Dudley and John Glascock ascended the Success Cleaver.

With several of the major glaciers and lesser ridges scaled, climbers tentatively began work on the steeper routes. In 1920 Hans and Heinie Fuhrer, Peyton Farrer, Joseph Hazard, Thomas Hermans, Harry M. Meyers, and Roger W. Tull climbed the Kautz Glacier and a steep snow coulior that came to be know as the Fuhrer Finger. Finally, on September 7 and 8, 1935, Wolf Bauer and Jack Hossack hacked their way up the hard ice of Ptarmigan Ridge.

Later the same month, Jim Borrow, Arnie Campbell, and Ome Daiber scaled the striking Liberty Ridge, considered, at the time, an actual ascent of Willis Wall. Technically speaking, the actual Willis Wall, which is capped by a three-quarter-mile-wide ice cliff, is situated between Curtis and Liberty

Mount Rainier from the north. Liberty Ridge is slightly to the right of center

Ridges. The climbers approached the 5000-foot north wall of the mountain from Carbon River and Cataract Creek carrying overnight gear, a 100-foot lead rope, a 50-foot smaller line, a homemade blizzard tent, clothing, and food for four days. That evening they made camp at 6000 feet at the base of Curtis Ridge and shared two sleeping bags between the three of them.

On September 29 the trio spent hours weaving in and around the séracs on the Carbon Glacier. Borrow felt the séracs were tedious, and probably would have been impossible if not for Daiber. He relates, "Ome proved his ability by skillfully cutting steps up fifty feet of almost vertical ice." From the Carbon the climbers fought their way up Liberty Ridge to 11,000 feet. After much chopping, the tired group produced a three-foot ledge in the ice and crawled into their tent and cooked supper. To save weight, they had cached their sleeping bags at Curtis Ridge, and thus they endured an even colder night out.

In the morning the three men ate a quick breakfast and strapped on crampons for the ascent. A short way above their camp, Daiber spent a long time leading an ice-glazed chute of rotten rock. He describe the difficult ascent, saying, "As I left one set of foot and hand holds and went on to another, everything that I had been standing on gave way and went tumbling down the mountain."

Above, the climbers reached the base of the prow where they chose a bit of rock work to avoid traversing steep hard ice. Although the high-angle ridge tapered off around 13,800 feet, two large crevasses blocked the group's progress. By using a modified shoulder stand, Borrow and Campbell hurled Daiber to the other side of the first big crack, where he jammed his ax in the snow. The second crevasse was easily skirted around one end. With Liberty Ridge scaled, the three climbers spent a third night out on the summit and descended to Paradise on the fourth day.

Forty-one years later, in 1976, Shari Kearney and I made our way to the base of Liberty Ridge during the month of July. We never even got on the ridge, since the warm weather sent volleys of rocks down, and snow avalanches poured off either side. Hoping for colder conditions in the springtime, Shari, Monty Mayko, and I returned during April of 1979 for another crack at the route. Snow fell continuously and Liberty Ridge was all but invisible.

I was discouraged by those attempts on Rainier and didn't climb the mountain again until April of 1990. Sue Harrington and I had cold spring conditions on the Ingraham Glacier and carried skis nearly to the summit. Our choice of routes for a ski descent wasn't the best, and we were forced to carry our boards down to 11,000 feet before enjoying good turning.

In February of 1993 I enlisted Dean Hagin to join me in an attempt on Liberty Ridge. We camped at the Carbon River entrance on a Friday night and awoke to light rain in the morning. Not anxious to carry huge packs fourteen miles, we drove home in time for Dean to enter a local climbing competition. Two weeks later Dean's brother, Dana, joined the two of us for another try; the weather looked good, although a front was moving in on Monday. We hoped to be off the route by then.

The approach was a grueling two-day affair in winter, since we had to walk five miles of road beyond a locked gate. Using Friday and all day Saturday, we reached the 8400-foot level of the Carbon Glacier on skis. Not a cloud

marred the sky, and Liberty Ridge swept upward in a grand line between Willis Wall and Liberty Wall.

Rainier's north side in February is a place of solitude without even any tracks of other climbers or skiers. Our only company was the rumbling and crashing of ice from the adjacent ice walls.

Dean and Dana hadn't explained to their girlfriends that our adventure might take and extra day (they said they would be home Sunday night), and there was some anxiety over this logistic faux pas. Although the approach had taken longer than we anticipated, no one mentioned skiing back out without trying the ridge. The plan was to go up—we hoped someone wouldn't initiate a search party.

Following hours of snow-melting for drinks and filling the bottles for the climb, we slept until 3:30 A.M. We each packed a bivy sack and insulated jackets, and divided group equipment of one shovel, a stove, cook pot, and drinks—the bare minimum for spending a night on a big mountain in winter.

Upon reaching the route's base, or while on the ridge, conditions were not as good as I had hoped they would be. Dana led out from camp, punching holes in snow that reached our knees in places. Once on the ridge I took over, sinking in to my thighs. Beyond Thumb Rock we began to encounter hard ice beneath the snow, and our progress slowed even more. We moved together and constantly placed Stoppers, slings over horns, and an occasional ice screw.

The climbing was always interesting and not extremely cold, but we were always aware that it was winter. Hands rewarmed slowly, toes were constantly on the edge of comfort, and the afternoon breeze sent fingers of icy spindrift down the slopes and into chinks in our clothing. Although the weather was still good, we chose 3 P.M. as our turnaround time, and from the top of the climb started back down. It would have been nice to have summited, but owing to the conditions and our slow progress, we had to be satisfied with our 13,000-foot high point.

It had taken us nine hours to climb 4600 feet from camp, and seven hours to descend the same route. Extra care was necessary in the dark; the leader would search the slope carefully with his headlamp looking for our tracks, and placing anchors. One desperate little pitch consisting of steep flakes

Opposite: *Dana Hagin at 12,500 feet on Liberty Ridge in February*

plastered with snow was especially frustrating because we couldn't quite see what our feet were doing.

We finally made the tent at 10 P.M. and struggled with frozen gaiters and laces before soothing our throats with soup, cocoa, and lots of water. During the night the storm hit, battering the tent with snow and wind. We were mighty glad not to have carried our gear up and over to the Emmons Glacier. A night stuck inside some miserable crevasse with snow pouring in would have been ugly.

On Monday the blizzard howled across the Carbon Glacier. Once we reached Curtis Ridge the wind gusts threatened to knock us flat. We made it to the car at 8 P.M. but there was no sign of the mountain—it had disappeared into its own storm cloud as snow sloughed down the precipitous walls. Dean and Dana's girlfriends had called my wife to see about our being late; she had assured them we were probably okay, but had been slowed up by the weather.

In June that same year I finally did complete the climb of Liberty Ridge with three friends. It had taken me only seventeen years.

Mount Rainier: Liberty Ridge

First ascent: Jim Borrow, Arnie Campbell, and Ome Daiber; September 29–30, 1935

Difficulty: Grade III or IV, snow and ice to 40–50 degrees and some rock

Equipment: Flukes, pickets, screws, and slings. Ice ax and crampons. A few pieces of rock pro as well.

Permit: A permit for climbing and overnight use is required in the park; it is available at Carbon River Ranger Station. For additional information contact Mount Rainier National Park, Tahoma Woods, Star Route, Ashford, WA 98304 (360-569-2211).

Access: From Buckley, take Highway 165 to Carbonado. South of Carbonado turn left to Fairfax and then drive the Carbon River Road 5.8 miles to the Carbon River entrance. Drive 5 more miles to Ipsut Creek Campground and the trailhead. Hike the Carbon River Trail (Wonderland Trail) 6 miles to Moraine Park. From Moraine Park, continue up the lower Curtis Ridge to 7500 feet where it's possible to drop down onto the Carbon Glacier and wind around crevasses to the base of Liberty Ridge. There is level camping at 8800 feet near the base of the ridge.

Alternate: Once the road to the White River Campground on the east side is open for the season, it is preferable to approach this way, as you begin hiking 2000 feet higher and the mileage is less. From the White River Campground hike the Glacier Basin Trail 3.5 miles into Glacier Basin. Traverse over St. Elmo's Pass and across the lower Winthrop Glacier to Moraine Park.

Route: Head straight for Willis Wall, then angle right to Liberty Ridge and attain the ridge up the east side 200 to 300 feet above the toe. Climb the right side of the ridge above Thumb Rock, then climb rightward on firn or ice to a gully in a rock step. Climb the gully up to the ridge crest, move leftward, and climb to the top of the Black Pyramid. Continue up the ridge until it merges with Liberty Cap Glacier and climb westward over a bergschrund to circumvent ice cliffs. Continue on to Liberty Cap.

Descent: From Liberty Cap traverse 1.5 miles east-southeast to the Emmons Glacier. (Be careful not to descend northeastward too soon, going down the steeper and badly crevassed upper Winthrop Glacier.) Descend the Emmons and Inter Glaciers, traverse up over St. Elmos Pass, and across the lower Winthrop Glacier back to Moraine Park. If approaching from the White River Campground, descend the Emmons and Inter Glaciers down to Glacier Basin, then proceed on out to the campground.

Maps: Green Trails: Mount Rainier West No. 269 and Mount Rainier East No. 270; USGS: Mount Rainier West, Mount Rainier East, Mowich Lake, and Sunrise

Reference: *CAG 1: Columbia River to Stevens Pass*

46 MOUNT ST. HELENS
Monitor Ridge

DURING THE FIRST ASCENT OF MOUNT ST. HELENS in 1853 by Thomas Dryer and his three companions there was evidence the mountain was an active volcano. "The 'smoke' was continually issuing from its [crater] mouth," Dryer wrote, "giving unmistakable evidence that the fire was not extinguished." The party ascended the south slopes of the peak after a long journey by horseback from Portland.

"A small, billowy, white cloud appeared over the summit ridge, then a huge, dirty, roiling mass towered above,"

The 37,000 year old volcano has been most animated in the last thousand years, during which time eruptions built a cone to a height of 9677 feet. Between 1831 and 1857, settlers in the region reported numerous eruptions; during one, ash fell sixty-four miles to the southeast in The Dalles, Oregon. Until 1980, the mountain had a uniform cone-shaped appearance because of its youth and lack of erosion.

Most people feel the mountain was more beautiful prior to the shattering May 1980 eruption that made the peak so famous. Downed timber does not make St. Helens an ugly destructive menace. It is man who presumed the environment around the mountain would remain intact for his consumption and pleasure. The present day crater is an awesome and striking example of the planet's forces—a reminder that as humans we do not control nature.

In 1961, when I first climbed the peak with my parents, I was ten years old. St. Helens was my third summit. The view from the top was incredible, but I wasn't fond of the sulphur fumes that came from the crater. My dad had pioneered our route up the Southeast Ridge from a high camp in the lava fields he named Moonbase Camp. He felt that the flat camping area surrounded by a circular ring of jagged lava rocks resembled a moon crater.

It was a tortuous two-mile hike across the lava beds to reach the camp, where, in the summer, the black lava radiated an unbelievable amount of heat. By the time I, my parents, and our friends, the Kurtz family and the Allworth's, finished the climb and hiked back across the lava to the car, I was one tired

Mount St. Helens. Monitor Ridge is slightly to the left of center

kid. I made five more ascents of St. Helens between 1967 and 1975, and decided that springtime was better, as then the lava flows are covered with snow.

In March of 1980, when the mountain began its recent eruptive phase, climbers and hikers wanted to scale the mountain to see it in action. Ancil Nance and Pete Reagan made a March ascent that year. Reagan described a small eruption as they neared the summit. "A small, billowy, white cloud appeared over the summit ridge, then a huge, dirty, roiling mass towered above," Reagan related. "Occasional puffs of wind brought hissing clouds of ash blowing across the slopes, but the eruptions themselves were quiet." The air that day was filled with a dozen light planes and helicopters, sightseeing and photographing the volcano. St. Helens was no longer a place to find wilderness solitude.

Many people wait until July or August to make an ascent, when the seasonal snow has melted and they can walk up a lava and cinder path. In 1992, my 69-year-old mother wanted to go up, so I obtained a permit. July was the target date. Mom and Dad had witnessed the May 18th, 1980 eruption from a scant seven miles to the west; St. Helens had become a significant part of their lives. My parents were avid climbers from 1945 to 1970. Mom was especially keen to climb to the top of the active volcano. We

Sue Harrington on Mount St. Helen's crater rim

planned it months in advance and Mom began doing hikes up to twelve miles in length every weekend with a group of her women friends in Vancouver, Washington. During an excited phone call she told me she felt ready to make the climb. A few weeks later she suffered second-degree burns from scalding water on her back, left arm, and upper left leg. The doctor instructed her to avoid intense sun while the skin healed. Unfortunately, this is often difficult on a high mountain.

On July 29th Mom was apprehensive, but conscientiously donned long clothing and put on plenty of sun cream. We had perfect sunny weather, and that day we were two of the mass of over a hundred people on the mountain. We were slow, but we still managed to pass a number of parties. All those years of climbing and hiking had given Mom strong legs. I kept our rest breaks to a minimum so we could maintain a steady pace.

At the false summit we beheld the immense 1.3 mile-wide and 1400-foot-deep crater. The edge was festooned with video camera-toting tourists, kids rolling rocks, and (unbelievably) entire families who had made the 4500-foot climb. Most people were content to remain at the 8281-foot point, but Mom and I had to trudge to the very top, eighty-four feet higher and a quarter-mile to the west. There, away from the crowd, we watched wind-driven plumes of dust and steam blow up out of the crater. Mom was overjoyed to have made the climb and related her ascent by ham radio to Dad and friends in Vancouver.

It was a hot hike down, not unlike that first climb thirty-one years before. When we reached the car I opened the cooler and produced cold drinks. High on Monitor Ridge we could make out tiny puffs of dust as late starters continued to descend.

Mount St. Helens: Monitor Ridge

First ascent: Thomas J. Dryer, Drew, Smith, and Wilson; August 27, 1853

Difficulty: Gentle to moderate snow in early season, lava and cinders later on. From April through June you can have more of a "mountaineering experience," and enjoy excellent skiing on the southern slopes.

Equipment: Ice ax and crampons for early season climbs.

Permit: Permits are required. Between May 15 and October 31 they can be obtained by mail from Mount St. Helens National Volcanic Monument Headquarters, 42218 NE Yale Bridge Road, Amboy, WA 98601 (360-247-5800). Seventy permits are issued per day; an additional forty permits are issued in person at Jack's Restaurant, 24 miles east of Woodland on Highway 503. Between November 1 and May 14 register only at Jack's Restaurant.

Access: From Woodland take Highway 503 for 36.2 miles past the town of Cougar to Road No. 83. Turn left on Road No. 83; at 1.7 miles keep right. At 3.1 miles go left on No. 8100 and right at 4.8 miles on No. 830. Follow No. 830 2.8 miles to the road end. Hike trail No. 216a for 2 miles through woods and cross trail No. 216. Hike 0.2 mile more to the start at Monitor Ridge (named for the seismic monitors once placed on the ridge).

Route: Follow Monitor Ridge 2 miles to the crater rim at 8281 feet. The true summit is ¼ mile to the west. Drop 150 feet to a saddle, then make a rising traverse to the highest point at 8365 feet. Although easy, early season ascents will have slippery snow and possible avalanches, and more rockfall as the snow melts. The crater rim is heavily corniced in spring and early summer and unstable at all times of the year. High people-traffic has not reduced any of the mountain hazards.

Descent: Descend via the same route.

Maps: Green Trails: Mount St. Helens NW No. 364 and No. 364s; USGS: Mount St. Helens

Reference: *CAG 1: Columbia River to Stevens Pass*

47 MOUNT ADAMS
Adams Glacier

I CAN REMEMBER, AS A LITTLE CHILD, seeing it sixty miles away. Cold and white and lone it was, more like a cloud than a part of solid earth." That was how Claude Ewing Rusk described his first view of 12,276-foot Mount Adams. Rusk later was to spend two decades exploring and naming features of the peak. As with other Northwest volcanoes, most viewers are struck by the sheer massiveness of the mountain and its singular nature.

"We lay and shivered as long as we could stand it, then we rose and walked back and forth to restore the circulation."

Volcanoes were obvious challenges to early mountaineers; in the summer of 1854 A.G. Aiken, Edward Allen, and Andrew Burge climbed Adams via the North Ridge. The now popular South Spur route was established in 1863 by Henry Coe, Julia Johnson, and a Mr. Phelps. In 1919 Rusk attempted the Wilson Glacier, Lava Ridge, and Victory Ridge. In each case Rusk scaled the hardest part of the route and was eager to continue on to the summit, but was forced back by unwilling partners. Finally, in 1921, Rusk and six others climbed the Rusk Glacier and The Castle. This was the third new route on the mountain, and the first up the East Face.

Rusk and W.E. Richardson had Swiss ice axes, while the remainder of the party used seven-foot alpenstocks. Without crampons of any kind, it was necessary to cut steps for their hobnailed boots. Getting over the bergschrund of the upper Rusk Glacier was difficult. As Rusk described, "Foot by foot, with my Swiss ice ax, I hewed steps along the sharp top of the brittle ice, the fragments rattling down into the frozen caverns with an ominous sound."

Once onto the rock wall of The Castle, the climbing was dangerous. The party had to be careful, as dragging their 100-foot rope across the slope dislodged rocks. The seven climbers reached the top of The Castle at 11,500 feet at 4 P.M., just in time for a hailstorm. Rusk thought it prudent to spend the night at the col between The Castle and the upper slopes rather than to try for the summit.

Mount Adams. The Adams Glacier is the shadowed glacier on the right

Without bivouac gear, the group spent a cold night out. "When it was dark we huddled together in our rocky nest beneath the overhanging cliff and tried to sleep," he related. "We lay and shivered as long as we could stand it, then we rose and walked back and forth to restore the circulation." The next day the men climbed in and around séracs and crevasses, reaching the top after nearly five hours of strenuous effort.

Three years later, Lindsley Ross, John Scott, and Fred Stadter ascended the Northwest Ridge. In 1938, Joe Luethold, Russ McJury, and Wendell Stout climbed the Klickitat Glacier.

The Adams Glacier fell to Fred Beckey, Dave Lind, and Robert Mulhall in July of 1945. The trio left 4000-foot Killen Creek at midnight and tramped to the start of the icefall by daylight. They strapped on crampons, roped up at 8500 feet, and began climbing up an avalanche path to the first bergschrund. Due to a heavy snow year, conditions through the icefall were good and the party found numerous bridges over crevasses.

Two 50-degree slopes led to 10,000 feet where the climbers worked their way up the left side of the icefall. Several short, steep, ice walls barred the upper glacier, but they quickly cramponed up them to finish their new route by 9:15 A.M. After a leisurely stay on the summit, the climbers descended the North Ridge back to Killen Creek.

In July of 1972 I attempted the Adams Glacier with Mike Murray. At that time we had little experience, and had never finished those climbs that would have provided us with more skills. Part way up the glacier our confidence waned. Although the weather was perfect, we retreated.

I returned the following summer with Bill McGruder and Avery Tichenor from Stevenson, Washington. Avery was full of enthusiasm for rock and alpine climbs—anywhere and anytime. Bill was interested in climbing, but didn't have the same drive or commitment as Avery. We hiked the Killen Creek Trail past timberline and made camp within sight of the Adams Glacier.

Early the next morning we cramponed toward the glacier in the cold shadow of the huge mountain. When you have previously failed on a route, there are two barriers to overcome: as on the first try, you don't know what difficulties lie above, and you must also break through the mental wall of failure. This time our group looked strong and my only concern was that Avery intended to carry both a Nikon and a heavy Mamiya 6x6 camera up the route. I chastised him, but that was before I was aware of his unstoppable strength.

We surmounted a number of short ice pitches, stretched across crevasses, and crawled over and through teetering séracs for several hours. When the sun finally reached us, the difficulties were over; the upper glacier sloped easily to the top. Avery stopped to change film right in the middle of a crevasse field. I just wanted to keep moving, to get up and back down. His comment was, "If you're serious about photography you gotta shoot a lot of film. Wait'll you see the great shots I get from this climb."

Bill McGruder at camp below the Adams Glacier

I was new to photography, using a cheap Petri 35mm compact, and had no concept of what he meant. Naturally, Avery's photos were superior to mine and his greater physical speed more than made up for the times he paused to change film. Avery went on to become a highly skilled rock climber in the 1980s, then suddenly succumbed to hepatitis. The few routes we shared were memorable experiences, and the Adams Glacier was the best.

Mount Adams: Adams Glacier

First ascent: Fred Beckey, Dave Lind, and Robert Mulhall; July 1945

Difficulty: Grade II, snow and ice to moderate steepness

Equipment: Pickets and ice screws. Ice ax and crampons.

Permit: A permit for overnight use in the Mount Adams Wilderness area is available from the USFS, Mount Adams District, Trout Lake, WA, 98650 (509-395-2501).

Access: From Trout Lake drive north on the Mount Adams Recreational Area Road for 4.7 miles to the Randle–Trout Lake Road, No. 23. Turn left, then drive 18.9 miles to Takhlakh Lake. Turn right onto the Midway Loop Road, No. 2329. Drive 4.6 miles to the Killen Creek Trail, just before a campground. Hike 3.5 miles to the Pacific Crest Trail. Continue southeast along a ridge for another mile to campsites at 6880 feet.

Route: The glacier climb mainly involves crevasse problems and short ice walls. The path through and up will vary greatly, depending on the season. Get an early start; avoid climbing too close to active adjacent slopes where rockfall has occurred, or areas where icefall is noticeable.

Descent: Descend the North Ridge back to camp.

Maps: Green Trails: Mount Adams West No. 366, and Blue Lake No. 344; USGS: Mount Adams West

Reference: *CAG 1: Columbia River to Stevens Pass*

48 MOUNT HOOD
North Face

FROM PORTLAND, OREGON, MOUNT HOOD'S STRIKING PYRAMID
has often been called the city's barometer. During the 1970s a television
weatherman read a letter on the air sent to him by a viewer. It said, "If you
can't see Mount Hood it's raining. If you can
see Mount Hood it's *going* to rain." The
11,239-foot peak dons a lenticular cloudcap
that often presages storms. Moist air rising
and condensing over the summit creates these peculiar phenomena.

The fog eventually cleared, revealing glare ice over the holds.

Hot magma lies deep within the dormant volcano, and steam and sulphur fumes are noticeable at Crater Rock, within the remnants of the crater.
The best time of year to ascend the peak is winter and spring, since even by
early summer rockfall can be horrendous off the crumbling, snow-free, volcanic walls. During the months of April and May the mountain has unleashed
its worst weather, with extreme winds and storms that lasted five to eight
days. The gentle appearance of the peak's south side belies the mountain
hazards that are always present. In fact, my dad chastised his dad (Grandpa
Kearney) for climbing Hood in street shoes and carrying a sweater and bag
lunch. Grandpa's response was sage. "If the weather's not good, I don't climb,"
he announced. Take along all the breathable, waterproof clothing you want,
but if you don't use some common sense it won't do you a bit of good.

Mount Hood was first climbed up the south side on August 6, 1857 by
W.L. Buckley, W.L. Chittenden, James Dierdorff, Henry Pittock, and L.J.
Powell. In July of 1872 J.W. Blakeney, O.D. Doane, C.C. Grimes, E.B.
McFarland, and O.D. Miller climbed the Wy'east route, after several previ-
ous parties had failed. Fifteen years later Newton Clark, J. Elmer Rand, and
William Smith established the Cathedral Ridge route. In 1891 Will and Doug
Langille climbed Cooper Spur. The latter route became popular for climbers
approaching the peak from the north. One year later, in September, Will
Langille and G.W. Graham made the first ascent of the Sunshine Route.

On August 26, 1928, local guide Mark Weygandt led two brothers

The North Face of Mount Hood from Cooper Spur

(Arthur and Orville Emmons, on vacation from Massachusetts) up the unclimbed North Face. Although Weygandt claimed the face had previously been climbed once, in 1902, no evidence has been found to support that statement. With an ice ax and hobnail boots, Weygandt short-roped the youths to him and carried 60 feet of extra line over his shoulder. The trio started up the rock rib between the two prominent North Face gullies where the climbing was tricky. He later wrote, "Much of the climb was finger and toe work, and sometimes the porous rock was treacherous."

Part way up, a fog enveloped the face. Fingers became damp and cold. Describing their difficulties, Weyandt wrote, "The younger Emmons boy several times climbed the rope and was within a few inches of the point at which the rope was anchored, but each time his hands were so cold that he could not grasp the edge of the ledge." The leader finally tossed him a length of spare rope so he could reach the belay. The fog eventually cleared, revealing glare ice over the holds. Weygandt laboriously scraped each hold clear of verglas and in two more hours the climbers reached the summit.

Because of the hazardous conditions and late hour, Weygandt led the Emmons brothers down the south side instead of descending one of the north side routes. Even today this practice is preferable, although it means hiking back up to Cooper Spur to retrieve cached gear.

I first climbed Mount Hood with the Mazamas climbing club in 1965, following the South Side route. As a fourteen-year-old, it was acceptable to my parents for me to go climbing with a big group, especially since Mom and Dad had done all of their climbs with the same club. When I got to the top, another party had climbed the West Face (now named Leuthold Couloir), which sounded more exciting to me. For six years I climbed with the club until finally cutting loose (to the horror of my parents), and attempting climbs with another student my age.

While living in Portland in the late 1970s, I frequented Hood in the winter. Relatively easy access made the peak ideal for practicing winter skills. Conditions on the mountain were always testy—never much pro and always weird layers of wind crust over powder snow or ice. I climbed the right-hand gully of the North Face in 1975 and two years later, in January, Jeff Thomas and I set out to do the left-hand couloir.

It was clear and cold as we hiked up from the old Cloud Cap Inn before dawn. A rosy-orange morning light airbrushed the Eliot Glacier

Jeff Thomas on the North Face of Mount Hood

and Mount Adams and St. Helens to the north. Good cramponing took us across the steep slopes above the glacier. We roped up for the couloir just below the bergschrund. As it was a dry winter, we found hard ice in places and little snow.

Jeff, powered by his huge thighs, climbed upwards at locomotive speed, rarely stopping to fidget with protection. Higher in the gully I took the lead and front-pointed up a short bulge of gleaming ice, pausing to twist in a screw. Once over the hardest climbing Jeff suggested we unrope, as there was no protection anyway. I was not in favor of this plan, but would learn my lesson the hard way four months later, in Alaska. On a small peak near Mount McKinley, three of us slid about 500 feet on steep snow, but were unhurt. One climber slipped and pulled the other two off, as there were no anchors.

I probably still had the large group mentality from my youth ingrained in my head; it was hard to think otherwise. I'd learned, "The rope is safety." Or is it, "The family that ties together dies together."? It is definitely the latter when crevasses, and knife-edge ridges do not fit into the equation. If you have good belay anchors, it's okay to be roped together.

After a brief stop on the summit we chugged some water and began descending the Cooper Spur route. Due to the route's angle, its lack of anchors, and the consequences of a slip, it took nearly as long as climbing the North Face. As the sun passed behind the peak we hiked down sparse snow patches and cinders to Cloud Cap and my van. Because of the dry year we had been able to drive to Cloud Cap instead of hiking there, and we made it back to Portland in a few hours.

Mount Hood: North Face

First ascent: Mark Weygandt, Arthur and Orville Emmons; August 26, 1928
Difficulty: Grade III, snow and ice up to 55–60 degrees
Equipment: Flukes, pickets, and screws. A few Stoppers and runners for frozen boulders. Ice ax and crampons.
Access: From Portland, drive Highway 26 52 miles to beyond Government Camp. Turn left on Highway 35 and follow it 20 miles to the Cooper Spur Road and the Cloud Cap Road, No. 3512. Turn left and drive 2.5 miles to the Cooper Spur Ski Area Road. Go left for nearly a mile. At the first fork go right, then right again at the second fork. Follow a dirt road 9 miles to Cloud Cap Inn, then hike the path up Cooper Spur,

paralleling the Eliot Glacier. Drop onto the glacier where feasible; follow it to the North Face. The Cloud Cap Road is open only from June to (sometimes) early November. Call or write the Zigzag Ranger District, 70220 East Highway 224, Zigzag, OR 97049, (503) 668-1704 for road conditions.

When the road is closed you must follow the road to the Cooper Spur Ski Area and park below at the Sno-Park, then follow the Cloud Cap Road 100 feet to the start of the Cooper Spur Ski Trail No. 643. It is 3 miles to Cloud Cap Inn. Less experienced skiers will want to hike the trail back down or ski the 9-mile Cloud Cap Road.

Route: From the Eliot Glacier surmount the bergschrund, then ascend the right-hand gully on the North Face. If the first rock band has little ice, climb around it on the left, then continue up a gully to the second rock band. Climb it directly if there is enough ice, or climb around it on the left. From the top of the rockband, go behind Cathedral Spire and continue directly to the summit, or do a rising left traverse to the top of Cooper Spur, then go up to the top.

Descent: Descend the Sunshine Route, then traverse back across the Eliot Glacier to the Cooper Spur. Or, descend the South Side Route after carrying all your gear up and over, then hitch back to your car. A third descent option is to access the route by traversing the Newton Clark Glacier and Cooper Spur from Mount Hood Meadows, climb the North Face, then descend the South Side and the White River Glacier back to Mount Hood Meadows. This latter approach and descent requires the climbers be in good shape, as you are circumnavigating half the mountain and climbing it in a single day.

Maps: USGS: Mount Hood North and Mount Hood South

Reference: *OH*

49 MOUNT JEFFERSON
Jefferson Park Glacier

MOUNT JEFFERSON IS OREGON'S SECOND HIGHEST SUMMIT, rising to 10,497 feet. The peak is draped by four active glaciers, whose carving was responsible for the conspicuous andesite summit pinnacle. The western

Jefferson's final pinnacle is highly fractured, loose, and often complicated by a layer of rime or snow.

side of the mountain lies within the Mount Jefferson Primitive Area and Wilderness, while the east side is in the Warm Springs Indian Reservation. Although the Whitewater Glacier Route is within the reservation, it is open to climbing. All approaches to the east side of the peak, however, are strictly prohibited.

The approach from the northwest goes through spectacular Jefferson Park, an idyllic collection of tarns and flowered meadows. As with all such spots, the terrain is fragile. You should use only established campsites or go higher onto the rocky moraine. Jefferson's final pinnacle is highly fractured, loose, and often complicated by a layer of rime or snow. One of my most rewarding alpine experiences was climbing the Whitewater Glacier Route in September of 1983, delicately cramponing up the rime-coated summit.

Ray Farmer and E.C. Cross first climbed Jefferson via the South Ridge on August 12, 1888. In 1903 Sidney Mohler climbed the North Ridge alone, after his partners retreated in a lightning storm. Lucius Hicks related, "Mr. Mohler, who climbs like a monkey, continued undaunted up the precipice, but the others, after warning him that he was on his way to certain death, decided to descend."

Three years later Mohler and Hicks scaled the Russell Glacier during August. In 1914 Andrew Montgomery and William Montgomery climbed the North Milk Creek Gully. In 1917 W.E. Stone and his wife climbed the West Rib. The now-popular Whitewater Glacier Route was established on August 25, 1921 by F.H. Jane and R. Nyden. The East Spur, described by Jeff Thomas as a "forgettable rib of rock" was first climbed by Peter Parsons in 1924, solo.

Carl Kurath and A.B. Metcalf put up the Jefferson Park Glacier Route

Mount Jefferson from Olallie Butte

on August 22, 1931. A Mazama group led by John Scott completed the second ascent in 1932, finding the climb "challenging and interesting." Scott, B. McNeil, Harold Roberts, and Paul Spangler left Jefferson Park at 5 A.M. on August 15th and hiked to the glacier, where they strapped on crampons. They climbed the right side of the glacier, then surmounted a bergschrund at the base of the western pinnacle. Skirting the spire, they encountered a second huge bergschrund, which they avoided by climbing steep rock to one side. They gained an ice gully that required 300 to 400 feet of step cutting to reach a rock ridge. The knife-edge ridge was exposed, but firm. "We found solid rock, offering plenty of good hand and foot holds," said Scott. "While it was good, it was also very precipitous."

In an hour the group reached the base of the summit pinnacle, where they ate lunch before making the final ascent. Once back at the north saddle, they downed a lunch dessert of pineapple and lemon sherbet before descending the east side to camp.

I first climbed Mount Jefferson with a Mazama group at the age of seventeen and mostly remember my painful hike into Jefferson Park. Dad had loaned me his army rucksack, with a steel frame and no waistband or padding whatsoever. I loaded up this instrument of cruelty with overnight gear and weekend food and fell in line with the other ten Mazamas. By the time we reached camp, I had bruises on my shoulders and hips that would last for weeks. My memory about the climb itself is vague, but I think it went all right.

In August of 1974 I joined Avery Tichenor for an ascent of the Jefferson Park Glacier. In the six years since my first climb of Jefferson I had obtained

a red nylon and aluminum REI Cruiser pack. This forty-dollar miracle invention produced no bruises, and even had a hipbelt. Avery considered the approach, then, unlike our Adams Glacier climb, decided to take only his Nikon camera gear, leaving behind his heavy Mamiya twin-lens reflex. I was amazed, since he usually carried everything.

We marched into Jefferson Park on a Saturday, made camp by one of the glittering lakes, then tried to cook and sleep with the mosquitoes. Up early, we reached the first of two big schrunds on the glacier and were stymied as to how to get over it. We finally chose to climb vertical rock and ice on the extreme left side of the first bergschrund, just below the Mohler Tooth. This proved exciting, as Avery was able to practice his dance steps dodging the rocks and ice that I sent down.

Avery Tichenor below the Mohler Tooth on Mount Jefferson

Once up the upper ice slope and second big crack, we scrambled up the slender rock ridge leading to the North Saddle. The ridge was solid and sporting. Soon we were grappling with the unstable blocks of the summit pinnacle. At the top, we each performed heroics for the camera and checked our 110-foot Goldline rope for cuts and nicks. After a snack we descended from the summit, traversed the western slope across to Red Saddle, then on down to the Whitewater Glacier.

On the hike out I stopped frequently to photograph the beargrass and shooting star blossoms, but Avery scolded me for pausing and wasting film. "The light's no good for flowers today, you need an overcast sky," he chided. My climbing skills were moving right along, but it was obvious I still had much to learn about photography.

Mount Hood: Jefferson Park Glacier

First ascent: Carl Kurath and A.B. Metcalf; August 22, 1931

Difficulty: Grade III. Snow and ice and low 5th class rock

Equipment: Some pickets, screws, and rock pro (large runners are most useful). Ice ax and crampons.

Permit: Pick up a permit for overnight use in the Mount Jefferson Wilderness at the USFS Ranger Station in Mill City or, by mail from the Detroit Ranger District, HC-73 Box 320, Mill City, OR 97360, 503-854-3366.

Access: From Salem drive Highway 22 for 22 miles to Mill City. Drive another 40 miles on Highway 22 to the Whitewater Road, No. 2243 and turn left. Drive 7.5 miles to the road end, then hike the Whitewater Trail for 1.5 miles to a junction and turn right. Go 2.5 miles to the Pacific Crest Trail and turn left. Follow the PCT a mile to Jefferson Park.

Route: Ascend the east side of the glacier to the first of two bergschrunds below the Mohler Tooth–Smith Rock saddle. If the schrunds are insurmountable, directly climb the rock on either side, the right side being more stable. Climb the 45-degree slope to the col, then ascend the knife-edge ridge leading east. The 5.1 ridge joins the North Ridge, which is followed to the west side of the summit pinnacle. Climb the west face of the North Horn (the highest summit), 4th or 5th class.

Descent: Descend the summit pinnacle and traverse the west slope to the Red Saddle, then proceed down to the Whitewater Glacier and back to Jefferson Park.

Map: USGS: Mount Jefferson

Reference: *OH*

50 ELEPHANT'S PERCH
Mountaineers Route

JUST OVER A MILE SOUTHWEST OF IDAHO'S REDFISH LAKE is the Elephant's Perch, with its imposing 1200-foot west face and 10,000-foot summit. Most Sawtooth peaks are craggy affairs with sharp tops, whereas the Perch stands out as one of the few wall-like features in the range. In the summer of 1960 a group of seventy-six Iowa Mountaineers camped

The Mountaineers Route climbs up the left side of the conspicuous feature known as the Cobra Head and follows beautiful cracks and corners for eight pitches.

on the shore of Redfish Lake and made numerous climbs in the vicinity. The north summit of Chockstone Peak, Flat Rock Needle, Quartzite Peak, Black Aiguille, and the Elephant's Perch were all first ascents.

Climbers who were on these ascents included Paul Bloland, Claire Brown, Wilbur and Cornelia Davis, Bill Echo, Hans Gmoser, Rodney Harris, James Lure, Dean Millsap, James Ross, Stanton Taylor, John Walker, and Jack Wilson.

In 1960, Seattle climber Steve Marts eagerly accepted an invitation to climb in the Sawtooths with Fred Beckey, Dan Davis, and Eric Bjornstad. It was in the Sawtooths that the inexperienced Marts first did longer technical routes with seasoned partners. "Even though I had done a little bit of climbing before," Marts stated, "it was fairly conservative." After Bjornstad left, Beckey, Davis, and Marts spent ten more days in the area around Monte Verita Ridge where, Marts claimed, "We practically just climbed everything in sight."

Three years later Marts returned to the Sawtooths with Beckey and Herb Swedlund and put up the West Face (or Beckey Route) on the Perch. The climbers used fixed ropes on the ascent of the twelve-pitch line that, like the Mountaineers Route, has become a classic. In 1967, Yosemite veterans T.M. Herbert and Dennis Henneck, along with Gordon Webster, established a grade III route on the Northwest Face. Their Mountaineers Route climbs up the left side of the conspicuous feature known as the Cobra Head and follows beautiful cracks and corners for eight pitches.

Opposite: *Elephant's Perch. The Mountaineers Route turns the left side of the Cobra Head*

Bob Kandiko ascends solid flakes on the Mountaineers Route

I paid a visit to the Sawtooths in 1976, climbing a long route on the North Face of Mount Heyburn. From the Heyburn summit, Shari Kearney and I could just make out the striking outline of Elephant's Perch to the south. We returned in October of 1977 to climb Packrat Peak, following a long road trip through Colorado and Utah. Although clear, it was cold and the rock was dusted with fresh snow. Hiking the trail back to Redfish Lake, after climbing Packrat's East Ridge, the wall of Elephant's Perch loomed large and tantalizing. The Perch remained on my list since then, but I did not return for sixteen years.

During a 1992 trip with Bob Kandiko, Sue Harrington, and Karen Neubauer, we climbed Warbonnet Peak and two other summits before hiking back down to attempt Elephant's Perch. The packs were a little lighter, what with some food gone, but they still seemed heavy as we ascended the dusty climbers' path to a camp at Saddleback Lakes. Early Sawtooth settlers called the Perch Saddleback Peak until the Mountaineers' name stuck in 1960.

Bob and I were constantly watching for other parties planning to climb the eight-pitch route. We decided to hike to the base the night before and cache the climbing gear in a garbage bag. As there was a threat of rain, our purpose was twofold: to keep the gear dry and get to the route quickly in the early morning.

At the lakes a couple of strange tents alarmingly popped up. In hushed tones we reset our chrono-watches for an even earlier wake-up, suspicious of the newcomer's objectives. The morning weather did not look promising, but at least the mosquitoes had subsided. Sue was a short way up the first pitch, stuffing pro into cold cracks when the competition arrived. Actually, the two climbers were locals who had hiked in from the lake early that morning to do the route. They amicably stated they would try another line on a nearby peak. Good chaps, I thought, for they looked as though they could have easily climbed right over us and sped on to the top.

With no further interference, the four of us had a great day on the quality route. It had every type of climbing—wild exposure across underclings, face climbing up smooth slabs, and an overhanging hand crack at the top. The threat of rain persisted all day as the sun strobed a staccato pattern on the granite wall. Dark clouds of precipitation hammered the surrounding peaks, but never managed to reach us. It was mostly cool and breezy, and any inactivity quickly brought on shivers. From the top of the steep climbing we scrambled across and up huge exfoliated slabs of granite to the summit.

The only downer occurred when Bob and Karen got a small cam stuck on the third pitch and were not able to retrieve it. When we returned to camp they told a pair of climbers planning to do the route the following day about the lost pro and gave them their address. Bob said to me later, "I don't expect to see that number 2 again." Imagine his surprise when it showed up in the mail two weeks later with a note. Finally, a story involving climbing gear with a good ending.

Elephant's Perch: Mountaineers Route

First ascent: T.M. Herbert, Dennis Henneck and Gordon Webster; 1967
Difficulty: Grade III, 5.9
Equipment: A standard rack up to a 4-inch cam.
Access: Continue on Highway 75 past the Decker Flat Road about 7 miles to the Redfish Lake turnoff. Turn left and drive to the Redfish Lake Lodge (208-774-3536). Get a ride on a resort boat ($5.00 per person, one way) or walk 6 miles along the north side of the lake to the south end. The boat goes on demand for two or more people and makes scheduled pickups at the transfer dock at the lake's south end at 9 in the morning and 2, 5, and 7 in the afternoon. From the transfer dock begin hiking the Redfish Creek–Baron Creek Trail No. 101 for 2 miles to an unmarked climbers' path that crosses Redfish Creek on a makeshift bridge

of logs. The path climbs uphill for a mile to Saddleback Lakes below Elephant's Perch, where there are good campsites. To reach the Mountaineers Route, make a rising traverse towards the Perch to gain a long big ledge at the base of the West Face. Follow the ledge north to below the Cobra Head and the start of the route.

Route: The route begins in a gully with a chockstone. **[1]** Climb the gully/chimney past the chockstone to a belay ledge (5.5). **[2]** Continue up a chimney 30 feet, exit left via a mantle (5.8), then climb a small corner to a tree and a short chimney to a pedestal belay. **[3]** Climb a crack and a left-facing corner to a ledge and a tree, then move left and climb a long hand crack (5.8) to a hanging belay below a big roof. **[4]** Undercling and face climb left (5.7) to gain a crack and a shallow chimney leading nearly to the Cobra Head. **[5]** Work up and left across the face left of Cobra Head (5.7) to a belay on its left side. **[6]** Climb a face, then a crack (5.8). Move right at the top of the pitch to a belay ledge. **[7]** Climb flakes and a crack in a long left-facing corner (5.9). At the end of the crack, where it overhangs and widens, step left to a sloping belay stance. **[8]** Climb a wide crack (5.6), then easier grooves and a face up to class 3 terrain.

Descent: Drop into the first major gully, 400 yards east of the summit. There is one 75-foot rappel from a tree at the bottom.

Map: USGS: Mount Cramer

Reference: CM No. 204, pp. 52–63.

51 WARBONNET PEAK
South Face

WARBONNET PEAK AND ITS FIVE SHARP SUMMITS arch back like feathers in an Indian chief's headdress, hence the name. Viewed from Packrat Peak, the rocky pinnacles rise 1400 feet above Feather and Bead Lakes to the 10,200-foot main summit of Warbonnet. The setting is pristine, with lush green meadows, deep blue lakes, and glacial polished slabs of gleaming granite.

"The view from Warbonnet is breathtaking. Quite understandably so, since a stone dropped from one point will fall for nine seconds before disintegrating on the boulder fields below."

An Iowa Mountaineers party that included Bruce Adams, Cole Fisher, Bob Merriam, Paul Pedzoldt, John Speck, and Cal Wilcox first climbed Warbonnet in 1947. They followed the meandering West Face up cracks and chimneys to the exposed summit fin. The final blade of clean white rock was cleaved away on two sides, forcing the climbers to stay composed on the nervy pitch. Pedzoldt felt the climb was challenging, since no easy way existed to the top. "This mountain should be classified with the few really difficult summits in the country," he wrote.

The second route established on the peak was up the South Face (now considered the normal route) in 1957 by Louis Stur, B. Ring, N. Bennett, and S. Franke. The six-pitch route had a variety of climbing, up a series of connecting chimneys. It was, according to Stur, ". . . tough enough to be fun, but yet within class 4 range." This route also finished via the spectacular final pitch, which, like the climbers from ten years earlier, elicited comments and exclamations from the participants.

Stur wrote later in the American Alpine Journal, "The sheer walls on both sides of the 'rooftop' overhang menacingly into nothingness down below; holds are a bare minimum and piton cracks zero. The view from the top of Warbonnet is exceptionally breathtaking. Quite understandably so, since a stone dropped from one point will fall for nine seconds before disintegrating on the boulder fields below."

My interest in the Sawtooths was piqued in 1971 while in college, as I was eager to learn all about climbing and do more of it. I was still a member of the Mazama climbing club in Portland, Oregon, and had read an article by Lyman Dye about those granite pinnacles over in Idaho. There was a photo of this older guy (an adult) climbing up the smooth arête of Warbonnet's summit in sneakers, with a rope tied around his waist. In my naive youth, I somehow had an idea that people a lot older couldn't possibly be capable of technical climbing. Now, thirty years later, I am still climbing and enjoying it.

In July of 1992, after climbing Finger of Fate, Sue Harrington, Bob Kandiko, Karen Neubauer, and I took the boat down Redfish Lake and began our march to Alpine Lake and the Feather Lakes below Warbonnet Peak. Now that everyone had warmed up on the 5.10 route of the Finger of Fate, we had perfect weather for our climb of a 5.6 route. Late in the afternoon we crested the final pass below Packrat Peak and began the descent into the Feather Lakes. Just as I noted that we had the place to ourselves, a lone hiker made his way through the talus toward us.

The stranger was Seattle climber Pat Gallager who, with his partner, had been climbing routes in the area for a week. His information about one line we wanted to try on Cirque Lake Peak proved invaluable; Sue and I had him draw us a topo. Once the four of us had erected our tents near one of the lakes we spent the afternoon relaxing and rubbing pack-sore backs and shoulders.

In the morning we headed out early to climb Warbonnet. We crossed over to Bead Lakes and climbed up scree and talus to the saddle between Warbonnet and its Central Tower to the east. It was clear and breezy; any belayer stuck in the shade wished for more clothing. Bob led up the first pitch of steep flakes to a large ledge as the rest of us pranced about trying to stay warm. Soon we were all in motion, clambering across ledges and writhing up easy chimneys.

Near the summit ridge we had to climb inside a giant slot, which from below looked improbable. Within the granite chasm we found excellent face holds and cracks for chilled fingers, as well as anchors. From the notch, Bob quickly stepped across the void and onto the steep, smooth, summit fin. Pro was scarce at the start, but higher up there were a few fixed pins and a couple of bolts. When it was Sue's turn to lead the pitch she had a hard time making that first step, even though Bob was lobbing down the time-worn phrase, "It's not that bad."

Opposite: *Warbonnet Peak and the South Face Route*

I wouldn't let her back out of the lead. I worked my way through an entire bag of M&M's and pulled my windshirt tight around my face at the belay. After several tentative moves, Sue moved up and clipped the first piece with a sigh of relief. From there to the top was a pure joy, as I also soon discovered. There were a lot of cameras clicking and exclamations about the

Bob Kandiko on the summit of Warbonnet Peak

pointed summits in every direction. Mostly, though, we were eager to get down out of the wind, return to camp and, with a hot brew in hand, look back at Warbonnet and say, "Yup, we climbed that!"

Warbonnet Peak: South Face

First ascent: Louis Stur, N. Bennet, S. Franke and B. Ring; 1957
Difficulty: Grade II, 5.6
Equipment: A light rack up to a 3-inch cam. An ice ax for early season approach.
Access: Approach as for Elephant's Perch, described previously, and hike 3.5 miles farther on trail No. 101 to Alpine Lake. From the lake, follow the Baron Lake Trail up to the second switchback at 8600 feet. Leave the trail and hike west-southwest across meadows, then up a long talus slope. Ascend a wide snow gully to a col at 9480 feet, between two 9700-foot peaks due east of Packrat Peak. Drop 200 feet, contour west a short way and climb 100 feet up to a second col below the northeast ridge of Packrat. From here you can descend easily to Feather Lakes, southwest of Warbonnet, and camp. To reach the route, hike over to the Bead Lakes, ascend talus northwest, then go north up to the large saddle on Warbonnet's southeast side.
Route: From the saddle, start up the Southeast Face and work around to the South Face. **[1]** Climb easy cracks and flakes 100 feet to a good ledge with a tree (5.3). **[2]** Traverse left and down a brushy ramp and around a corner to the base of three chimneys. **[3]** Climb the left chimney for 120 feet, then exit left and climb a short diagonal crack (5.6). Then work up and right in a talus-filled gully. **[4]** Follow the talus gully into a large chimney and a belay at a fork. **[5]** Climb a large curving chimney (giant slot) on the left to the ridge crest (5.3), then continue up the crest and go right to a notch below the summit fin. **[6]** Climb the right edge of the summit arête to the top (5.6).
Descent: Rappel and downclimb the route.
Map: USGS: Warbonnet Peak
Reference: *AAJ* 1958, pp. 299–301

References

Cascade Alpine Guide, 1: Columbia River to Stevens Pass (second edition), Fred Beckey. The Mountaineers Books, Seattle, 1986.

Cascade Alpine Guide, 2: Stevens Pass to Rainy Pass (second edition), Fred Beckey. The Mountaineers Books, Seattle, 1989.

Cascade Alpine Guide, 3: Rainy Pass to Fraser River (second edition), Fred Beckey. The Mountaineers Books, Seattle, 1995.

Cascade-Olympic Natural History, Daniel Mathews. Raven Editions, Portland, 1988.

Challenge of the North Cascades, Fred Beckey. The Mountaineers Books, Seattle, 1969.

Climbers Guide to the Olympic Mountains, Olympic Mountain Rescue. The Mountaineers Books, Seattle, 1972.

Fifty Classic Climbs of North America, Steve Roper and Allen Steck. Sierra Club Books, San Francisco, 1979.

Glacier Travel and Crevasse Rescue, Andy Selters. The Mountaineers Books, Seattle, 1990.

Koma Kulshan, The Story of Mt. Baker, John C. Miles. The Mountaineers Books, Seattle, 1984.

North Cascades Rock, Sport and Alpine Routes, Bryan Burdo. Rhinotopia Productions, Seattle, 1996.

One Man's Mountains, Tom Patey. Victor Gollancz Ltd., London, 1975.

Oregon High, A Climbing Guide, Jeff Thomas. Keep Climbing Press, Portland, 1991.

Secrets of Warmth, Hal Weiss. Cloudcap Books, Seattle, 1991.

Tales of a Western Mountaineer, C. E. Rusk. The Mountaineers Books, Seattle, 1978.

Index

INDEX

About the Author

Photo by Carl Skoog

Alan Kearney grew up in the Northwest and began hiking, skiing, and climbing mountains at the age of seven. He has been publishing photographs and writing articles about the outdoors since 1975. His work has appeared in Climbing, Rock and Ice, Men's Health, Newsweek and Outside. His first book, *Mountaineering In Patagonia*, was published in 1993. He resides in Bellingham, Washington, and writes and shoots photos full time.